THE VOICE OF ADVAITA VEDANTA

Insights into Non-Duality

BR. PRASANNA SWAROOPA

PUBLISHERS & DISTRIBUTORS (P) LTD

7/22, Ansari Road, Darya Ganj, New Delhi
Tel.: +91-11-4077 5252, 2327 3880
E-mail: orders@atlanticbooks.com
Web: www.atlanticbooks.com

Reprint 2026

Published by Atlantic Publishers & Distributors (P) Ltd.

Printed & bound in India by Atlantic Print Services

To

those who aspire:

to seek the Truth
which lies beyond the words,

to realise the Truth
behind the world phenomena,

to see this world
as beautiful and enriching,

to lead a life of
happiness, peace and contentment.

Preface

Verses in Sanskrit always fascinated me for their poetry, message, succinctness and, above all, the beauty and serenity derived from the chanting of the verses. One of the earliest books I possessed that had a lasting impact on me was 'Altar Flowers: A Bouquet of Choicest Sanskrit Hymns' published by Advaita Ashrama. The section from this book with small compositions of Adi Shankarāchārya was of particular interest to me.

This collection of Sanskrit verses cultivated a fondness in me for Sanskrit poetry and chanting. I had memorized many of the verses from the book, and they were my frequent companions.

In recent years, some friends have enquired if there is a book which contains a collection of works associated with Vedanta. Many often wonder about the ideal starting point for the exploration of the subject of Vedanta. I, too, have long imagined a compilation of Sanskrit verses from across different texts in one book.

Thus was born the idea of this book!

The intent was to provide a collection (with translation) that covers some of the important works on Vedanta for those aspiring to discover the Truth. For the selection, I have included the ones that have guided me and have had a profound impact on my journey.

This isn't a complete collection by any stretch of imagination. That would mean a vast library. I have compiled the texts and the verses with the intent of keeping it all within one volume.

I have put this book together with the fond hope that it will benefit the readers by exposing them to Advaita Vedanta and serve as a constant companion in their journey to seek the Truth. I hope I have been able to do justice to the task!

Br. Prasanna Swaroopa
Chennai, India
March 2024

Acknowledgements

I feel a deep sense of gratitude to our Nation's great culture, which has shaped the thoughts and lives of its people for thousands of years and will continue to do so for eternity through the richness of its knowledge tradition. It is this tradition that has preserved all these scriptures and ensured that even today we have access to them.

My deepest gratitude to my guru, Swami Bhoomananda Tirtha, who initiated me into the spiritual path and thus inducted me into the Advaita Vedanta tradition. Swamiji's continued stress on the importance of scriptures and frequently quoting them furthered my interest in our scriptures.

I wish to express my salutations and deepest gratitude to Adi Shankarāchārya, who has greatly enriched us by giving commentaries on the three canonical texts of Vedanta (the Brahma Sutras, Bhagavad Gīta and the Upanishads) while enriching us with numerous other compositions.

My deepest gratitude to my mother Smt. Savitri Neelakantan and father Late Sri. N. R. Neelakantan, for having ensured that I received sufficient exposure during my childhood to the culture and tradition of this land and for having ensured that chanting was a part of my upbringing.

I wish to express my sincere gratitude to my brother, N. N. Subramanian, for offering valuable suggestions from time to time. This book would not have been possible, but for my sister Mala Sridhar's painstaking efforts to review and proofread the contents meticulously.

Br. Prasanna Swaroopa

Notes to the Reader

- Throughout this book, the term Vedanta has been used to refer to the Advaita Vedanta school of philosophy.
- For every verse (in Sanskrit), a translation has been presented (in English). Therefore, even if you do not know Sanskrit, you can benefit from this book.
- In this book, only the translation of verses has been presented. As and when readers develop an interest in a particular text, they may look for that specific text along with detailed commentary on the text and the meaning of individual words.
- Abbreviations have been used in place of the full name of the text. For example, BG has been used to refer to the Bhagavad Gīta. Refer to the Appendix for the complete list of Abbreviations used in this book.
- Across the book, some Sanskrit terms have been used (with transliteration) because there are no equivalent words in English. (e.g., *samādhi*)
- For some of the frequently used terms (in Sanskrit), a section called 'Glossary' has been provided at the end of this book. This section explains the terms, rather than just giving a one-word meaning for the same.
- In the English translation across the book, usage of words like This, It, That, His and Supreme (with the first letter in capitals), refer to Brahman (the Supreme Reality).
- Care must be taken when mixing and matching concepts from different texts discussed in this book. There may be some subtle differences in the usage of these terms depending on the context.
- The third section of this book covers the following texts: Bhagavad Gīta, Kathopanishad, Muṇḍakopanishad, Ashtāvakra Samhita (also called Ashtāvakra Gīta), Avadhūta

Gīta and Vivekacūḍāmaṇi. Covering all these texts in full would have called for many volumes; hence, an abridged version of these texts, with selected verses, has been presented in this book.

- Knowledge of the Self (as discussed in Vedanta, the Upanishads) is attained by *shruti-yukti-anubhava. Shruti* refers to listening (or study); *yukti* refers to reason, and *anubhava* refers to one's own direct experience. This three-step process of the Vedantic pursuit has been discussed in the first section of this book.
- In certain places you will find that parentheses, i.e., '( )', have been used in the translation. This has been done to provide points that have been implied in the Sanskrit text and not mentioned. In some other places, brackets, i.e., '[ ]', have been used to provide additional notes. This is a general idea and may not have been strictly adhered to.
- Even though the text refers to 'he' or 'man' in some places, the reader may read this as applicable to both genders.

* * *

Contents

Section 4

Section 5

Section 6

Appendix

Introduction

Advaita Vedanta provides answers regarding the individual, creator, world and life. It guides seekers in leading a life of peace and happiness, unveiling the limitless potential within. It ultimately leads seekers on the path to liberation, i.e., everlasting peace and fulfilment.

Over the course of our culture's long history (i.e., in the context of Sanātana Dharma, popularly referred to as Hinduism), numerous authors have addressed the subject of spirituality in various ways based on their own experiences. Different philosophies evolved in due course of time, and thus numerous texts were written for each of the philosophies.

In the domain of Advaita Vedanta alone, there are hundreds of texts. Given this scenario, a spiritual seeker who is looking for guidance from the scriptures is faced with the following questions:

- What are the main texts?
- What is contained in these texts?
- Where do I begin the study of Vedanta?

Given the vastness of the landscape of the scriptures, this book is an attempt to provide answers to these questions.

This book focusses on Advaita Vedanta!

Why this book?

- The intention of this book is to provide some of the significant texts of Advaita Vedanta in one volume.
- There are many important ideas and concepts that form the foundation of Advaita Vedanta. This book presents selected verses from across different texts that explain these ideas.
- Everything is presented in the original voice of the scriptures, in Sanskrit, along with a translation in English.

- This book destroys the myths that there is something secretive hidden in the Upanishads and other texts and that the Advaita philosophy is somehow exclusively accessible to a few privileged groups of people.
- Since the reader has a first-hand exposure to what the scriptures have to say, mysteries and doubts regarding Advaita Vedanta should be well removed.
- Very importantly, this book has been compiled to be a constant companion and guide to any seeker, helping him/her through the entire journey on the spiritual path.

* * *

A Prayer

यतः सर्वाणि भूतानि प्रतिभान्ति स्थितानि च ।
यत्रैवोपशमं यान्ति तस्मै सत्यात्मने नमः ॥

Salutations to That (Supreme),
Who is of the nature of Truth,
From Whom all beings arise and become manifest,
In Whom all beings exist, and
In Whom all beings become extinct.

* * *

ज्ञाता ज्ञानं तथा ज्ञेयं द्रष्टा दर्शनदृश्यभूः ।
कर्ता हेतुः क्रिया यस्मात्तस्मै ज्ञस्यात्मने नमः ॥

Salutations to That (Supreme),
Who is of the nature of Pure Intelligence,
From Whom arise the Knower, Knowledge and the Known,
From Whom arise the Seer, the Seen and the Visible Universe, and
From Whom arise the Doer, the Cause and the Effect.

[*Source*: Yogavāsishtha 1.1.1-2]

* * *

Section 1

This section presents an introduction to the subject of Advaita Vedanta and discusses the three-step process of Vedantic pursuit.

1

What is Spirituality?

What is life?

We seek happiness through every interaction, activity, pursuit and situation. Whatever we seek must be in the context of our 'life'. For this, let us first try and understand LIFE.

As humans, we are not striving to answer this question in terms of the physiological definition of life. Instead, let's delve into life as a collection of 'experiences'.

We 'experience' life in terms of the following human emotions: happiness, sorrow, anxiety, fear, doubt, anger, kindness, compassion, jealousy, greed, envy and so on.

What gives rise to these experiences? Now, that gives us a clue to a perspective on how we can look at 'life'.

Life, in that sense, is a series of experiences resulting from:

- **Objects:** world of variety (of things) around us.
- **Situations** and challenges that the world presents.
- **Actions**, work and activities and their outcomes.
- **People** and the relationships and interactions that we have with them.
- **Thoughts**, feelings, etc., arising in the mind.
- **Desires**, expectations, aspirations and ambitions we have from the world around us.

Notion of Happiness Re-examined

In all the above experiences, we welcome ones that are favourable (what we like), and we avoid ones that are unfavourable (what we dislike). In every aspect of life, we want the favourable (agreeable) and shun the unfavourable (disagreeable).

Being humans, we want only one thing in this world–HAPPINESS. We may give it any other name, but eventually, that is the only thing we all want.

We believe happiness to be 'getting what we desire or getting what is favourable to us' and sorrow to be 'not getting what we desire or getting what is unfavourable'.

If we define happiness to be the state in which everything (viz. things, situations, activities and outcomes, people, desires) is always favourable to us, in that case, there is a good chance that happiness will be very elusive in life. In other words, if we expect that things will *always* be in our favour and we will *always* be happy, that will not happen.

Our World of Actions, Activities and Work

Right from setting foot in this world until our last breath, we are perpetually in action. There is not a second when we are not doing something. We may call it action, activity, work, endeavour, effort, project or anything else. At the most basic level, it is all 'action'.

Every action has an outcome or a result. Whenever an outcome is according to what we expect or desire, we call it success. And when the outcome is not as per our expectations, we call it a failure.

If we define success as something that makes us happy, we are likely to be unhappy often. This is because not every action will yield a favourable outcome.

In the context of work and activities, here are some of the problems we face:

- We end up being anxious much of the time, wanting favourable outcomes.
- The unexpected outcome makes us unhappy.
- The progress of the activity is not according to our expectations, and therefore, we are disturbed.
- The outcome is what we expected, but we do not get the rewards or recognition we feel we deserve. Therefore, we become unhappy.

- There are occasions when we get rewarded and recognized for the results, but we are disturbed because others, too, got rewarded for it.
- We face challenges or obstacles along the way, and they cause agitation.

These are just a few of the things that agitate us.

Afflictions are a Part of Life

In life, wc facc afflictions from the following (This is just a representative list):

- Since interactions with things, situations and people are not always favourable, we are left with an agitated mind.
- In the context of our actions or work (including the profession we engage in), we have numerous things that cause afflictions.
- Natural calamities (floods, volcanic eruptions, landslides, forest fires, etc.) result in the loss of lives and resources. We also face threats from other beings (including virus outbreaks).
- We also have bodily problems, viz. diseases and eventually death.
- Then, there are afflictions of the mind, like jealousy, greed, hatred, anger, fear, etc., that often leave the mind disturbed.

We experience most of the above problems and afflictions almost throughout life. No one in this world (irrespective of power and position) is free from these problems and the resultant agitation.

What are we Seeking in life?

We are constantly seeking the following:

- Happiness
- Freedom from suffering
- Freedom from other agitations of the mind
- Peace with everything and all
- Poise in interactions with the world around
- Joy at work and excellence in every endeavour

- Calmness in this diverse world of challenges

  Is this possible? Absolutely!

  The answer to 'HOW?' is provided by spirituality.

Spirituality addresses the following questions:

- How to attain the real goal of human life – freedom, liberation?
- How to be constantly free from agitations of the mind?
- How can one achieve a state of constant happiness and be free from suffering?
- How to realise the unlimited potential within us?
- How to attain freedom from all constrictions of the mind?
- How to realise one's true nature?

In short, spirituality shows us a practical way to cruise through life—with all its trials and tribulations—always remaining in a state of peace and equanimity.

Remember: The problems and challenges the world throws at us do not go away. But spirituality provides us with a way to remain in a state of peace and poise in and through all situations in life.

Note the following important points:

- All the experiences in life are seated in the mind.
- All the agitations and disturbances are but experiences in the mind.
- Peace and happiness, we seek, are also to be experienced in the mind alone.

When it comes to the realm of conquering the mind and realising the unlimited potential within, IT IS THE SAME MIND that makes it happen. The mind and intelligence are the levers we have to achieve this goal. In this pursuit, we are not dependent on the world around us; we do not need anything we don't already have.

Is it doable? Absolutely, and for everyone! No one is less qualified or more qualified. We all have equal access to that.

Some Myths regarding Spirituality

Myth – For the old and retired: Spirituality is a pursuit for those who have superannuated from active work life (profession, employment, etc.), and thus gives them something to occupy themselves with.

Correction: In fact, Spirituality means to be an excellent performer at whatever one does throughout life. Being exposed to this knowledge early helps us to navigate smoothly through life, even during its initial stages.

Myth – Give up family life: One cannot pursue the spiritual path while actively engaging in family life, having children, generating wealth, etc.

Correction: This is the biggest misconception. In fact, spirituality helps one face the challenges of household life with ease.

Myth – Join an ashram (monastery): Some think that to pursue spirituality wholesomely, one has to retire to a monastery, giving up all other pursuits.

Correction: Bhagavad Gīta, a beautiful handbook of life, talks about how Arjuna, a great warrior, is instructed on spiritual truths while remaining on the battlefield. More importantly, spiritual instructions were given to fight the war and not to get away from the war.

Myth – It is about mysticism: Certain individuals think spirituality is all about mysticism and gaining mystical powers, transcending ordinary understanding.

Correction: It is crucial to understand that spirituality is a rational pursuit of the mind and intelligence based on reason.

To Summarize:

Spirituality helps us:

- Lead a life of peace, free from worries
- Excel in every endeavour in life
- See and accept whatever the world throws at us without getting distressed

- Live in this world with an unagitated mind
- Be in a state of poise independent of the world around

'INDEPENDENT OF THE WORLD' is the key. The people, things and situations in the world around us may not change, but we can be in perfect peace with and in this world.

Being in complete control in this world and of all situations is all about being in complete control WITHIN, *independent of the world around.*

Is it possible?

Certainly, Vedanta shows us the way.

***

2

An Introduction to Vedanta

This chapter is an overview of the topic of Vedanta—a profound journey that essentially guides the seeker on the path to peace, happiness, fulfilment and, eventually, to liberation.

Meaning of the term 'Vedanta'

The word Vedanta literally means 'the end portion of the Vedas' [In Sanskrit, *Veda* = Veda, *anta* = end. Veda is the oldest scripture in Hinduism]. Vedanta refers to the wisdom of the Upanishads that form the end portion of the Vedas. It is also the 'culmination of all knowledge'. Vedanta is one of the six schools of philosophy in Hinduism in which Advaita (non-dual) Vedanta, Dvaita (dual) Vedanta, etc., are the different schools of Vedanta Philosophy.

Note that, in this book, the term Vedanta has been used to refer to the Advaita Vedanta.

In the Muṇḍaka Upanishad (1.1.3), a seeker presents the following question to his teacher: "What is that by knowing which all becomes known?" That is what the knowledge of Vedanta represents. This also suggests that there is nothing to be known beyond this. What is this knowledge? It is that knowledge (Self-knowledge or knowledge of the Self) by which the Supreme Truth is realised.

Aim of Vedanta

- To reveal our real nature to us.
- To show us a way to attain liberation (which is nothing but a state of eternal happiness, free from misery).
- To reveal to us the way to achieve contentment and fulfilment.

- To guide us in living a life that enables us to sail through challenges while maintaining a state of peace and equanimity.

The Scope of Vedanta

The various schools of Vedanta address the following:

- The cause of our suffering in the world
- The way to attain freedom from suffering
- Our true nature and identity
- The idea of the Ultimate Reality (Supreme Truth)
- The notion of liberation or freedom
- The role of body, mind, intelligence, sense organs
- The concept of the Self
- The notion of death and immortality
- The real nature of the world around
- The oneness of everything

Key points to note about Vedanta

- It is universal and rational in its approach and application.
- It is not an 'academic' philosophy but a practical approach to life.
- It is the knowledge that can be experienced at every step and need not be accepted just because the scriptures say so.
- Recognises that all paths lead to the same goal of liberation.
- Recognises that "the Truth is one; the wise express it variously".

Advaita Vedanta

Vedanta explores the true nature of the individual (*jīva*), Creator or God (*Īshvara*) and the world (*jagat*). In other words, it seeks to address the following questions:

- What is the true nature of the individual being?
- What is the true nature of the world or universe?
- What is the true nature of *Īshvara* (God)?
- What is the relationship between these three?

The term Advaita literally means non-duality. The essence of the philosophy of Advaita Vedanta is:

- Brahman (the Supreme Reality) alone is the one Reality
- The phenomenal universe is a mere appearance of Brahman
- The Individual Self is no different from Brahman.

In other words, Advaita addresses the identity or oneness of Brahman with the universe and the individual Self or the ONENESS of all existence.

The philosophy of Advaita is condensed in the following statement, by Adi Shankarāchārya:

ब्रह्म सत्यं जगन्मिथ्या जीवो ब्रह्मैव नापरः ।

"Brahman alone is truth, and the entire universe is a falsity. The individual Self is nothing but Brahman alone".

Canonical Texts

The following are the three *primary* sources of Vedantic knowledge:

1. Bhagavad Gīta: Contains the essence of all Upanishads.
2. Brahma Sutras: Presented as 500+ aphorisms.
3. Upanishads: More than 100 Upanishads are known to us today. Ten among them are referred to as principal Upanishads and are more popular.

These three are collectively referred to as Prasthānatrayī (literally 'three sources'), referring to the three canonical texts. Adi Shankarāchārya has written commentaries on the Bhagavad Gīta, Brahma Sutras and the ten principal Upanishads. Note that these are not the only texts on Vedanta; these three are the primary sources.

* * *

3

Three Steps in the Knowledge Pursuit of Vedanta

Vedanta (the wisdom of the Upanishads) addresses the knowledge about the nature of the individual human, the Supreme, the world and the relationship between these three. In this article, we discuss the steps in the process of realising the knowledge, as discussed in Brihadāraṇyaka Upanishad.

A typical situation in life

You have been experiencing fear on account of something and are unable to shake it off. When you look into the scriptures or seek guidance from someone, you learn that desires and attachment are the primary causes of fear. You have understood why you are so afraid and have found a ray of hope in getting rid of it. And in the days that follow, you feel just fine. However, after a few weeks, you find that you are back to square one with regard to fear.

The following thoughts come to mind: "I thought I had understood it very well. I felt I had finally figured out a way out of this constant fear. Even though I had understood it clearly, why am I not free from it. The knowledge I had acquired from the texts (or a person) was not having the desired result. Why?"

Not cognitive knowledge

In the context of external world phenomena, cognitive knowledge and understanding help us deal with them. But when it comes to knowledge regarding our inner personality and realising our true nature, cognition fails us in taking us all the way to the end.

This is not to say that cognition and reasoning are not important. We shall see the role of cognition in the knowledge pursuit. But for completely internalizing (or realising) this knowledge, we need to go beyond cognition. This internalising or realising is what we refer to (loosely) as 'becoming part of the DNA'.

I am not suggesting that it is a matter of faith or belief. It is something that everyone can experience. It is experiential!

While the above case referred to the idea of overcoming fear, in the Vedantic pursuit, we will be dealing with something far subtler than fear–the Self.

What is knowledge?

In spirituality, in the term 'knowledge pursuit', what is the meaning of 'knowledge'? Nirālamba Upanishad 24 gives us the meaning of knowledge, thus:

ज्ञानमिति च देहेन्द्रियनिग्रहसद्गुरूपासन-श्रवणमननिदिध्यासनैर्यद्यदृग्दृश्यस्वरूपं सर्वान्तरस्थं सर्वसमं घटपटादिपदार्थ-मिवाविकारं विकारेषु चैतन्यं विना किञ्चिन्नास्तीति साक्षात्कारानुभवो ज्ञानम् ।

"Knowledge is the direct realization that there is nothing other than Consciousness (Self). This Consciousness is of the nature of the seer (subject) and the seen (object), pervades everything in this universe, and is not subject to change like in the case of pots, clothes, etc. This direct realization is attained by restraining the body, senses and the mind, being in close association with a teacher, and by means of the process of listening, reflection and meditation".

In other words, knowledge is the 'knowledge of our true nature', i.e., the knowledge of the Self or the realisation that 'I am the Self'.

The Three-step Process

In the above statement, the Upanishad points out that knowledge is attained by 'listening, reflection and meditation'.

In the Brihadāraṇyaka Upanishad 2.4.5, 4.5.6, Yājñavalkya tells his wife Maitreyi:

"The Self alone is dear to all, dearer than anything else in this world. It is the only thing worth attaining. Therefore, the Self alone should be made the object of attainment in one's life".

Then, he says:

आत्मा वा अरे द्रष्टव्यः श्रोतव्यो मन्तव्यो निदिध्यासितव्यो मैत्रेयि, आत्मनो वा अरे दर्शनेन श्रवणेन मत्या विज्ञानेनेदं सर्वं विदितम् ॥

"O Maitreyi, the Self should be realized, should be heard of (from a preceptor and the scriptures), should be reflected upon and should be meditated upon. When the Self is realized, through the process of listening, reflection, and meditation, all this is known".

[**Note:** *The purport of 'all this is known' is that there is nothing more to be known, for everything is nothing but the Self.*]

What does 'all this is known' mean? In the very next statement, the Brihadāraṇyaka Upanishad (2.4.6) provides the answer:

"Everything–these worlds, these gods, these beings, and all these are nothing but the Self. For, everything arises from the Self, finds dissolution in and is the Self during its existence. There is nothing other than the Self. Everything is the Self".

Ātmabodha 66 says:

> "Having been heated in the fire of knowledge, kindled by the process of listening, reflection and meditation, the individual (*jīva*), is cleansed of all the impurities (in the form of desires in the mind) and shines by itself like gold".

Sarva-vedānta-siddhānta-sāra-sangrah 808-809 says:

> "Brahman (the Supreme Reality), that which is to be attained, which is spoken of in the Upanishads, is attained by subtle intellect. For those who do not have sharpness of subtle intellect, only by listening alone, and without constant practice of reflection and meditation, Brahman cannot be attained. Only by constantly devoting

oneself to listening, reflection and meditation is Brahman attained".

Let us now examine the three steps to Self-realisation (realisation of one's true nature):

1. *Shravaṇa* (hereafter referred to as Listening)
2. *Manana* (Reflection)
3. *Nididhyāsana* (Meditation)

Listening (*Shravaṇa*)

Vedānta-sāra 182 defines 'listening' thus:

श्रवणं नाम षड्विधलिङ्गैः अशेषवेदान्तानाम् अद्वितीयवस्तुनि तात्पर्यावधारणम् ॥

"The ascertainment of the purport of the statements of Vedanta (Upanishads), through six signs of knowledge that establishes the conviction in the non-dual Existence which is Brahman (Supreme Reality) is called listening" (The same idea is expressed in Sarva-vedānta-siddhānta-sāra-sangrah 811-812).

The six signs or characteristics of the texts that discuss this knowledge are: (1) commencement, introduction, conclusion and summing up; (2) repetition, practice; (3) uniqueness, unprecedented; (4) benefits of the text; (5) praise, eulogy regarding the text; (6) reason, proof, demonstration, evidence (These are discussed in Vedānta-sāra 183-190).

In Panchadashi 1.53, listening is defined thus: "Investigation (inquiry) and subsequent discovery of the purport of the statements of the Upanishads regarding one's true nature (i.e., regarding the Self and the Supreme) is referred to as listening".

The three primary sources of Vedantic knowledge are: (1) Bhagavad Gīta (2) Brahma Sutras (3) Upanishads. Though the term *shravaṇa* literally refers to 'listening', it essentially refers to the process of acquisition of knowledge through studying the scriptures and/or listening to the words of a preceptor.

For listening to be effective, it is important to have *shraddhā*, i.e., faith in the scriptures and in the words of the teacher.

Reflection (*Manana*)

"Scriptures are a burden to one who does not have the faculty of discrimination between the real and unreal. Knowledge is a burden to one who is attached", says Yoga-vāsishtha 1.14.13.

In this way, academic knowledge, i.e., mere listening to and studying the scriptures, is not enough. That is why reflection and meditation are critical.

Vedānta-sāra 191 defines 'reflection' thus:

मननं तु श्रुतस्य अद्वितीयवस्तुनः वेदान्तानुगुणयुक्तिभिः अनवरतम् अनुचिन्तनम् ॥

"Constantly introspecting over what has been listened to (from the preceptor and studied from the scriptures) about the non-dual Brahman (which is of the nature of the Self), by means of reasoning that is suitable to the statements of the Upanishads, is called reflection" (The same idea is expressed in Sarva-vedānta-siddhānta-sāra-sangrah 812-813).

"To establish by means of reason, the validity regarding what has been listened to (or studied), is called reflection". [Panchadashi 1. 53]

Thus, reflection is about deep introspection on the Self, resulting in conviction regarding our true nature (the Self). It is not just faith or belief. Reflection is supported by reason and removes all doubts.

The word 'reflect' originates from the Latin word which means "to bend back". And the word 'introspection' comes from the Latin word meaning "to look within".

Meditation (*Nididhyāsana*)

"The Self cannot be realised just by extensive study of the scriptures. Neither can it be attained by the capacity of the intellect (and by the retention power of memory) nor by listening to the expositions about the Self from the wise", says Kathopanishad 1.2.23.

Kenopanishad 1.3 says: "The eye does not go there (i.e., the Self cannot be perceived by the senses); speech does not go there (i.e., just by listening we cannot realise it); nor does the mind go there."

When listening and reflection of one's true nature (the Self) are effective, it will naturally lead us to the next step–meditation.

Vedānta-sāra 192 defines 'meditation' thus:

विजातीय-देहादि-प्रत्ययरहित-अद्वितीयवस्तु-सजातीय-प्रत्ययप्रवाहः निदिध्यासनम् ॥

"The steady flow of thoughts (like the uninterrupted flow of oil) regarding Brahman, to the exclusion of other thoughts alien to Brahman, like body, mind and anything else which is not the Self, is referred to as meditation. The mind should be completely absorbed in the Self, and be full with the Self" (The same idea is expressed in Sarva-vedānta-siddhānta-sāra-sangrah 813-814).

"Having brought the mind to a state of doubt-free conviction, by means of listening and reflection, to constantly establish the mind in the Self alone is called meditation". [Panchadashi 1. 54]

Through constant meditation upon the Self, one realises (attains) it.

If you ask, "What do I gain by realising the Self"? Here are the answers:

तरति शोकमात्मवित् ।

"The knower of the Self goes beyond sorrow". [Chandogya Upanishad 7.1.3]

सा विद्या या विमुक्तये ।

"Knowledge is that which liberates". [Vishnu-purana 1.19.41]

तमेव विदित्वाऽतिमृत्युमेति नान्यः पन्था विद्यतेऽयनाय ।

"Knowing Brahman alone, one transcends death; there is no other way". [Shvetāsvatara Upanishad 3.8]

The state that follows, where the meditator and the meditated upon become one, is described thus in Panchadashi 1.55:

"In meditation, there is the one who meditates, the act of meditation and the one meditated upon. When one gives up the idea of meditator and the act of meditation and becomes one with the object of meditation, that state is called Samādhi, which is like the flame of the lamp in a breezeless condition".

Conclusion

Knowledge of the Self (as discussed in Vedanta, the Upanishads) is attained by *shruti-yukti-anubhava*. *Shruti* refers to listening (or study); *yukti* refers to reason and *anubhava* refers to one's own direct experience.

This triad of *shruti-yukti-anubhava* relates to the three-step process that we discussed in this chapter. *Shruti* refers to the process of *shravaṇa* (listening). *Yukti* relates to the process of *manana* (introspection or reflection) and reason (*yukti*) is the means by which we attain conviction and become doubt-free. *Anubhava* relates to the process of *nididhyāsana* (meditation) and it is only through direct experience (*anubhava*) that we shall know that we have attained the goal of meditation.

* * *

Section 2

This section presents some of the commonly used peace invocations (*mantras*) from the Upanishads and their meanings.

4

Peace Invocation

(*Shānti Mantras*)

The Peace Invocation (or *Shānti Mantra*) is a prayer for peace. Any study of the scriptures or contemplation on the message of the texts is usually preceded by chanting of the peace invocations. This section presents some of the commonly used invocations from the Upanishads and their meanings.

These invocations:

- Remove agitation in the mind and have a soothing effect.
- Relieve the mind of any stress.
- Ready the mind and intellect for spiritual study.
- Prepare the mind for contemplation and meditation.
- Help the mind focus on the spiritual goal.
- Help the seeker integrate thoughts, speech and action.

When chanting these invocations, the word 'peace' is chanted thrice at the end. This is to remove the three kinds of afflictions of the human mind.

These afflictions are caused by the following factors:

आधिदैविक (*ādhidaivika*) – supernatural agencies

आधिभौतिक (*ādhibhautika*) – terrestrial beings, material things, the elements

आध्यात्मिक (*ādhyātmika*) – body, mind, intellect

ॐ असतो मा सद्गमय। तमसो मा ज्योतिर्गमय।
मृत्योर्मा अमृतं गमय। ॐ शान्तिः शान्तिः शान्तिः॥

Om. Lead. me from untruth to truth;
Lead me from darkness to light;
Lead me from death to immortality.
Om Peace. Peace. Peace.

[Brihadāraṇyaka Upanishad]

* * *

ॐ पूर्णमदः पूर्णमिदं पूर्णात्पूर्णमुदच्यते।
पूर्णस्य पूर्णमादाय पूर्णमेवावशिष्यते॥

Om. That (Supreme Brahman) is full.
This (the phenomenal universe) is full.
From that Brahman (which is full),
this fullness of the universe has emerged.
By removing the fullness from the infinite universe,
Brahman alone remains.

[Brihadāraṇyaka Upanishad]

* * *

ॐ सह नाववतु।
सह नौ भुनक्तु।
सह वीर्यं करवावहै।
तेजस्वि नावधीतमस्तु।
मा विद्विषावहै॥
ॐ शान्तिः शान्तिः शान्तिः॥

Om. May the Lord protect both of us.
May He nourish us both.
May we both strive with great vigour.

May our study be diligent and successful.
May we not hate each other.
Om. Peace! Peace! Peace!

(*NOTE: 'Both' here usually refers to the teacher and the taught.*)

[Katha Upanishad]

* * *

ॐ भद्रं कर्णेभिः शृणुयाम देवाः
भद्रं पश्येमाक्षभिर्यजत्राः ।
स्थिरैरङ्गैः तुष्टुवांसस्तनूभिः
व्यशेम देवहितं यदायुः ।
स्वस्ति न इन्द्रो वृद्धश्रवाः
स्वस्ति नः पूषा विश्ववेदाः ।
स्वस्ति नस्तार्क्ष्यो अरिष्टनेमिः
स्वस्ति नो बृहस्पतिर्दधातु ॥
ॐ शान्तिः शान्तिः शान्तिः ॥

Om! O Deities! With our ears, may we hear
what is auspicious!
O Deities who are worthy of worship!
With our eyes, may we see what is auspicious!
Possessed with bodies with firm and healthy limbs,
Praising Gods, may we live the life obtained,
In a manner beneficial to the divine forces!
May Indra, of great glories, bestow wellbeing on us!
May the all-knowing Pushān (Sun God)
Bestow wellbeing to us!
May Garuda, who protects from evil or harm,
Bestow wellbeing to us!
May Brihaspati, the Preceptor of Devas,

Bestow auspiciousness on us.
Om. Peace! Peace! Peace!

[Muṇḍaka Upanishad]

***

ॐ आप्यायन्तु ममाङ्गानि
वाक्प्राणश्चक्षुः श्रोत्रमथो बलमिन्द्रियाणि च सर्वाणि
सर्वं ब्रह्मौपनिषदं माहं ब्रह्म निराकुर्यां
मा मा ब्रह्म निराकरोत् अनिराकरणमस्तु अनिराकरणं मेऽस्तु
तदात्मनि निरते य उपनिषत्सु
धर्मास्ते मयि सन्तु
ते मयि सन्तु ॥
ॐ शान्तिः शान्तिः शान्तिः ॥

Om! May my limbs be strong;
Likewise, may my speech, life forces, vital energy,
Eyes, ears, vitality and all sense organs be strong.
All of existence is Brahman, mentioned in the Upanishads.
May I not reject Brahman.
May Brahman not reject me.
May there be acceptance by Brahman of me.
May there be acceptance of Brahman by me.
May the values which are proclaimed in the Upanishads,
Reside in me, who is established in the Self.
May they be in me.
Om! Peace! Peace! Peace!

[Kena Upanishad]

ॐ वाङ् मे मनसि प्रतिष्ठिता
मनो मे वाचि प्रतिष्ठितम् ।
आविरावीर्म एधि ।

वेदस्य म आणीस्थः श्रुतं मे मा प्रहासीः ।
अनेनाधीतेनाहोरात्रान् सन्दधामि ।
ऋतं वदिष्यामि सत्यं वदिष्यामि ।
तन्मामवतु तद्वक्तारमवतु ।
अवतु मामवतु वक्तारमवतु वक्तारम् ॥
ॐ शान्तिः शान्तिः शान्तिः॥

Om! May my speech be based on the mind
(i.e., may my speech be in accordance with the thoughts);
May my mind be based on the speech.
O Self-effulgent Supreme! May You reveal Yourself to me.
O speech and mind! May you bring the Vedas (and Upanishads) unto me.
May what I have heard never leave me.
May I join day and night through my study (of the scriptures).
(i.e., may my study continue day and night.)
May I be honest in my speech. May I be truthful in the mind.
May That Brahman protect me.
May That Brahman protect the speaker (the teacher).
May That Brahman protect the speaker.

[Aitareya Upanishad]

***

Section 3

This section presents selected verses
from the following six texts on Advaita Vedanta:

Bhagavad Gīta
Kathopanishad
Muṇḍakopanishad
Vivekacūḍāmaṇi
Ashtāvakra Samhita
Avadhūta Gīta

5

Bhagavad Gīta

(श्रीमद्भगवद्गीता)

Abridged Bhagavad Gīta

Bhagavad Gīta is a dialogue between Sri Krishna and Arjuna that took place on the battlefield of Kurukshetra. The following selected verses are the words of Sri Krishna.

मात्रास्पर्शास्तु कौन्तेय शीतोष्णसुखदुःखदाः ।
आगमापायिनोऽनित्यास्तांस्तितिक्षस्व भारत ॥ 2.14 ॥

The contact of the five senses (vision, hearing, smell, touch, taste) with the objects of the world gives rise to pairs of opposites like cold and heat, happiness and sorrow. These experiences and the resultant feelings come and go, being transient in nature. Forbear them. [The term 'object' includes things, situations, relationships, events, material resources, wealth, etc.]

यं हि न व्यथयन्त्येते पुरुषं पुरुषर्षभ ।
समदुःखसुखं धीरं सोऽमृतत्वाय कल्पते ॥ 2.15 ॥

O Arjuna, the wise one who is indeed not afflicted by these pairs of opposites (feelings of cold and heat, etc.) and to whom pain and pleasure (or sorrow and happiness) are alike, becomes fit for immortality.

नासतो विद्यते भावो नाभावो विद्यते सतः ।
उभयोरपि दृष्टोऽन्तः त्वनयोस्तत्त्वदर्शिभिः ॥ 2.16 ॥

The unreal never comes into existence. The real never goes out of existence. The knowers of the Supreme Truth indeed perceive the certainty or nature of these two.

अविनाशि तु तद्विद्धि येन सर्वमिदं ततम् ।
विनाशमव्ययस्यास्य न कश्चित्कर्तुमर्हति ॥ 2.17 ॥

Know that, the one by which all this is pervaded is indestructible. None can bring about the destruction of this Imperishable entity.

य एनं वेत्ति हन्तारं यश्चैनं मन्यते हतम् ।
उभौ तौ न विजानीतो नायं हन्ति न हन्यते ॥ 2.19 ॥

One who knows this (Self) to be the slayer, and one who thinks this (Self) to be slain or destroyed, both these do not know well. This (Self) neither kills nor is killed.

न जायते म्रियते वा कदाचिन्
नायं भूत्वा भविता वा न भूयः ।
अजो नित्यः शाश्वतोऽयं पुराणो
न हन्यते हन्यमाने शरीरे ॥ 2.20 ॥

The Self is neither born nor does it ever die. It is not that, being non-existent, it comes into existence. Then again, it is not that being in existence, it becomes non-existent. The Self is unborn, eternal, everlasting, ever-fresh (in the past, present and future) and is not killed even when the body is destroyed. [There are six kinds of modifications (changes) that apply to matter: is born, exists, grows, changes, decays and dies. These do not apply to the Self.]

वासांसि जीर्णानि यथा विहाय
नवानि गृह्णाति नरोऽपराणि ।
तथा शरीराणि विहाय जीर्णा-
न्यन्यानि संयाति नवानि देही ॥ 2.22 ॥

Just as the human sets aside old or worn-out clothes (dresses) and takes on (wears) others that are new, in the same manner, the embodied Self casts aside worn-out bodies and takes up (enters) others that are new.

अव्यक्तोऽयमचिन्त्योऽयमविकार्योऽयमुच्यते ।
तस्मादेवं विदित्वैनं नानुशोचितुमर्हसि ॥ 2.25 ॥

This (Self) is said to be inaccessible to the senses; This (Self) is unattainable by thought; This (Self) is unchanging (i.e., devoid of any change). Therefore, knowing the Self to be thus (as spoken above), you should not grieve (thinking that "I will kill them" or "they will be killed by me", etc.).

जातस्य हि ध्रुवो मृत्युर्ध्रुवं जन्म मृतस्य च ।
तस्मादपरिहार्येऽर्थे न त्वं शोचितुमर्हसि ॥ 2.27 ॥

Death is inevitable for the one that is born; for the one that is dead, birth is certain. Therefore, in something that is inevitable (and unavoidable), you ought not to grieve.

सुखदुःखे समे कृत्वा लाभालाभौ जयाजयौ ।
ततो युद्धाय युज्यस्व नैवं पापमवाप्स्यसि ॥ 2.38 ॥

Treating alike the pairs of opposites–happiness and sorrow, gain and loss and victory and defeat–get ready for battle. This way, you will not incur any sin.

नेहाभिक्रमनाशोऽस्ति प्रत्यवायो न विद्यते ।
स्वल्पमप्यस्य धर्मस्य त्रायते महतो भयात् ॥ 2.40 ॥

In this (in karma yoga), there is no wastage of any effort (even if not pursued to its end). Also, there is no contrary result (i.e., no adverse result comes about, which otherwise might happen in case of incomplete action). Observing even a bit of this dharma (yoga) will protect one from great fear.

त्रैगुण्यविषया वेदा निस्त्रैगुण्यो भवार्जुन ।
निर्द्वन्द्वो नित्यसत्त्वस्थो निर्योगक्षेम आत्मवान् ॥ 2.45 ॥

The Vedas are the subject matter of the three *guṇas* (*sattva*, *rajas*, *tamas*). O Arjuna! Be free from these three *guṇas* (i.e., be desireless); be free from the pairs of opposites (causing pleasure and pain); be ever-established in *sattva-guṇas*; be free from the endeavour of acquisition and preservation and be ever-established in the Self.

यावानर्थ उदपाने सर्वतः सम्प्लुतोदके ।
तावान्सर्वेषु वेदेषु ब्राह्मणस्य विजानतः ॥ 2.46 ॥

To the wise one who has known the Self, all the Vedas (i.e., the rituals prescribed for achieving various objectives in life) are as much use just as the utility of a well (or a small tank of water) when the place is filled with water in every direction.

कर्मण्येवाधिकारस्ते मा फलेषु कदाचन ।
मा कर्मफलहेतुर्भूर्मा ते सङ्गोऽस्त्वकर्मणि ॥ 2.47 ॥

Do not get attached to the action or its result. Your right is to the performance of the action alone. Let the fruits of action not be your motive to act. Perform the action without any desire to enjoy the fruits of action. When any action is performed, the outcome will follow, whether you think about the outcome or not. Also, do not become attached to inaction.

योगस्थः कुरु कर्माणि सङ्गं त्यक्त्वा धनञ्जय ।
सिद्ध्यसिद्ध्योः समो भूत्वा समत्वं योग उच्यते ॥ 2.48 ॥

O Arjuna! Perform all actions being established in yoga (as described in 2.47), giving up all attachment and treating success and failure alike. This evenness of the mind is called yoga.

बुद्धियुक्तो जहातीह उभे सुकृतदुष्कृते ।
तस्माद्योगाय युज्यस्व योगः कर्मसु कौशलम् ॥ 2.50 ॥

One who is endowed with the attitude of evenness (in pleasure and pain) gives up the idea (preference) of meritorious and evil deeds here, in this life itself (having the attitude of karma-yoga). Therefore, embrace the attitude of Yoga. Yoga is the very skill (which is equanimity in success and failure) for all actions.

श्रुतिविप्रतिपन्ना ते यदा स्थास्यति निश्चला ।
समाधावचला बुद्धिस्तदा योगमवाप्स्यसि ॥ 2.53 ॥

The mind gets perplexed by the conflicting opinions heard (read) regarding the varying tenets which explain the different aims in life and the means to attain them. Only when your mind stops being uncertain and bewildered from wandering in different directions and becomes fixed and steady and remains established in the Self (without distraction or doubt), then you will attain yoga or *samādhi* (where the mind is established in the Self).

प्रजहाति यदा कामान्सर्वान्पार्थ मनोगतान् ।
आत्मन्येवात्मना तुष्टः स्थितप्रज्ञस्तदोच्यते ॥ 2.55 ॥

O Arjuna, when one thoroughly casts off all desires that have taken root in the mind and becomes (and remains) content in the Self, by oneself without any dependence on external possessions, then he is said to be wise—one of established wisdom (in whom the awareness born of discrimination between the Real and unreal is firmly established).

दुःखेष्वनुद्विग्नमनाः सुखेषु विगतस्पृहः ।
वीतरागभयक्रोधः स्थितधीर्मुनिरुच्यते ॥ 2.56 ॥

One, whose mind is free from apprehension or disturbance and does not lose its equilibrium in the face of difficulties or adversities, who is free from hankering and covetousness in pleasures or happiness, and is free from attachment, fear and anger, then such a one is said to be of steady wisdom.

ध्यायतो विषयान्पुंसः सङ्गस्तेषूपजायते ।
सङ्गात्सञ्जायते कामः कामात्क्रोधोऽभिजायते ॥ 2.62 ॥

क्रोधाद्भवति सम्मोहः सम्मोहात्स्मृतिविभ्रमः ।
स्मृतिभ्रंशाद् बुद्धिनाशो बुद्धिनाशात्प्रणश्यति ॥ 2.63 ॥

In the case of the human being, thinking or brooding over objects of the senses leads to attachment with the objects;

from attachment arises longing or craving for the objects; from longing, anger is born; from anger arises delusion or wrong perception of the world (from lack of discrimination); from delusion, arises loss (or disturbance) of memory (regarding the spiritual goal); from the loss of memory arises destruction of reason (ability to discern right and wrong); finally from destruction of reason and understanding, the human being falls (and is unable to acquire the real object of human life).

रागद्वेषवियुक्तैस्तु विषयानिन्द्रियैश्चरन् ।
आत्मवश्यैर्विधेयात्मा प्रसादमधिगच्छति ॥ 2.64 ॥

The one in whom the mind and intelligence are in control, free from likes and dislikes (attachment and aversion), and with the senses under control though active in the world around, attains tranquility of the mind.

प्रसादे सर्वदुःखानां हानिरस्योपजायते ।
प्रसन्नचेतसो ह्याशु बुद्धिः पर्यवतिष्ठते ॥ 2.65 ॥

On attaining tranquility, there are no miseries or suffering due to unfavourable or sorrowful situations. Of such a one, whose mind is calm and serene, soon the intellect becomes steady and remains in equilibrium, firmly established in the Self.

या निशा सर्वभूतानां तस्यां जागर्ति संयमी ।
यस्यां जाग्रति भूतानि सा निशा पश्यतो मुनेः ॥ 2.69 ॥

That which is night for all the beings, in that the Self-restrained one is awake. In which the beings are awake, that is night for the wise one who has perceived the Supreme Reality.

आपूर्यमाणमचलप्रतिष्ठं
समुद्रमापः प्रविशन्ति यद्वत् ।
तद्वत्कामा यं प्रविशन्ति सर्वे
स शान्तिमाप्नोति न कामकामी ॥ 2.70 ॥

The ocean, which is firm, still and filled with water from all sides, continues to remain so without any change, even when the water of the various rivers flow into the ocean. In the same manner, one in whom, though remaining amidst the world of objects of senses, all desires come and dissolve without causing any change, such a one attains peace and not the one who constantly seeks enjoyment from the objects of the world.

विहाय कामान्यः सर्वान्पुमांश्चरति निःस्पृहः ।
निर्ममो निरहङ्कारः स शान्तिमधिगच्छति ॥ 2.71 ॥

Having abandoned all desires, the person who lives in this world free from longing and covetousness, free from the sense of "this is mine" (even regarding bare necessities of life), and free from egoism (sense of 'I'), such a one attains peace (leading to cessation of any suffering).

एषा ब्राह्मी स्थितिः पार्थ नैनां प्राप्य विमुह्यति ।
स्थित्वास्यामन्तकालेऽपि ब्रह्मनिर्वाणमृच्छति ॥ 2.72 ॥

This (as described thus far) is the state of Brahman, O Arjuna, having attained which, one is no longer deluded. Remaining in this state, even in the last stage of one's life, one attains oneness with the Supreme (liberation).

न कर्मणामनारम्भान्नैष्कर्म्यं पुरुषोऽश्नुते ।
न च संन्यसनादेव सिद्धिं समधिगच्छति ॥ 3.4 ॥

By just non-performance of action (secular or religious), one does not attain 'freedom from action' (*naishkarmya*). And by mere renunciation of action (without knowledge of the Self), one does not attain fruition ('freedom from action'). [It is the action that leads one to the purity of the mind, and that alone leads one to realise the true nature of the Self, i.e., actionlessness.]

न हि कश्चित्क्षणमपि जातु तिष्ठत्यकर्मकृत् ।
कार्यते ह्यवशः कर्म सर्वः प्रकृतिजैर्गुणैः ॥ 3.5 ॥

None can remain inactive, even for a moment. Because all are helplessly impelled to perform action by their respective *guṇas* (*sattva, rajas, tamas*) born of *Prakriti* (Nature).

यस्त्विन्द्रियाणि मनसा नियम्यारभतेऽर्जुन ।
कर्मेन्द्रियैः कर्मयोगमसक्तः स विशिष्यते ॥ 3.7 ॥

But, restraining the sense organs by the mind, the one who undertakes action by means of the organs of action (speech, hands, legs, anus and the genitals), governed by karma yoga, unattached (to the action and its outcome), such a one excels.

यस्त्वात्मरतिरेव स्यादात्मतृप्तश्च मानवः ।
आत्मन्येव च सन्तुष्टस्तस्य कार्यं न विद्यते ॥ 3.17 ॥

The one who delights in the Self alone (one who is completely devoted to Self-knowledge) and not in the objects of the senses, who is satisfied with the Self and does not go after the objects for satisfaction, and who is content in the Self, having realized that objects of the world cannot bestow happiness–for such a one who has realized the Self, there is nothing to be done in this world (i.e., there is nothing by way of responsibility, duty, etc.).

प्रकृतेः क्रियमाणानि गुणैः कर्माणि सर्वशः ।
अहङ्कारविमूढात्मा कर्ताहमिति मन्यते ॥ 3.27 ॥

All actions are executed by the *guṇas* (*sattva, rajas, tamas*) of Nature. One who is deluded by egoism thinks, "I am the doer". [The identification of the Self with the body-mind-senses aggregate is referred to as egoism.]

मयि सर्वाणि कर्माणि संन्यस्याध्यात्मचेतसा ।
निराशीर्निर्ममो भूत्वा युध्यस्व विगतज्वरः ॥ 3.30 ॥

Renouncing all actions unto Me, the Supreme (i.e., performing them as an offering to Me), with the mind established in the Self, without any expectations, and free from the sense of "this is mine", you must fight being free from affliction and anguish.

सदृशं चेष्टते स्वस्याः प्रकृतेर्ज्ञानवानपि ।
प्रकृतिं यान्ति भूतानि निग्रहः किं करिष्यति ॥ 3.33 ॥

Even a wise one (the one who has realised the knowledge of the Self) acts in accordance with his/her own nature. All beings are constantly under the influence of their own nature. What can restraint do?

इन्द्रियाणि पराण्याहुरिन्द्रियेभ्यः परं मनः ।
मनसस्तु परा बुद्धिर्यो बुद्धेः परतस्तु सः ॥ 3.42 ॥

The five senses (vision, hearing, etc.) are considered superior to (subtler than) the body, which is gross; the mind is superior to the senses, and the intellect is superior to the mind. The Self (the witness to the mind and intellect) is superior to (subtler than) the intellect. [Thus, knowing the Self to be superior to all, restrain the mind and senses, and become free from desires.]

वीतरागभयक्रोधा मन्मया मामुपाश्रिताः ।
बहवो ज्ञानतपसा पूता मद्भावमागताः ॥ 4.10 ॥

Freed from attachment, fear and anger, completely established in Me (i.e., who have realised the Supreme), having taken refuge in Me (i.e., being completely established in the Supreme) and purified by the fire of knowledge of the Supreme Truth, many have attained Me.

कर्मण्यकर्म यः पश्येदकर्मणि च कर्म यः ।
स बुद्धिमान्मनुष्येषु स युक्तः कृत्स्नकर्मकृत् ॥ 4.18 ॥

One who sees inaction in action, and one who sees action in inaction, is wise among humans and the real performer of actions.

यस्य सर्वे समारम्भाः कामसङ्कल्पवर्जिताः ।
ज्ञानाग्निदग्धकर्माणं तमाहुः पण्डितं बुधाः ॥ 4.19 ॥

One whose (defined in verse 4.18) all undertakings are free from desire and motives, and whose actions have been burnt by the fire of knowledge, the sages call that one a wise person.

त्यक्त्वा कर्मफलासङ्गं नित्यतृप्तो निराश्रयः ।
कर्मण्यभिप्रवृत्तोऽपि नैव किञ्चित्करोति सः ॥ 4.20 ॥

Giving up any attachment to the fruits of action, ever-content, free from any dependence on anything, even though engaged in action, such a one indeed does nothing at all.

निराशीर्यतचित्तात्मा त्यक्तसर्वपरिग्रहः ।
शारीरं केवलं कर्म कुर्वन्नाप्नोति किल्बिषम् ॥ 4.21 ॥

One who is free from desires, whose body, senses and mind are in control, and who has renounced all possessions, though performing bodily actions, does not incur any sin.

यदृच्छालाभसन्तुष्टो द्वन्द्वातीतो विमत्सरः ।
समः सिद्धावसिद्धौ च कृत्वापि न निबध्यते ॥ 4.22 ॥

Being content with whatever comes unsought, being free from the pairs of opposites (like happiness-sorrow, like-dislikes, favourable-unfavourable), being free from envy, and being even-minded in success and failure–such a one is free even though performing any action and does not become bound.

गतसङ्गस्य मुक्तस्य ज्ञानावस्थितचेतसः ।
यज्ञायाचरतः कर्म समग्रं प्रविलीयते ॥ 4.23 ॥

The action (karma) together with the results are dissolved of the one who is liberated, who is free from attachments, whose mind is abiding in the knowledge of the Self, and whose all undertakings are performed as a sacrifice (offering).

ब्रह्मार्पणं ब्रह्म हविर्ब्रह्माग्नौ ब्रह्मणा हुतम् ।
ब्रह्मैव तेन गन्तव्यं ब्रह्मकर्मसमाधिना ॥ 4.24 ॥

The instrument (e.g., ladle) by which the oblation is poured into the fire is Brahman (the Supreme Reality). The oblation poured into fire (e.g., clarified butter) is also Brahman. The one performing the sacrifice (pouring the oblation) is Brahman. The oblation is being poured into the fire that is nothing but Brahman. The act of pouring the oblation into the fire is also Brahman. Thus, by the performer who is absorbed in the performance, which is Brahman, the goal of Brahman alone is attained.

श्रेयान्द्रव्यमयाद्यज्ञाज्ज्ञानयज्ञः परन्तप ।
सर्वं कर्माखिलं पार्थ ज्ञाने परिसमाप्यते ॥ 4.33 ॥

Sacrifice (*yajña*) in the form of knowledge pursuit (involving listening, study, reflection, meditation, etc., regarding knowledge of the Self) is referred to as *jñāna-yajña* (or knowledge-sacrifice). *Jñāna-yajña* is superior to sacrifice performed using various material means. (This is because sacrifice performed with material objects results in bondage.) O Arjuna, all actions ultimately culminate in knowledge alone (for knowledge is the means to liberation).

यथैधांसि समिद्धोऽग्निः भस्मसात्कुरुतेऽर्जुन ।
ज्ञानाग्निः सर्वकर्माणि भस्मसात्कुरुते तथा ॥ 4.37 ॥

O Arjuna, just as well-kindled fire burns and reduces fuel (firewood, etc.) to ashes, in the same manner, the fire of the knowledge of the Self reduces all karma to ashes. [Reducing karma to ashes: Any action, because of attachment, results in *prārabdha*, *sanchita* and *āgāmi* karma. Knowledge burns all of *sanchita* and *āgāmi* karma to ashes.]

न हि ज्ञानेन सदृशं पवित्रमिह विद्यते ।
तत्स्वयं योगसंसिद्धः कालेनात्मनि विन्दति ॥ 4.38 ॥

There indeed exists nothing in this world that is purifying like knowledge. In the course of time, one who has attained success in karma yoga attains that knowledge oneself in one's own self.

श्रद्धावाँल्लभते ज्ञानं तत्परः संयतेन्द्रियः ।
ज्ञानं लब्ध्वा परां शान्तिमचिरेणाधिगच्छति ॥ 4.39 ॥

One fully endowed with *shraddhā*, fully devoted and who has fully restrained the senses attains knowledge. Having attained the knowledge, very soon, he/she attains supreme peace.

नैव किञ्चित्करोमीति युक्तो मन्येत तत्त्ववित् ।
पश्यञ्शृण्वन्स्पृशञ्जिघ्रन्नश्नन्गच्छन्स्वपञ्श्वसन् ॥ 5.8 ॥

प्रलपन्विसृजन्गृह्णन्नुन्मिषन्निमिषन्नपि ।
इन्द्रियाणीन्द्रियार्थेषु वर्तन्त इति धारयन् ॥ 5.9 ॥

Even though engaged in seeing, listening, touching, smelling, eating, moving, sleeping, breathing, speaking, releasing, holding and opening and closing the eyes–the one who has realised the Self, being established in the Self, thinks, "I do nothing at all", with the attitude (mindset) that only the sense organs are moving among the objects of the world.

ब्रह्मण्याधाय कर्माणि सङ्गं त्यक्त्वा करोति यः ।
लिप्यते न स पापेन पद्मपत्रमिवाम्भसा ॥ 5.10 ॥

One who performs all actions, giving up attachment and having offered them to Brahman (offered them to God), is not tainted by any sin, just as a lotus leaf is not smeared by water.

न कर्तृत्वं न कर्माणि लोकस्य सृजति प्रभुः ।
न कर्मफलसंयोगं स्वभावस्तु प्रवर्तते ॥ 5.14 ॥

Neither the state of being the performer or author of anything, nor the actions, nor the connection between action and its fruits or results of the people are created by the Lord. One's own nature prevails in this regard.

न प्रहृष्येत्प्रियं प्राप्य नोद्विजेत्प्राप्य चाप्रियम् ।
स्थिरबुद्धिरसम्मूढो ब्रह्मविद् ब्रह्मणि स्थितः ॥ 5.20 ॥

The knower of Brahman (the one who has realised the omnipresent Brahman), being established in Brahman, with steady and unwavering understanding (that the Self in all beings is one) and free from delusion, does not exult (rejoice) on obtaining something pleasant and also does not grieve on getting something unpleasant.

ये हि संस्पर्शजा भोगा दुःखयोनय एव ते ।
आद्यन्तवन्तः कौन्तेय न तेषु रमते बुधः ॥ 5.22 ॥

O Arjuna, all enjoyments born of contacts with objects of the world are generators of sorrow alone and have a beginning and an end. The wise one does not delight in them.

शक्नोतीहैव यः सोढुं प्राक्शरीरविमोक्षणात् ।
कामक्रोधोद्भवं वेगं स युक्तः स सुखी नरः ॥ 5.23 ॥

The one who is able to overcome the agitations or impulses arising from desires and anger before dropping the body is a yogi. Such a one is happy.

योऽन्तःसुखोऽन्तरारामस्तथान्तर्ज्योतिरेव यः ।
स योगी ब्रह्मनिर्वाणं ब्रह्मभूतोऽधिगच्छति ॥ 5.24 ॥

The one who finds happiness in the Self, the one who delights (rejoices) in the Self and whose Self alone is the light (effulgence), such a yogi, becoming Brahman (the Supreme Reality), attains liberation (attains the bliss of Brahman).

यदा हि नेन्द्रियार्थेषु न कर्मस्वनुषज्जते ।
सर्वसङ्कल्पसंन्यासी योगारूढस्तदोच्यते ॥ 6.4 ॥

When an individual is neither attached to the objects of the senses nor is attached to the actions performed (or their results) and has renounced all intentions or volitions (in the form of desires that lead to actions), such a one is said to have attained yoga.

उद्धरेदात्मनात्मानं नात्मानमवसादयेत् ।
आत्मैव ह्यात्मनो बन्धुरात्मैव रिपुरात्मनः ॥ 6.5 ॥

The seeker should lift oneself (from the chains and sufferings in life) by one's own self. The seeker should not weaken or degrade oneself; i.e., one should not be the cause of one's own downfall, trapped and continuing to suffer in this world. Lifting oneself would mean lifting oneself from the 'limited' identity to realizing the 'infinite' identity of oneself, which is free and unbounded. The self alone is one's friend, for there is no other friend in the world who can raise one trapped in bondage. And the self alone is the enemy of oneself.

ज्ञानविज्ञानतृप्तात्मा कूटस्थो विजितेन्द्रियः ।
युक्त इत्युच्यते योगी समलोष्टाश्मकाञ्चनः ॥ 6.8 ॥

The one who is satiated (i.e., nothing more is to be known) with knowledge (of the Self) and in the personal experience (realisation), who is unshaken (well-established in the knowledge), who has conquered the senses and to whom a lump of clay, a stone and gold are the same, such a one is a yogi.

सुहृन्मित्रार्युदासीनमध्यस्थद्वेष्यबन्धुषु ।
साधुष्वपि च पापेषु समबुद्धिर्विशिष्यते ॥ 6.9 ॥

Such a one (among the yogis) excels (is liberated) who is of equal vision (equanimous) towards the following: the good-hearted (well-wishers), friends, foes, the indifferent (strangers), the ones who are neutral, the hateful ones, the relatives, the virtuous and the sinful.

तत्रैकाग्रं मनः कृत्वा यतचित्तेन्द्रियक्रियः ।
उपविश्यासने युञ्ज्याद्योगमात्मविशुद्धये ॥ 6.12 ॥

Seated comfortably (on a seat and in a comfortable posture), making the mind one-pointed and withdrawing the mind and the senses (and restraining them), one should practise yoga for the purification of the mind.

शनैः शनैरुपरमेद् बुद्ध्या धृतिगृहीतया ।
आत्मसंस्थं मनः कृत्वा न किञ्चिदपि चिन्तयेत् ॥ 6.25 ॥

Gradually withdraw, by means of understanding and reason, endowed with the steadiness of the intellect and establish the mind completely in the Self. (The idea of gradually means with gradual practice imbued with patience). And the seeker should not think of anything else. "Establish the mind in the Self" means the Self is everything, and there is nothing else to be thought of. If the mind wanders away, let the seeker restrain the mind and bring it under the control of the Self.

सर्वभूतस्थमात्मानं सर्वभूतानि चात्मनि ।
ईक्षते योगयुक्तात्मा सर्वत्र समदर्शनः ॥ 6.29 ॥

With the mind steadfast in yoga and with the vision of oneness everywhere (regarding everything), he perceives the Self as abiding in all beings and all beings (everything) abiding in one's own Self.

यो मां पश्यति सर्वत्र सर्वं च मयि पश्यति ।
तस्याहं न प्रणश्यामि स च मे न प्रणश्यति ॥ 6.30 ॥

One who sees Me in all beings and sees all beings in Me, I am never separated from such a one, and he is never separated from Me.

सर्वभूतस्थितं यो मां भजत्येकत्वमास्थितः ।
सर्वथा वर्तमानोऽपि स योगी मयि वर्तते ॥ 6.31 ॥

Always abiding in the oneness, one who worships Me residing in all beings that yogi abides in Me, even though adopting any mode of life.

आत्मौपम्येन सर्वत्र समं पश्यति योऽर्जुन ।
सुखं वा यदि वा दुःखं स योगी परमो मतः ॥ 6.32 ॥

One who sees the pleasure and pain in every other being by the same standards as one sees in oneself, that yogi (wise one) is considered supreme. [In other words, just as pain is disagreeable to me, it will also be disagreeable to other beings. Similarly, just as pleasure is delightful to me, it will be pleasing to others too.]

यो यो यां यां तनुं भक्तः श्रद्धयार्चितुमिच्छति ।
तस्य तस्याचलां श्रद्धां तामेव विदधाम्यहम् ॥ 7.21 ॥

Whoever wants to worship whichever form of deities or gods (depending on their natural tendencies or preferences) with *shraddhā*, I make the *shraddhā* of that devotee unwavering (firm).

अव्यक्तोऽक्षर इत्युक्तस्तमाहुः परमां गतिम् ।
यं प्राप्य न निवर्तन्ते तद्धाम परमं मम ॥ 8.21 ॥

That which is said to be unmanifested and imperishable is alone considered the supreme abode (highest goal). Having attained that goal, none returns to the state of suffering in this worldly existence. That is My supreme abode.

अवजानन्ति मां मूढा मानुषीं तनुमाश्रितम् ।
परं भावमजानन्तो मम भूतमहेश्वरम् ॥ 9.11 ॥

Not knowing My supreme state as the Universal Self of all beings, some who lack discrimination (between the real and unreal) disregard Me, dwelling in the human form (body).

अनन्याश्चिन्तयन्तो मां ये जनाः पर्युपासते ।
तेषां नित्याभियुक्तानां योगक्षेमं वहाम्यहम् ॥ 9.22 ॥

Those individuals who think of Me, considering Me as the Supreme Being, as not separate from one's own Self and worship Me, to them (who have perceived the Supreme Reality), ever steadfast, I cause to provide that which they lack and preserve that which has been acquired.

यत्करोषि यदश्नासि यज्जुहोषि ददासि यत् ।
यत्तपस्यसि कौन्तेय तत्कुरुष्व मदर्पणम् ॥ 9.27 ॥

Whatever you do, whatever you eat, whatever you offer in sacrificial rites, whatever you give and whatever you perform as austerity, O Arjuna, you do that as an offering unto Me.

मन्मना भव मद्भक्तो मद्याजी मां नमस्कुरु ।
मामेवैष्यसि युक्त्वैवमात्मानं मत्परायणः ॥ 9.34 ॥

You fix your mind on Me, be devoted to Me, offer your worship or sacrifice (offering) to Me and bow down reverentially to Me. Having thus made the mind steadfast in Me, and having Me as Supreme Goal or abode, you shall attain Me.

अहमात्मा गुडाकेश सर्वभूताशयस्थितः ।
अहमादिश्च मध्यं च भूतानामन्त एव च ॥ 10.20 ॥

O Gudākesha! I am the Self, residing in the hearts of all beings. I am the beginning (the cause, the source), the middle (existence) and the end (death) of all beings. [Arjuna is being referred to as Gudākesha, meaning the one who has conquered sleep.]

मत्कर्मकृन्मत्परमो मद्भक्तः सङ्गवर्जितः ।
निर्वैरः सर्वभूतेषु यः स मामेति पाण्डव ॥ 11.55 ॥

O Arjuna! One who performs all actions for Me, who considers Me as the supreme goal, who is devoted to Me, who is free from attachment and free from enmity towards any being, such a one attains Me.

श्रेयो हि ज्ञानमभ्यासाज्ज्ञानाद्ध्यानं विशिष्यते ।
ध्यानात्कर्मफलत्यागः त्यागाच्छान्तिरनन्तरम् ॥ 12.12 ॥

Knowledge is better than the practice of concentration without discrimination (*viveka*–discrimination between the real and the unreal). Better than just knowledge is meditation accompanied by knowledge. Better than meditation accompanied by knowledge is renunciation of the fruits of action (not attached to the result of the action). From the renunciation of fruits of action, there arises peace immediately. Peace is nothing but the complete cessation of misery or suffering in the world.

अद्वेष्टा सर्वभूतानां मैत्रः करुण एव च ।
निर्ममो निरहङ्कारः समदुःखसुखः क्षमी ॥ 12.13 ॥
सन्तुष्टः सततं योगी यतात्मा दृढनिश्चयः ।
मय्यर्पितमनोबुद्धिर्यो मद्भक्तः स मे प्रियः ॥ 12.14 ॥

The one who is completely free from hatred towards any being, is ever-friendly towards all, is compassionate towards all, is free from the feeling of "mine" towards anything in the world, is free from egoism, is even-minded (equanimous) in pleasure and pain alike, is patient (forgiving, endowed with forbearance), is always content, has a collected mind, is self-controlled (self-possessed), is of firm conviction (regarding ideas related to the Self) and has offered (surrendered) the mind and intelligence unto Me–such a one, devoted to Me, is dear to Me.

यस्मान्नोद्विजते लोको लोकान्नोद्विजते च यः ।
हर्षामर्षभयोद्वेगैर्मुक्तो यः स च मे प्रियः ॥ 12.15 ॥

The one by whom the world is not agitated, who is not agitated by the world, and who is free from exultation (excessive joy obtaining something very dear), impatience (or anger), fear and anxiety–such a one is dear to Me.

अनपेक्षः शुचिर्दक्ष उदासीनो गतव्यथः ।
सर्वारम्भपरित्यागी यो मद्भक्तः स मे प्रियः ॥ 12.16 ॥

One who is free from wants or expectations, who is pure, dexterous, unbiased, and free from fear, renouncing all undertakings that lead to desires or those that are free from selfish motives, such a one who is (thus) devoted to Me, is dear to Me.

यो न हृष्यति न द्वेष्टि न शोचति न काङ्क्षति ।
शुभाशुभपरित्यागी भक्तिमान्यः स मे प्रियः ॥ 12.17 ॥

One who neither rejoices nor hates, nor grieves, nor desires, who has renounced the idea of auspicious and inauspicious, such a devotee is dear to me.

समः शत्रौ च मित्रे च तथा मानापमानयोः ।
शीतोष्णसुखदुःखेषु समः सङ्गविवर्जितः ॥ 12.18 ॥
तुल्यनिन्दास्तुतिर्मौनी सन्तुष्टो येन केनचित् ।
अनिकेतः स्थिरमतिर्भक्तिमान्मे प्रियो नरः ॥ 12.19 ॥

One who is the same to an enemy and a friend, in honour and dishonour, who is the same in cold (unfavourable circumstances) and heat (favourable circumstances), same in happiness and sorrow, who is free from attachment, who is the same in reproach and praise, who is silent, content, not attached to any place, is of a steady mind, and endowed with devotion–such a one is dear to Me.

ध्यानेनात्मनि पश्यन्ति केचिदात्मानमात्मना ।
अन्ये साङ्ख्येन योगेन कर्मयोगेन चापरे ॥ 13.24 ॥

Some behold (realise) the Self, by the Self, in the Self by means of meditation. Some others behold the Self by following the path of Sānkhya. And there are others who follow the path of action to realise the Self. [Withdrawal of the senses from their respective objects, withdrawing the mind, and then fixing the mind in the Self, and then the uninterrupted contemplation on the Self is meditation, says Adi Shankarāchārya in his commentary here.]

समं सर्वेषु भूतेषु तिष्ठन्तं परमेश्वरम् ।
विनश्यत्स्वविनश्यन्तं यः पश्यति स पश्यति ॥ 13.27 ॥

He who sees the One Supreme Being equally abiding in all beings is the one who has the real vision. Everything in this world is perishable, and the Supreme Being is imperishable. Thus, the one who sees the Supreme in all beings, i.e., sees the One Imperishable in all perishable beings, is the one who realizes the Truth.

नान्यं गुणेभ्यः कर्तारं यदा द्रष्टानुपश्यति ।
गुणेभ्यश्च परं वेत्ति मद्भावं सोऽधिगच्छति ॥ 14.19 ॥

When the seer (the witness) perceives that it is the three *guṇas* that are responsible for all actions and knows That (Self) which is distinct and beyond them, then such a one attains to My being (nature). Only the one with a deluded mind with egoism thinks "I am the doer".

गुणानेतानतीत्य त्रीन्देही देहसमुद्भवान् ।
जन्ममृत्युजरादुःखैः विमुक्तोऽमृतमश्नुते ॥ 14.20 ॥

Having transcended the three *guṇas* (*sattva, rajas, tamas*), which form the seed from which this body is evolved, the embodied one is liberated from birth, death, decay and suffering while still alive and attains immortality.

समदुःखसुखः स्वस्थः समलोष्टाश्मकाञ्चनः ।
तुल्यप्रियाप्रियो धीरस्तुल्यनिन्दात्मसंस्तुतिः ॥ 14.24 ॥
मानापमानयोस्तुल्यस्तुल्यो मित्रारिपक्षयोः ।
सर्वारम्भपरित्यागी गुणातीतः स उच्यते ॥ 14.25 ॥

The one who is the same in pleasure and pain, who is established in his Self, to whom a lump of clay, a stone and gold are the same, to whom the dear ones and the disliked ones are the same, who is wise, to whom censure (blame) and praise are the same, who is alike in honour and dishonour, who is same to friends and foe alike, and who has given up all endeavours (except those which are required to sustain the body)–such a one is said to have transcended the three *guṇas*.

निर्मानमोहा जितसङ्गदोषा
अध्यात्मनित्या विनिवृत्तकामाः ।
द्वन्द्वैर्विमुक्ताः सुखदुःखसंज्ञैर्-
गच्छन्त्यमूढाः पदमव्ययं तत् ॥ 15.5 ॥

One who is free from pride (egoism) and delusion (e.g., wrong perception regarding one's identity and the real source of happiness), who has conquered the vice of attachment, who is ever-established in the Self, whose desires have ceased, who is completely freed from the pairs of opposites like pleasure and pain, likes-dislikes and success-failure–such a one attains the imperishable state of oneness with the Universal Self.

सत्त्वानुरूपा सर्वस्य श्रद्धा भवति भारत ।
श्रद्धामयोऽयं पुरुषो यो यच्छ्रद्धः स एव सः ॥ 17.3 ॥

The *shraddhā* of every individual, O Arjuna, is in accordance with their inherent nature (and impressions that are latent in the mind). Each individual is made up of (or of the nature of) the *shraddhā* he possesses. Whatever the *shraddhā* is that the individual is.

आयुःसत्त्वबलारोग्यसुखप्रीतिविवर्धनाः ।
रस्याः स्निग्धाः स्थिरा हृद्या आहाराः सात्त्विक प्रियाः ॥ 17.8 ॥

The foods that are conducive to and promote vital power (long life), energy, vigour (strength), good health (freedom from disease), comfort and gratification (satisfaction), and are savoury (juicy and tasty), tender (soft), lasting, and agreeable and pleasant (to the body and mind) are the foods that are dear to individuals of *sāttvic* nature.

यज्ञदानतपःकर्म न त्याज्यं कार्यमेव तत् ।
यज्ञो दानं तपश्चैव पावनानि मनीषिणाम् ॥ 18.5 ॥
एतान्यपि तु कर्माणि सङ्गं त्यक्त्वा फलानि च ।
कर्तव्यानीति मे पार्थ निश्चितं मतमुत्तमम् ॥ 18.6 ॥

Yajña (sacrifice), *dāna* (charity) and *tapas* (austerity)–these three kinds of actions should not be given up. They should verily be performed. Sacrifice, charity and austerity are the purifiers in the case of the wise. But these (three) actions should also be performed by relinquishing attachment towards them and without any desire for the fruits of these actions. This, O Arjuna, is My principal and certain view.

यस्य नाहङ्कृतो भावो बुद्धिर्यस्य न लिप्यते ।
हत्वाऽपि स इमाँल्लोकान्न हन्ति न निबध्यते ॥ 18.17 ॥

The one who is free from egoism regarding the action (i.e., performs the action free from the notion of "I am the doer"), whose inner faculties (the seat of thought and feeling, the mind) are not tainted (thinking that this is good or this is sinful action), even though killing these people (these warriors in the battle), he 'does not kill', nor is he bound (to ideas associated with the evil outcome of the *adhārmic* act of killing).

अहङ्कारं बलं दर्पं कामं क्रोधं परिग्रहम् ।
विमुच्य निर्ममः शान्तो ब्रह्मभूयाय कल्पते ॥ 18.53 ॥

Having become free from egoism, power, arrogance, lust, anger, desire and sense of ownership, becoming free from the notion of "mine" and being peaceful–one attains deservingness for becoming Brahman.

भक्त्या मामभिजानाति यावान्यश्चास्मि तत्त्वतः ।
ततो मां तत्त्वतो ज्ञात्वा विशते तदनन्तरम् ॥ 18.55 ॥

Through devotion, he knows Me–what I am (as having manifold manifestations) and who I am in essence (free from all limitations, I am the all-pervading Consciousness that is unborn, immortal, non-dual). Then, having known Me in my true nature, he immediately enters into the Supreme reality that is Me.

ईश्वरः सर्वभूतानां हृद्देशेऽर्जुन तिष्ठति ।
भ्रामयन्सर्वभूतानि यन्त्रारूढानि मायया ॥ 18.61 ॥

O Arjuna, the Lord resides in the hearts of all beings, causing them to revolve by the power of *māyā* as if the beings are all mounted on a machine.

सर्वधर्मान्परित्यज्य मामेकं शरणं व्रज ।
अहं त्वा सर्वपापेभ्यो मोक्षयिष्यामि मा शुचः ॥ 18.66 ॥

Forsaking all dharmas (including *adharma*), take refuge in Me (the Self of all, the One abiding equally in all beings) alone. I will liberate you from all sins; do not grieve.

* * *

6
Kathopanishad
(कठोपनिषद्)

Abridged Kathopanishad

Kathopanishad is a dialogue between the Lord of Death (Yama) and Nachiketa.

येयं प्रेते विचिकित्सा मनुष्ये-
ऽस्तीत्येके नायमस्तीति चैके ।
एतद्विद्यामनुशिष्टस्त्वयाऽहं
वराणामेष वरस्तृतीयः ॥ 1.1.20 ॥

Nachiketa said: When a man dies, there is a doubt that arises. Some people say, "The Self exists", and some others say, "The Self does not exist". This I would like to know, with your instruction. Of the boons, this is the third one.

तं दुर्दर्शं गूढमनुप्रविष्टं
गुहाहितं गह्वरेष्ठं पुराणम् ।
अध्यात्मयोगाधिगमेन देवं
मत्वा धीरो हर्षशोकौ जहाति ॥ 1.2.12 ॥

Yama said: Having entered the being, the Self, the effulgent one, is hidden (veiled because of ignorance) deep inside. Existing within the body, it is seated in the cave of the heart. This Self, the old (everlasting) one, is difficult to perceive (realize). The wise one, by means of meditation upon the Self, goes beyond happiness and sorrow.

अन्यत्र धर्मादन्यत्राधर्मादन्यत्रास्मात् कृताकृतात् ।
अन्यत्र भूताच्च भव्याच्च यत्तत्पश्यसि तद्वद ॥ 1.2.14 ॥

Nachiketa said: That which You see, as different from *ādharma* and adharma, as different from cause and effect, as different from past and future, do tell me That.

The following selected verses are the words of the Lord of Death (Yama).

सर्वे वेदा यत्पदमामनन्ति
तपांसि सर्वाणि च यद्वदन्ति ।
यदिच्छन्तो ब्रह्मचर्यं चरन्ति
तत्ते पदं सङ्ग्रहेण ब्रवीम्योमित्येतत् ॥ 1.2.15 ॥

Yama said: The goal which all Vedas proclaim, which all austerities declare and desiring which they practice Brahmacharya, I tell It to you, briefly–it is Om.

एतद्ध्येवाक्षरं ब्रह्म एतद्ध्येवाक्षरं परम् ।
एतद्ध्येवाक्षरं ज्ञात्वा यो यदिच्छति तस्य तत् ॥ 1.2.16 ॥

This syllable (Om) alone is Brahman; this syllable is indeed the Supreme; having known this syllable (the Imperishable, Supreme Reality), whatever one desires, he attains that.

एतदालम्बनं श्रेष्ठमेतदालम्बनं परम् ।
एतदालम्बनं ज्ञात्वा ब्रह्मलोके महीयते ॥1.2.17 ॥

The support (i.e., Om) of this is most excellent; the support of this is supreme. Knowing (realising) this support, one is revered (worshipped) in the world of Brahman.

न जायते म्रियते वा विपश्चिन्
नायं कुतश्चिन्न बभूव कश्चित् ।
अजो नित्यः शाश्वतोऽयं पुराणो
न हन्यते हन्यमाने शरीरे ॥ 1.2.18 ॥

The Self (literally, 'intelligent', since it is of the nature of Consciousness) is not born, nor does It (the Self) die. The Self did not come into existence from any other cause, nor has something come into existence from It (the Self). The Self is unborn, eternal, everlasting and ancient. And the Self is not destroyed when the body is destroyed.

हन्ता चेन्मन्यते हन्तुं हतश्चेन्मन्यते हतम् ।
उभौ तौ न विजानीतो नायं हन्ति न हन्यते ॥ 1.2.19 ॥

If the killer (destroyer) thinks that he kills (destroys) the Self, and the killed (the one who is being killed) thinks that he is being killed, then both of them do not know the true nature of the Self. The Self does not kill, nor is the Self killed.

अणोरणीयान्महतो महीया-
नात्माऽस्य जन्तोर्निहितो गुहायाम् ।
तमक्रतुः पश्यति वीतशोको
धातुप्रसादान्महिमानमात्मनः ॥ 1.2.20 ॥

The Self is smaller (subtler) than the smallest; it is greater (in dimensions) than the greatest. And it is established (resides) in the heart (innermost core) of every creature in this universe. The desireless one (free from desires regarding the objects of the world) sees the glory of the Self (through direct experience as 'I am the Self') through the tranquility of the mind and senses and becomes free from suffering.

अशरीरं शरीरेष्वनवस्थेष्ववस्थितम् ।
महान्तं विभुमात्मानं मत्वा धीरो न शोचति ॥ 1.2.22 ॥

Having realised the Supreme all-pervading one, which is without a body and dwells in all the transient (perishable) bodies, the wise do not grieve.

नायमात्मा प्रवचनेन लभ्यो
न मेधया न बहुना श्रुतेन ।

यमेवैष वृणुते तेन लभ्यः
तस्यैष आत्मा विवृणुते तनूं स्वाम् ॥ 1.2.23 ॥

The Self has been extensively discussed in the scriptures and subsequently commented upon. But the Self cannot be realised just by extensive study of the scriptures (including the Upanishads). Neither can it be attained by the capacity of the intellect (by the retention power of memory) nor by listening to the expositions about the Self from the wise. Thus, the Self is attained by one who yearns for it over everything else (i.e., by renouncing everything else), and to such a seeker with exclusivity in yearning, the Self reveals itself. [The Self is our real identity. Therefore, in the true sense, it does not have to be attained. Only the ignorance veiling it has to be removed.]

आत्मानं रथिनं विद्धि शरीरं रथमेव तु ।
बुद्धिं तु सारथिं विद्धि मनः प्रग्रहमेव च ॥ 1.3.3 ॥

Know the Self (*ātmā*) to be the master of the chariot and the body to be the chariot. Know the intellect to be the charioteer and the mind to be the rein indeed.

इन्द्रियाणि हयानाहुर्विषयांस्तेषु गोचरान् ।
आत्मेन्द्रियमनोयुक्तं भोक्तेत्याहुर्मनीषिणः ॥ 1.3.4 ॥

The sense organs are said to be the horses (drawing the chariot); the sense objects are said to be the path (or road) for the senses. The Self, identified with the sense organs and mind, is referred to as the enjoyer (experiencer) by the wise ones.

यस्त्वविज्ञानवान्भवत्ययुक्तेन मनसा सदा ।
तस्येन्द्रियाण्यवश्यानि दुष्टाश्वा इव सारथेः ॥ 1.3.5 ॥

For one who is always with an uncontrolled mind and without *viveka* (the right understanding to discriminate between the real and unreal), his sense organs become uncontrolled, like the case of the wicked horses of the charioteer.

यस्तु विज्ञानवान्भवति युक्तेन मनसा सदा ।
तस्येन्द्रियाणि वश्यानि सदश्वा इव सारथेः ॥ 1.3.6 ॥

But, for one who has the right understanding (with the faculty to discriminate between the real and unreal) and has a controlled mind (ever-restrained), his senses are controlled, like the case of good horses of a charioteer.

यस्त्वविज्ञानवान्भवत्यमनस्कः सदाऽशुचिः ।
न स तत्पदमाप्नोति संसारं चाधिगच्छति ॥ 1.3.7 ॥

One who lacks the right understanding (discrimination), who lacks self-restraint and who is always impure, never attains the supreme state. He attains *samsāra*, remaining trapped in worldly existence.

यस्तु विज्ञानवान्भवति समनस्कः सदा शुचिः ।
स तु तत्पदमाप्नोति यस्माद्भूयो न जायते ॥ 1.3.8 ॥

One who has the right understanding (discrimination), who has self-restraint, and who is always pure, attains the supreme state and is not born again (is liberated from the bondage of *samsāra*, worldly existence).

विज्ञानसारथिर्यस्तु मनः प्रग्रहवान्नरः ।
सोऽध्वनः पारमाप्नोति तद्विष्णोः परमं पदम् ॥ 1.3.9 ॥

The one who has discriminating intellect as the charioteer and has a well-controlled mind for reins, such a one attains the destination (freed from all the bondages) and attains the supreme abode of Vishnu (the all-pervading Brahman, the Supreme Reality).

इन्द्रियेभ्यः परा ह्यर्था अर्थेभ्यश्च परं मनः ।
मनसस्तु परा बुद्धिर्बुद्धेरात्मा महान्परः ॥ 1.3.10 ॥
महतः परमव्यक्तमव्यक्तात्पुरुषः परः ।
पुरुषान्न परं किञ्चित्सा काष्ठा सा परा गतिः ॥ 1.3.11 ॥

The sense objects are superior to the senses; the mind is superior to the sense objects; the intelligence is superior to the mind, and the great Self is superior to the intelligence. The unmanifest is superior to the great Self; the *Purusha* (the Supreme Being) is superior to the unmanifest. There is nothing superior to the *Purusha*; That is the summit and That is the Supreme Abode.

एष सर्वेषु भूतेषु गूढोऽऽत्मा न प्रकाशते ।
दृश्यते त्वग्र्यया बुद्ध्या सूक्ष्मया सूक्ष्मदर्शिभिः ॥ 1.3.12 ॥

This Self remains hidden in all beings and does not shine (does not reveal itself to all due to ignorance). But, by those who have an eye for the subtle Truth, by means of the subtle intellect, refined (made subtle) by the power of meditation, it is seen (realized).

यच्छेद्वाङ्मनसी
प्राज्ञस्तद्यच्छेज्ज्ञान आत्मनि ।
ज्ञानमात्मनि महति नियच्छेत्
तद्यच्छेच्छान्त आत्मनि ॥ 1.3.13 ॥

The wise one should establish (merge) the speech (including all sense perceptions) in the mind (by withdrawing from the sense objects). Then that mind should be merged with the intellect. Let the intellect then merge in the 'great Self', the *Hiranyagarbha* (i.e., the intellect should shine in its own true nature, as the Self). Finally, he should merge the 'great-Self' with the 'peaceful-Self'(The peaceful Self is the one without any attributes, which is the witness).

उत्तिष्ठत जाग्रत
प्राप्य वरान्निबोधत ।
क्षुरस्य धारा निशिता दुरत्यया
दुर्गं पथस्तत्कवयो वदन्ति ॥ 1.3.14 ॥

O human! Arise, awake (from the sleep of ignorance)! Awaken to the Self (realise the Self) by approaching the wise ones (who have realised the Truth). The wise say that the path (leading to the Self) is unfathomable (inscrutable) and difficult to traverse, like the sharp razor's edge.

अशब्दमस्पर्शमरूपमव्ययं
तथाऽरसं नित्यमगन्धवच्च यत् ।
अनाद्यनन्तं महतः परं ध्रुवं
निचाय्य तन्मृत्युमुखात् प्रमुच्यते ॥ 1.3.15 ॥

The Self is soundless (beyond sound), beyond touch, formless, imperishable and also tasteless, eternal and odourless. It is beginningless, endless and distinct from the *Mahat* Principle (the intellect in the Sānkhya Philosophy, being the nature of Knowledge), and is immutable. Having realised the Self, one is liberated from the jaws of death (attains immortality).

पराञ्चि खानि व्यतृणत् स्वयम्भू-
स्तस्मात्पराङ्पश्यति नान्तरात्मन् ।
कश्चिद्धीरः प्रत्यगात्मानमैक्ष-
दावृत्तचक्षुरमृतत्वमिच्छन् ॥ 2.1.1 ॥

The self-existing One (Brahmā) has designed the sense-organs with defects, resulting them in going outward (into the world). Therefore, the human only sees the external phenomenal world, not the inner Self. However, some wise ones, desiring to realize their immortal nature, turn their eyes inward and perceive the inner Self.

येन रूपं रसं गन्धं शब्दान् स्पर्शांश्च मैथुनान् ।
एतेनैव विजानाति किमत्र परिशिष्यते ।
एतद्वै तत् ॥ 2.1.3 ॥

By the Self alone, the human knows form, taste, smell, sound, touch and sexual pleasure. What else is left here, in this world (that cannot be known by the Self)? This, indeed, is That (the goal or the highest state sought by the seeker).

स्वप्नान्तं जागरितान्तं चोभौ येनानुपश्यति ।
महान्तं विभुमात्मानं मत्वा धीरो न शोचति ॥ 2.1.4 ॥

It is by knowing (realising) the great and splendorous Self, by means of which one sees the objects of the dream state and the objects of the wakeful state, that the wise one does not grieve.

मनसैवेदमाप्तव्यं नेह नानाऽस्ति किंचन ।
मृत्योः स मृत्युं गच्छति य इह नानेव पश्यति ॥ 2.1.11 ॥

By the mind (which is pure) alone, Brahman is attained. Once it is attained, there is no differentiation there (i.e., everything is the Brahman, and there is nothing else there). But one who perceives difference or variety (out of ignorance), he goes from death to death.

यथोदकं शुद्धे शुद्धमासिक्तं तादृगेव भवति ।
एवं मुनेर्विजानत आत्मा भवति गौतम ॥ 2.1.15 ॥

O Gautama! Just as when pure water poured into pure water remains the same, in the same manner, the Self of the wise one who knows becomes the Self (The Self becomes one with the Universal Self).

अग्निर्यथैको भुवनं प्रविष्टो
रूपं रूपं प्रतिरूपो बभूव ।
एकस्तथा सर्वभूतान्तरात्मा
रूपं रूपं प्रतिरूपो बहिश्च ॥ 2.2.9 ॥

Fire, though being one, having entered this world, takes on different forms in accordance with the forms and shapes of the different objects it burns (combustibles like wood, etc.). In the same manner, the Self, though being one (the Universal Self or indwelling Self of all beings), exists in all beings, appearing in different forms according to the being and is also outside it.

सूर्यो यथा सर्वलोकस्य चक्षुः
न लिप्यते चाक्षुषैर्बाह्यदोषैः ।
एकस्तथा सर्वभूतान्तरात्मा
न लिप्यते लोकदुःखेन बाह्यः ॥ 2.2.11 ॥

The sun, the eye of the entire world, is not tainted by the defects and impurities of the external world it sees. In the same manner, the one Self, which is the indwelling Self of all beings, is not tainted (affected) by the misery in the world, for the misery is outside.

एको वशी सर्वभूतान्तरात्मा
एकं रूपं बहुधा यः करोति ।
तमात्मस्थं येऽनुपश्यन्ति धीराः
तेषां सुखं शाश्वतं नेतरेषाम् ॥ 2.2.12 ॥

The Supreme Being is One, the controller (the Lord), the indwelling Self of all beings (the Universal Self), and though being one, creates the manifoldness around. The eternal (everlasting) happiness belongs to the wise ones who perceive this Supreme Being as their own Self and does not belong to the others.

नित्योऽनित्यानां चेतनश्चेतनानाम्
एको बहूनां यो विदधाति कामान् ।
तमात्मस्थं येऽनुपश्यन्ति धीराः
तेषां शान्तिः शाश्वती नेतरेषाम् ॥ 2.2.13 ॥

He is the Eternal (indestructible) among the non-eternals (destructibles); He is the Consciousness among the conscious beings. Though one, He dispenses to all the results of their actions. The eternal (everlasting) peace belongs to the wise ones who perceive this Supreme Being as their own Self and not to others.

न तत्र सूर्यो भाति न चन्द्रतारकं
नेमा विद्युतो भान्ति कुतोऽयमग्निः ।
तमेव भान्तमनुभाति सर्वं
तस्य भासा सर्वमिदं विभाति ॥ 2.2.15 ॥

[The Self-effulgent Brahman]: The sun (that illuminates everything in the world) does not shine there (i.e., it cannot illuminate Brahman); the moon, the stars and lightning do not shine there. Where is the question of fire shining there (illuminating it)? In fact, it is by the light of Brahman that all these luminaries shine. All this, the entire universe shines after the light of Brahman. Brahman alone is real.

इह चेदशकद्बोद्धुं प्राक् शरीरस्य विस्रसः ।
ततः सर्गेषु लोकेषु शरीरत्वाय कल्पते ॥ 2.3.4 ॥

If one is able to know (realise) the Truth (Brahman) here, before the fall of the body, then one is liberated from all bondages of the world. If one fails to know the Truth, then he takes on a body in the world of creations.

इन्द्रियाणां पृथग्भावमुदयास्तमयौ च यत् ।
पृथगुत्पद्यमानानां मत्वा धीरो न शोचति ॥ 2.3.6 ॥

The wise one knows that the senses originated from their causes (the five elements) and are of a different nature (compared to the nature of the Self). The wise one also knows about the constant rising and setting (i.e., the transience) of the sense objects (i.e., being created and destroyed in the waking and dream states) and that these objects belong to the senses, not to the Self. Knowing these, the wise one does not grieve.

न सन्दृशे तिष्ठति रूपमस्य
न चक्षुषा पश्यति कश्चनैनम् ।
हृदा मनीषा मनसाऽभिक्लृप्तो
य एतद्विदुरमृतास्ते भवन्ति ॥ 2.3.9 ॥

His (referring to the all-pervading Supreme Being devoid of attributes) nature is not perceptible to the senses (the verse says 'not in the scope of vision'). None sees Him with the eyes (or perceive with other senses). This Supreme Being is revealed (illuminated) through meditation by the heart (intellect) that has the mind in control. Those who realize Him become immortal (i.e., become liberated).

यदा पञ्चावतिष्ठन्ते ज्ञानानि मनसा सह ।
बुद्धिश्च न विचेष्टते तामाहुः परमां गतिम् ॥ 2.3.10 ॥

When the five knowledge senses (having withdrawn from the respective sense objects of the world) come to rest along with the mind (in the Self), and the intellect (withdrawing from its activities), too, is at rest, such state is called the Supreme One. [Knowledge sense organs are ear, skin, eyes, tongue and nose.]

तां योगमिति मन्यन्ते स्थिरामिन्द्रियधारणाम् ।
अप्रमत्तस्तदा भवति योगो हि प्रभवाप्ययौ ॥ 2.3.11 ॥

That (the control of the senses described above) is considered to be yoga. In that state, the Self shines in its true nature. The mind of the yogi becomes free from all distractions. (The yogi must practice concentration on the Self to remain free from distraction from objects of the world.) For, the state of yoga can be attained and lost.

नैव वाचा न मनसा प्राप्तुं शक्यो न चक्षुषा ।
अस्तीति ब्रुवतोऽन्यत्र कथं तदुपलभ्यते ॥ 2.3.12 ॥

The Self can never be attained by speech, nor by the mind, nor by the eyes (including all senses). It can be attained only by the one who believes "It (the Self) exists". How can anyone else attain It?

यदा सर्वे प्रमुच्यन्ते कामा येऽस्य हृदि श्रिताः ।
अथ मर्त्योऽमृतो भवत्यत्र ब्रह्म समश्नुते ॥ 2.3.14 ॥

When all the desires dwelling in the heart are destroyed, then the mortal (human) becomes immortal and attains the Supreme Brahman here, in this world (while living) itself.

* * *

7

Muṇḍakopanishad
(मुण्डकोपनिषद्)

Abridged Muṇḍakopanishad

शौनको ह वै महाशालोऽङ्गिरसं विधिवदुपसन्नः पप्रच्छ ।
कस्मिन्नु भगवो विज्ञाते सर्वमिदं विज्ञातं भवतीति ॥ 1.1.3 ॥

Shaunaka, the distinguished householder, approached Sage Angiras, observing the prescribed injunctions in the tradition and enquired: "Revered sir, knowing what, all this (everything in this world) becomes known"?

तस्मै स होवाच । द्वे विद्ये वेदितव्ये इति ह स्म
यद्ब्रह्मविदो वदन्ति परा चैवापरा च ॥ 1.1.4 ॥

Sage Angira responded to him thus: "The knowers of Brahman have said that the knowledge to be known is of two kinds–the higher knowledge and the lower knowledge".

तत्रापरा ऋग्वेदो यजुर्वेदः सामवेदोऽथर्ववेदः
शिक्षा कल्पो व्याकरणं निरुक्तं छन्दो ज्योतिषमिति ।
अथ परा यया तदक्षरमधिगम्यते ॥ 1.1.5 ॥

There (of these two), the inferior knowledge consists of the four Vedas (Rigveda, Yajurveda, Samaveda, Atharvaveda), phonetics, codes of rituals, grammar, etymology, prosody and astronomy. The higher knowledge is that by which the Imperishable (Indestructible Brahman) is attained.

यत्तदद्रेश्यमग्राह्यमगोत्रमवर्ण-
मचक्षुःश्रोत्रं तदपाणिपादम् ।
नित्यं विभुं सर्वगतं सुसूक्ष्मं
तदव्ययं यद्भूतयोनिं परिपश्यन्ति धीराः ॥ 1.1.6 ॥

That which is imperceptible (cannot be perceived by the senses), ungraspable, which is without a source or origin, devoid of any classification into a species or caste, which has neither eyes nor ears, nor hands and feet, and that which is eternal, equally present in all, all-pervading (like ether), extremely subtle, unchanging (undiminishing), and that which is the womb (source) of all beings–the wise ones perceive That (the Self, the higher knowledge) everywhere.

यथोर्णनाभिः सृजते गृह्णते च
यथा पृथिव्यामोषधयः सम्भवन्ति ।
यथा सतः पुरुषात् केशलोमानि
तथाऽक्षरात् सम्भवतीह विश्वम् ॥ 1.1.7 ॥

Just as a spider (a living entity) spins a web from within itself and also withdraws the same into itself, as the plants and herbs (that are animate) sprout and grow from the earth (which is inert), and as the hairs (which are inert) grow on the head and body of man (a living entity), in the same manner from the Imperishable Brahman, the universe is born.

यः सर्वज्ञः सर्वविद् यस्य ज्ञानमयं तपः ।
तस्मादेतद् ब्रह्म नाम रूपमन्नं च जायते ॥ 1.1.9 ॥

He (described in verse 7 above) is all-knowing (omniscient), whose austerity is of the nature of knowledge (and not action). From Him (the omniscient) is born Brahmā (the creator of all creations), all names, forms and food.

तदेतत् सत्यं मन्त्रेषु कर्माणि कवयो
यान्यपश्यंस्तानि त्रेतायां बहुधा सन्ततानि ।
तान्याचरथ नियतं सत्यकामा एष वः
पन्थाः सुकृतस्य लोके ॥ 1.2.1 ॥

The various rites and rituals (prescribed in the Vedas) conceived by the wise are true. They have a certain efficacy in the context of the worldly desires of human beings (but are subject to transience). May you, desirous of true results, perform them diligently to attain the desired and prescribed outcomes. These actions are the path to your attainment of worldly fruits.

प्लवा ह्येते अदृढा यज्ञरूपा
अष्टादशोक्तमवरं येषु कर्म ।
एतच्छ्रेयो येऽभिनन्दन्ति मूढा
जरामृत्युं ते पुनरेवापि यन्ति ॥ 1.2.7 ॥

[Description of the limitations of rituals]: These rituals, sacrifices, etc. (described in 1.2.1) involving eighteen components are being compared to rafts that are infirm and unstable. All these inferior acts rest on these rafts. The ignorant ones (unaware of the shortcomings) praise these rituals as the means to the highest attainment (auspiciousness). And these ignorant ones fall into the cycle of old age and death again and again.

अविद्यायामन्तरे वर्तमानाः
स्वयं धीराः पण्डितं मन्यमानाः ।
जङ्घन्यमानाः परियन्ति मूढा
अन्धेनैव नीयमाना यथान्धाः ॥ 1.2.8 ॥

Present among the deluded ones, considering themselves intelligent and wise (enlightened), undergoing afflictions (suffering) again and again, these ignorant ones wander about like the blind leading the blind.

अविद्यायां बहुधा वर्तमाना
वयं कृतार्था इत्यभिमन्यन्ति बालाः ।
यत् कर्मिणो न प्रवेदयन्ति रागात्
तेनातुराः क्षीणलोकाश्च्यवन्ते ॥ 1.2.9 ॥

Steeped in ignorance, blindly engrossed in the manifold inferior actions (rituals, etc.), they think ignorantly (lit. childishly), "We are blessed and have achieved the highest good". Since they are attached to the actions (the rituals), they do not know the 'real' greater attainment in the form of Self-knowledge. And therefore, they fall down into affliction once their merits are exhausted.

इष्टापूर्तं मन्यमाना वरिष्ठं
नान्यच्छ्रेयो वेदयन्ते प्रमूढाः ।
नाकस्य पृष्ठे ते सुकृतेऽनुभूत्वेमं
लोकं हीनतरं वा विशन्ति ॥ 1.2.10 ॥

[Description of ignorance]: The ignorant ones think that these rites and rituals and acts like service to fellow beings (like digging wells, feeding, etc.) are the most excellent. They are unaware of the other one of the greatest good (the path of knowledge leading to liberation). Staying with their rituals (and other acts) and reaping and enjoying the benefits of the rituals, they continue in this world of misery and suffer and even fall into the lower worlds.

परीक्ष्य लोकान् कर्मचितान् ब्राह्मणो
निर्वेदमायान्नास्त्यकृतः कृतेन ।
तद्विज्ञानार्थं स गुरुमेवाभिगच्छेत्
समित्पाणिः श्रोत्रियं ब्रह्मनिष्ठम् ॥ 1.2.12 ॥

[Approaching the guru]: The seeker of Truth, after having carefully examined all these worlds that are gained by the various actions and rituals, should attain indifference towards them because nothing everlasting (peace, happiness, the abode of Brahman) is ever attained by performing rituals. In other words, whatever is attained by any action is ephemeral. To know the Supreme (that which bestows the eternal abode), one should, with humility, approach a guru, who is well-versed in the scriptures and is completely established in Brahman.

तस्मै स विद्वानुपसन्नाय सम्यक्
प्रशान्तचित्ताय शमान्विताय ।
येनाक्षरं पुरुषं वेद सत्यं
प्रोवाच तां तत्त्वतो ब्रह्मविद्याम् ॥ 1.2.13 ॥

The wise one (the guru), to that seeker of Truth who has approached him–who is of a tranquil mind and whose senses have been restrained–the guru should impart the knowledge of Brahman (*Brahma-vidyā*) in its very essence, knowing which one realizes the indestructible Supreme Being.

दिव्यो ह्यमूर्तः पुरुषः स बाह्याभ्यन्तरो ह्यजः ।
अप्राणो ह्यमनाः शुभ्रो ह्यक्षरात् परतः परः ॥ 2.1.2 ॥

The Supreme Being (*Purusha*) is indeed resplendent (being self-effulgent), is without form, is within and without, in unborn, devoid of *prāṇa* (vital air) and mind, is pure (since it is beyond the mind) and is greater than even the Unmanifested.

पुरुष एवेदं विश्वं कर्म तपो ब्रह्म परामृतम् ।
एतद्यो वेद निहितं गुहायां सोऽविद्याग्रन्थिं विकिरतीह सोम्य ॥ 2.1.10 ॥

The Supreme Being alone is all this, including rituals, austerity, etc. (there is nothing apart from the Supreme Being). O gentle one! The one who knows the Supreme, immortal Brahman, as residing in the cavern of the heart, destroys the knot of ignorance, here in this world itself.

आविः सन्निहितं गुहाचरं नाम
महत्पदमत्रैतत् समर्पितम् ।
एजत्प्राणन्निमिषच्च यदेतज्जानथ
सदसद्वरेण्यं परं विज्ञानाद्यद्वरिष्ठं प्रजानाम् ॥ 2.2.1 ॥

That Brahman is effulgent, established within, shining through all experiences (of the world in the form of hearing, seeing, etc.) in the heart of all beings. It is the great goal, the great refuge of all. All the beings that move, breathe and wink are established in Brahman (supported by It.) Realize (know) this clearly as your Self–that which is both gross and subtle, which is the most desirable of all, is the most excellent and is distinct from the knowledge of all creatures.

धनुर् गृहीत्वौपनिषदं महास्त्रं
शरं ह्युपासा निशितं सन्धयीत ।
आयम्य तद्भावगतेन चेतसा
लक्ष्यं तदेवाक्षरं सोम्य विद्धि ॥ 2.2.3 ॥

Lifting the bow, the great weapon described in the Upanishads, fix the arrow sharpened by worship (constant meditation). Drawing the string (withdrawing the mind and senses from external objects) with the mind established (focussed) on the thought of Brahman alone, strike the target, the Indestructible Brahman.

प्रणवो धनुः शरो ह्यात्मा ब्रह्म तल्लक्ष्यमुच्यते ।
अप्रमत्तेन वेद्धव्यं शरवत् तन्मयो भवेत् ॥ 2.2.4 ॥

The syllable Om (*praṇava*) is the bow; the Self is indeed the arrow; Brahman is said to be the target. The target should be struck by the undistracted (undeluded) mind (unattached to the objects of the world). And just like the arrow becoming one with the target, the Self should become one with Brahman.

यस्मिन् द्यौः पृथिवी चान्तरिक्षमोतं
मनः सह प्राणैश्च सर्वैः ।
तमेवैकं जानथ आत्मानमन्या
वाचो विमुञ्चथामृतस्यैष सेतुः ॥ 2.2.5 ॥

In Whom (the Indestructible Supreme Being), the sky, the earth, the intermediate space (between heaven and earth), along with the mind, and *prāṇa* (the five vital airs) are all interwoven, as the substratum of all, know Him (the Supreme Being) alone to be the one (non-dual) Self within. Abandon all other ideas and talk about anything else (for they are all inferior to this). This (Self) alone is the bridge leading to immortality (liberation).

अरा इव रथनाभौ संहता यत्र नाड्यः ।
स एषोऽन्तश्चरते बहुधा जायमानः ।
ओमित्येवं ध्यायथ आत्मानं
स्वस्ति वः पाराय तमसः परस्तात् ॥ 2.2.6 ॥

Like the spokes of a chariot-wheel that come together at the hub of the wheel, and just as the nerves (arteries) meet in the heart, in the same manner, this Self resides within (as the witness), becoming the manifold experiences (in the form of experiences of the mind). Meditate upon this Self as Om. May there be no hindrance in this, to reach the goal (lit. to the other side of the darkness or delusion). May everything be auspicious for you.

यः सर्वज्ञः सर्वविद् यस्यैष महिमा भुवि ।
दिव्ये ब्रह्मपुरे ह्येष व्योम्न्यात्मा प्रतिष्ठितः ॥
मनोमयः प्राणशरीरनेता
प्रतिष्ठितोऽन्ने हृदयं सन्निधाय ।
तद् विज्ञानेन परिपश्यन्ति धीरा
आनन्दरूपममृतं यद् विभाति ॥ 2.2.7 ॥

He who is all-wise, omniscient, to whom belongs all the glory on this earth, He–the Self–resides in the sky of the heart, in the splendorous city of Brahman. He is the nature of the mind, and He is the lord of the life forces and body. Established in the food, he resides in the heart. By means of Self-knowledge, the wise realize Him, who shines as the nature of bliss and immortality.

भिद्यते हृदयग्रन्थिश्छिद्यन्ते सर्वसंशयाः ।
क्षीयन्ते चास्य कर्माणि तस्मिन् दृष्टे परावरे ॥ 2.2.8 ॥

When one sees (realizes) the Supreme–that one Supreme Reality which is both the high (as the cause) and the low (as the effect)–then all knots of the heart (ideas caused by ignorance, e.g., thoughts such as "I am this body", "my house", "I am sad") are disentangled (eliminated); all doubts (regarding what is to be known in the context of the world) are destroyed; and all effects of karma (all except the *prārabdha-karma*) are destroyed. Also, all outcomes in the form of merits and demerits (*puṇya* and *pāpā*) in the context of actions are also destroyed.

हिरण्मये परे कोशे विरजं ब्रह्म निष्कलम् ।
तच्छुभ्रं ज्योतिषां ज्योतिस्तद् यदात्मविदो विदुः ॥ 2.2.9 ॥

The indivisible (without parts) Brahman (the Supreme Reality) is seated in the supreme effulgent sheath (as a result of the light of knowledge). He is pure and is the light of all lights that shine, and is the Self of all. He is that which the knowers of the Self realise.

न तत्र सूर्यो भाति न चन्द्रतारकं
नेमा विद्युतो भान्ति कुतोऽयमग्निः ।
तमेव भान्तमनुभाति सर्वं
तस्य भासा सर्वमिदं विभाति ॥ 2.2.10 ॥

[The Self-effulgent Brahman]: The sun that illuminates everything in the world does not shine there (i.e., it cannot illuminate Brahman), nor do the moon, the stars and lightning shine there. Where is the question of this fire shining there (illuminating it)? In fact, it is by the light of Brahman that all these luminaries shine. All this, the entire universe shines after the light of Brahman. Brahman alone is real.

द्वा सुपर्णा सयुजा सखाया
समानं वृक्षं परिषस्वजाते ।
तयोरन्यः पिप्पलं स्वाद्वत्त्य-
नश्नन्नन्यो अभिचाकशीति ॥ 3.1.1 ॥

Two birds, associated with each other in an intimate relationship, with similar names (identities), are in the same tree. [The two birds are the *jīva* and *Īshvara*, and the tree here refers to the body.] Of the two birds, one (*jīva*) eats (experiences) the different fruits (i.e., outcomes in the form of happiness and sorrow) of the various actions. The other bird simply watches without eating (i.e., the *Īshvara* remains the eternal witness).

समाने वृक्षे पुरुषो निमग्नो-
ऽनीशया शोचति मुह्यमानः ।
जुष्टं यदा पश्यत्यन्यमीशमस्य
महिमानमिति वीतशोकः ॥ 3.1.2 ॥

On the same tree, one of the birds, the Individual Self, (*jīva*), experiencing the fruits of action, is plunged in grief (because of delusion and attachment). [The delusion is the result of wrong identification with the body, mind, ego, etc. And the grief is the result of the wrong perception regarding oneself.] However, when it sees the other (the *Īshvara*), the worshipful Lord and His glories, it becomes free from grief and suffering.

यदा पश्यः पश्यते रुक्मवर्णं
कर्तारमीशं पुरुषं ब्रह्मयोनिम् ।
तदा विद्वान् पुण्यपापे विधूय
निरञ्जनः परमं साम्यमुपैति ॥ 3.1.3 ॥

When the witness (seer) sees (realises) the radiant One, the original source of Brahmā (the progenitor of all), the creator, the Lord and the Supreme Being, then the wise one forsaking merits and demerits, becomes pure (free from desires) and attains oneness with the Supreme Brahman.

सत्येन लभ्यस्तपसा ह्येष आत्मा
सम्यग्ज्ञानेन ब्रह्मचर्येण नित्यम् ।
अन्तःशरीरे ज्योतिर्मयो हि शुभ्रो
यं पश्यन्ति यतयः क्षीणदोषाः ॥ 3.1.5 ॥

Truthfulness, austerity (withdrawing the mind and senses from the world of objects and focusing it on the Self), the right knowledge (of the Self) and continence–by constantly engaging in these, the Self is attained. Which is this Self? It is that Self which is within the body, which the pure-minded wise ones aspire for and which the wise realise within.

सत्यमेव जयते नानृतं
सत्येन पन्था विततो देवयानः ।
येनाऽऽक्रमन्त्यृषयो ह्याप्तकामा
यत्र तत् सत्यस्य परमं निधानम् ॥ 3.1.6 ॥

Truth alone triumphs and not untruth (Can also be interpreted as: 'the truthful alone triumphs'). By truth alone, the path of the gods (path to liberation) is spread wide open, by which the wise ones, free from desires, ascend to the Supreme Abode of Truth (Brahman).

बृहच्च तद् दिव्यमचिन्त्यरूपं
सूक्ष्माच्च तत् सूक्ष्मतरं विभाति ।
दूरात् सुदूरे तदिहान्तिके च
पश्यन्त्विहैव निहितं गुहायाम् ॥ 3.1.7 ॥

That (Brahman, the Supreme Reality) is great (infinite, all-pervading), divine (self-effulgent) and is beyond imagination (not perceptible to the senses in terms of a form). It (Brahman) shines as subtler than the subtlest and is far beyond the farthest. It is perceived by the wise ones, hidden within, in the innermost core of the heart.

न चक्षुषा गृह्यते नापि वाचा
नान्यैर्देवैस्तपसा कर्मणा वा ।
ज्ञानप्रसादेन विशुद्धसत्त्व-
स्ततस्तु तं पश्यते निष्कलं ध्यायमानः ॥ 3.1.8 ॥

The Self (being formless) is not perceived by the eyes; it cannot be described by using speech (as it is indescribable), and it cannot be apprehended by the other senses. Also, it cannot be reached through any form of action (rites, rituals, ceremonies, etc.) or austerity. When the mind is purified by the knowledge, through meditation, one perceives (realises) the Self that is devoid of any parts (i.e., sees it as the Absolute One).

कामान् यः कामयते मन्यमानः
स कामभिर्जायते तत्र तत्र ।
पर्याप्तकामस्य कृतात्मनस्तु
इहैव सर्वे प्रविलीयन्ति कामाः ॥ 3.2.2 ॥

Yearning for the various objects of desire, the one who is constantly thinking of them is born here and there, along with one's desires for the fulfilment of those desires. However, for one whose desires have completely been fulfilled (having attained contentment, self-satisfaction) through the realization of the knowledge of the Self, all the desires are destroyed here in this world itself.

नायमात्मा प्रवचनेन लभ्यो
न मेधया न बहुना श्रुतेन ।
यमेवैष वृणुते तेन लभ्य-
स्तस्यैष आत्मा विवृणुते तनूं स्वाम् ॥ 3.2.3 ॥

The Self has been extensively discussed in the scriptures and subsequently commented upon. But the Self cannot be realised just by extensive study of the scriptures (including the Upanishads). Neither can it be attained by the capacity of the intellect (by the retention power of memory) nor by listening to the expositions about the Self from the wise. [The Self is our real identity. Therefore, in a true sense, it does not have to be attained. Only the ignorance veiling it has to be removed.] Thus, the Self is attained by one who yearns for it over everything else (i.e., by renouncing everything else), and to such a seeker with exclusivity in yearning, the Self reveals itself.

नायमात्मा बलहीनेन लभ्यो
न च प्रमादात् तपसो वाप्यलिङ्गात् ।
एतैरुपायैर्यतते यस्तु विद्वां-
स्तस्यैष आत्मा विशते ब्रह्मधाम ॥ 3.2.4 ॥

This Self is not attained by one who lacks mental strength (fortitude, confidence, etc.). It (the Self) is not attained by one who is intoxicated with attachment towards the objects of the world. It is not attained by means of austerity (of knowledge) that lacks the necessary characteristics (renunciation of desires). But the seeker who strives with these three qualities (mental strength, freedom from attachment and proper austerities) enters the abode of Brahman.

वेदान्तविज्ञानसुनिश्चितार्थाः
संन्यासयोगाद् यतयः शुद्धसत्त्वाः ।
ते ब्रह्मलोकेषु परान्तकाले
परामृताः परिमुच्यन्ति सर्वे ॥ 3.2.6 ॥

Having attained the object of the knowledge described in the Upanishads (Vedantic scriptures), having purified their minds through the yoga of renunciation (*sannyāsa-yoga*), the ascetics, who have realised the oneness with the immortal Brahman, become liberated at the time of enlightenment (realization).

यथा नद्यः स्यन्दमानाः समुद्रे-
ऽस्तं गच्छन्ति नामरूपे विहाय ।
तथा विद्वान् नामरूपाद्विमुक्तः
परात्परं पुरुषमुपैति दिव्यम् ॥ 3.2.8 ॥

The various rivers (having different sizes, colours, names, etc.), giving up their names and forms, lose their identity on merging with the ocean (and become one with the large expanse). In the same manner, the wise one (who has realised the Self), having given up the name and form (the different identities that the ignorant one takes up), attains the Supreme Being (Purusha), who is greater than the greatest divinity.

स यो ह वै तत् परमं ब्रह्म वेद
ब्रह्मैव भवति नास्याब्रह्मवित्कुले भवति ।
तरति शोकं तरति पाप्मानं
गुहाग्रन्थिभ्यो विमुक्तोऽमृतो भवति ॥ 3.2.9 ॥

The one who knows (realises) the Supreme Brahman (as "I am Brahman"), indeed becomes Brahman Itself. In the family of such a one (who has known Brahman), one who does not know Brahman is not born. Also, the knower of Brahman goes beyond grief, suffering, virtue and vice. The knots of the heart (in the form of ignorance, delusion) are destroyed, and the knower of Brahman attains immortality (liberation).

***

8

Ashtāvakra Gīta

(अष्टावक्र गीता)

Abridged Ashtāvakra Gīta

This text is in the form of a dialogue between Sage Ashtāvakra and King Janaka. [Also called Ashtāvakra Samhita]

कथं ज्ञानमवाप्नोति कथं मुक्तिर्भविष्यति ।
वैराग्यं च कथं प्राप्तं एतद् ब्रूहि मम प्रभो ॥ 1.1 ॥

Please tell me, O Lord! How does one acquire knowledge of the Self? How does one become liberated? How is *vairāgya* (non-attachment) attained?

मुक्तिं इच्छसि चेत्तात विषयान् विषवत्त्यज ।
क्षमार्जवदयातोषसत्यं पीयूषवद् भज ॥ 1.2 ॥

If liberation is what you desire, my dear, avoid sense objects as if you would avoid poison. Seek forbearance, straightforwardness, compassion, contentment, and truthfulness as if they are nectar.

यदि देहं पृथक् कृत्य चिति विश्राम्य तिष्ठसि ।
अधुनैव सुखी शान्तो बन्धमुक्तो भविष्यसि ॥ 1.4 ॥

Having detached yourself from the body (being free of the notion that "I am the body"), if you establish yourself in the Consciousness, immediately (now itself), you will be happy, tranquil and free from all bondages.

न त्वं विप्रादिको वर्णो नाश्रमी नाक्षगोचरः ।
असङ्गोऽसि निराकारो विश्वसाक्षी सुखी भव ॥ 1.5 ॥

You (your true nature or identity) are not a *brāhmaṇa*, *kshatriya* (warrior) or any other such castes; you do not belong to any of the four stages of life (like *brahmacharya*, etc.). You are not perceptible to the senses. You are unattached, formless and the witness of the entire universe. Be happy!

धर्माधर्मौ सुखं दुःखं मानसानि न ते विभो ।
न कर्तासि न भोक्तासि मुक्त एवासि सर्वदा ॥ 1.6 ॥

O Great One! *Dharma* and *adharma* (good and evil, or virtue and vice), happiness and sorrow (pleasure and pain) are of the mind and do not belong to you. You are not the doer, and you are not the experiencer (enjoyer or sufferer). You are forever free indeed!

एको द्रष्टासि सर्वस्य मुक्तप्रायोऽसि सर्वदा ।
अयमेव हि ते बन्धो द्रष्टारं पश्यसीतरम् ॥ 1.7 ॥

You are the One seer (witness) of all; you are always free. Not seeing yourself as the witness, you consider someone else to be the seer (witness). This is your bondage.

यत्र विश्वमिदं भाति कल्पितं रज्जुसर्पवत् ।
आनन्दपरमानन्दः स बोधस्त्वं सुखं चर ॥ 1.10 ॥

You are That superimposed in whom the entire universe (the visible phenomena) shines (appears), as in the case of the snake appearing in place of a rope. You are That bliss, supreme bliss, Consciousness. Live in this world happily.

मुक्ताभिमानी मुक्तो हि बद्धो बद्धाभिमान्यपि ।
किंवदन्तीह सत्येयं या मतिः सा गतिर्भवेत् ॥ 1.11 ॥

One who regards himself as free is indeed free. And, one who regards himself to be in bondage is indeed bound. The common saying: "as one thinks, so he becomes" is true indeed. [By its very nature, the Self is ever-free.]

आत्मा साक्षी विभुः पूर्ण एको मुक्तश्चिदक्रियः ।
असंगो निःस्पृहः शान्तो भ्रमात्संसारवानिव ॥ 1.12 ॥

The Self (*ātmā*) is a witness, omnipresent (all-pervading), full (complete), One (non-dual, absolute), free, Consciousness, non-doer (actionless), unattached, devoid of desires and tranquil. But, because of delusion (ignorance), the Self appears to belong to the world (active, limited, manifold, bound by the world, desireful, etc.).

देहाभिमानपाशेन चिरं बद्धोऽसि पुत्रक ।
बोधोऽहं ज्ञानखड्गेन तन्निकृत्य सुखी भव ॥ 1.14 ॥

Dear child, by the fetters of superimposition upon the body (considering oneself to be the body), you are forever in bondage. By the sword of the awakening that "I am Consciousness", cutting (destroying) that delusion, be happy.

एकं सर्वगतं व्योम बहिरन्तर्यथा घटे ।
नित्यं निरन्तरं ब्रह्म सर्वभूतगणे तथा ॥ 1.20 ॥

Just as there exists the same all-pervading ether (space), inside and outside the pitcher, in the same manner, the eternal and omnipresent (lit. uninterrupted) Brahman (the Supreme Reality) exists in all beings.

यथा न तोयतो भिन्नास्तरंगाः फेनबुद्बुदाः ।
आत्मनो न तथा भिन्नं विश्वमात्मविनिर्गतम् ॥ 2.4 ॥

Just as waves, froth and bubbles are not different from water, in the same manner, the universe that has sprung forth from the Self is no different from the Self.

तन्तुमात्रो भवेदेव पटो यद्वद्विचारितः ।
आत्मतन्मात्रमेवेदं तद्वद्विश्वं विचारितम् ॥ 2.5 ॥

Just as, when investigated, it is discovered that the garment is nothing but thread, in the same manner, when investigated, the universe is nothing but the Self.

आत्माज्ञानाज्जगद्भाति आत्मज्ञानान्न भासते ।
रज्ज्वज्ञानादहिर्भाति तज्ज्ञानाद्भासते न हि ॥ 2.7 ॥

It is because of the ignorance of the Self that the entire world appears, and it is because of the knowledge of the Self that the universe disappears. This is just as, the snake appears because of the ignorance of the rope and the snake disappears because of the knowledge of the rope.

प्रकाशो मे निजं रूपं नातिरिक्तोऽस्म्यहं ततः ।
यदा प्रकाशते विश्वं तदाहं भास एव हि ॥ 2.8 ॥

My real nature is light (effulgence); I am nothing different from that. When the universe appears (manifest), in reality, it is the "I" that shines.

मत्तो विनिर्गतं विश्वं मय्येव लयमेष्यति ।
मृदि कुम्भो जले वीचिः कनके कटकं यथा ॥ 2.10 ॥

The universe that sprung forth (out of ignorance) from me, dissolves into me indeed, just as the pot (of clay) dissolves into clay, the wave into the water, and the bracelet (of gold) dissolves into gold.

ज्ञानं ज्ञेयं तथा ज्ञाता त्रितयं नास्ति वास्तवम् ।
अज्ञानाद्भाति यत्रेदं सोऽहमस्मि निरञ्जनः ॥ 2.15 ॥

The three–knowledge, the knowable and the knower–are not real. I am that blemish-less Self in whom these three appear because of ignorance.

द्वैतमूलमहो दुःखं नान्यत्तस्यास्ति भेषजम् ।
दृश्यमेतन्मृषा सर्वं एकोऽहं चिद्रसोऽमलः ॥ 2.16 ॥

Alas! All grief and sufferings are rooted in duality. There is no other cure for these except the realisation that the entire visible world phenomenon is unreal (illusory) and that I (the Self) am one (non-dual), pure, Consciousness and blissful.

शरीरं स्वर्गनरकौ बन्धमोक्षौ भयं तथा ।
कल्पनामात्रमेवैतत् किं मे कार्यं चिदात्मनः ॥ 2.20 ॥

Body, heaven and hell, bondage and liberation and fear–these are mere forms indeed in the imagination. What business do I, the Pure Consciousness, have with any of these?

विश्वं स्फुरति यत्रेदं तरङ्गा इव सागरे ।
सोऽहमस्मीति विज्ञाय किं दीन इव धावसि ॥ 3.3. ॥

This universe springs forth from the Self, just as the waves arise from the ocean. Then, realizing the truth, "I am That", why are you still running around (in this world) like someone who is miserable and afflicted?

चेष्टमानं शरीरं स्वं पश्यत्यन्यशरीरवत् ।
संस्तवे चापि निन्दायां कथं क्षुभ्येत् महाशयः ॥ 3.10 ॥

The wise one sees (witnesses) his own body (which is doing everything in this world) as someone else's body. How can such a wise one be agitated when praised or censured (blamed)?

मायामात्रमिदं विश्वं पश्यन् विगतकौतुकः ।
अपि सन्निहिते मृत्यौ कथं त्रस्यति धीरधीः ॥ 3.11 ॥

This entire universe is merely an illusion (*māyā*). Seeing this truth about the universe, all the pleasure and curiosity from it disappear. How then can one of steady wisdom be fearful when death is near?

अन्तस्त्यक्तकषायस्य निर्द्वन्द्वस्य निराशिषः ।
यदृच्छयागतो भोगो न दुःखाय न तुष्टये ॥ 3.14 ॥

One who has renounced all defects in the form of attachments from the mind, who has gone beyond the pairs of opposites (like success and failure, happiness and sorrow) and who is free from desires, such a one neither experiences sorrow nor elation with regard to anything that comes to him by chance.

तज्ज्ञस्य पुण्यपापाभ्यां स्पर्शो ह्यन्तर्न जायते ।
न ह्याकाशस्य धूमेन दृश्यमानापि सङ्गतिः ॥ 4.3 ॥

The seat of thoughts and feelings (the mind) of one who has realized the Truth is untouched by *puṇya* and *pāpā* (merit and demerit, good and bad, virtue and vice). Even though the smoke appears to be in contact with the sky, the sky is untouched (unaffected) by the smoke in the sky.

न ते सङ्गोऽस्ति केनापि किं शुद्धस्त्यक्तुमिच्छसि ।
सङ्घातविलयं कुर्वन्नेवमेव लयं व्रज ॥ 5.1 ॥

You are Pure. You have no attachment to anything in this world. What, then, are you trying to renounce? Thus, getting rid of delusion (identifying the Self with the body, mind, etc.), attain the oneness with the Supreme (i.e., attain liberation).

समदुःखसुखः पूर्ण आशानैराश्ययोः समः ।
समजीवितमृत्युः सन्नेवमेव लयं व्रज ॥ 5.4 ॥

You are full (complete); you are even-minded in pleasure and pain, even-minded in hope and despair and equable in birth and death. Being thus, attain the oneness with the Supreme (attain liberation).

आकाशवदनन्तोऽहं घटवत् प्राकृतं जगत् ।
इति ज्ञानं तथैतस्य न त्यागो न ग्रहो लयः ॥ 6.1 ॥

Like the sky (or space), I am unbounded (limitless, omniscient). And like the pitcher, the world of phenomena is limited, transient and bounded in nature. [The pitcher is of material nature and thus comes into existence and also is destroyed.] This is true knowledge. Therefore, for the Self, there is neither renunciation, attainment, nor any destruction.

मय्यनन्तमहाम्भोधौ जगद्वीचिः स्वभावतः ।
उदेतु वास्तमायातु न मे वृद्धिर्न च क्षतिः ॥ 7.2 ॥

In me (the Self), the eternal great ocean, the universe is but a wave, and in a natural manner, the universe appears and disappears. The rising of the wave does not cause any increase in me, and the subsidence of the wave does not cause any loss to me (for the Self is ever-full and complete).

तदा बन्धो यदा चित्तं किञ्चिद्वाञ्छति शोचति ।
किञ्चिन्मुञ्चति गृण्हाति किञ्चिद्धृष्यति कुप्यति ॥ 8.1 ॥

Whenever the mind desires anything or grieves over something, rejects or accepts anything, delights in something or is angry at something, it is in bondage.

तदा मुक्तिर्यदा चित्तं न वाञ्छति न शोचति ।
न मुञ्चति न गृह्णाति न हृष्यति न कुप्यति ॥ 8.2 ॥

When the mind does not desire anything or grieve for anything, does not reject or accept anything, and does not delight over anything and is not angered by anything, then it is liberation.

तदा बन्धो यदा चित्तं सक्तं कास्वपि दृष्टिषु ।
तदा मोक्षो यदा चित्तमसक्तं सर्वदृष्टिषु ॥ 8.3 ॥

When the mind is attached to anything 'seen' (sense objects of the world), then it is in bondage. And when the mind is free from attachment towards all sense objects, then it is liberation.

यदा नाहं तदा मोक्षो यदाहं बन्धनं तदा ।
मत्वेति हेलया किञ्चित् मा गृहाण विमुञ्च मा ॥ 8.4 ॥

When the "I" (egoism, or identification of the Self with the body and mind) does not exist, then it is liberation. When there is the sense of "I", then it is bondage. Thinking thus, be free from rejecting anything or accepting anything (free from aversion and attachment).

वासना एव संसार इति सर्वा विमुञ्च ताः ।
तत्त्यागो वासनात्यागात् स्थितिरद्य यथा तथा ॥ 9.8 ॥

Only desires are the cause of the *samsāra* (worldly existence). Therefore, you should give up all your desires. The renunciation of desires alone leads to the renunciation of *samsāra*. After this (having given up desires), you may live and move about anywhere in the world, free from affectation.

तृष्णामात्रात्मको बन्धस्तन्नाशो मोक्ष उच्यते ।
भवासंसक्तिमात्रेण प्राप्तितुष्टिर्मुहुर्मुहुः ॥ 10.4 ॥

Bondage is nothing but the presence of desires; the elimination of desires is called liberation. By being unattached to the objects of the world alone, one attains the state of constant contentment (because of the realisation of the Self).

चिन्तया जायते दुःखं नान्यथेहेति निश्चयी ।
तया हीनः सुखी शान्तः सर्वत्र गलितस्पृहः ॥ 11.5 ॥

Misery (or suffering) in this world is born of the constant thought of the objects of the world; nothing else causes misery. The one who is of this realisation is free from misery, is happy, tranquil and free from desires everywhere.

नाहं देहो न मे देहो बोधोऽहमिति निश्चयी ।
कैवल्यं इव सम्प्राप्तो न स्मरत्यकृतं कृतम् ॥ 11.6 ॥

"I am not the body, and the body is not mine. I am the Consciousness"–the one who has this established realisation attains liberation (*kaivalya*). He does not think about what is to be accomplished or what has been accomplished (i.e., he has no attachment to work, past, present or future).

आब्रह्मस्तम्बपर्यन्तमहमेवेति निश्चयी ।
निर्विकल्पः शुचिः शान्तः प्राप्ताप्राप्तविनिर्वृतः ॥ 11.7 ॥

"From a blade of grass till Brahmā, I alone am in everything"– the one who has this established realisation is pure, tranquil, becomes free from any waveringness in thought and becomes free from any attachment towards accomplishments or non-accomplishments.

हेयोपादेयविरहादेवं हर्षविषादयोः ।
अभावादद्य हे ब्रह्मन्नेवमेवाहमास्थितः ॥ 12.4 ॥

Revered Sir! Being free from happiness and sorrow as a result of the absence of the notions of rejection and acceptance (of anything in this world), I am firmly established in the Self now.

कर्मानुष्ठानमज्ञानाद्यथैवोपरमस्तथा ।
बुध्वा सम्यगिदं तत्त्वमेवमेवाहमास्थितः ॥ 12.6 ॥

Performance of action (religious or secular) is the result of ignorance. In the same manner, cessation (avoidance) of action is also the result of ignorance. Realizing this truth well, I am firmly established in the Self now.

कुत्रापि खेदः कायस्य जिह्वा कुत्रापि खिद्यते ।
मनः कुत्रापि तत्त्यक्त्वा पुरुषार्थे स्थितः सुखम् ॥ 13.2 ॥

Somewhere, there is an affliction of the body; elsewhere, there is an affliction of the tongue; somewhere else, there is an affliction of the mind. Having renounced all these three, being firmly established in the goal of life (i.e., liberation), be happy.

कृतं किमपि नैव स्यादिति सञ्चिन्त्य तत्त्वतः ।
यदा यत्कर्तुमायाति तत्कृत्वासे यथासुखम् ॥ 13.3 ॥

In reality, there is nothing to be done (by the Self). Thinking this way (having realized this truth), doing whatever needs to be done (doing whatever comes up by itself), I live happily.

क्व धनानि क्व मित्राणि क्व मे विषयदस्यवः ।
क्व शास्त्रं क्व च विज्ञानं यदा मे गलिता स्पृहा ॥ 14.2 ॥

When one is free from desires (following the realization of the Self), where is wealth (riches), where are friends, where is the question of thieves in the form of objects (of the senses), where are scriptures, and where is knowledge?

विज्ञाते साक्षिपुरुषे परमात्मनि चेश्वरे ।
नैराश्ये बन्धमोक्षे च न चिन्ता मुक्तये मम ॥ 14.3 ॥

Realizing the Universal Self, which is of the nature of the witness and is the Supreme Lord (*Īshvara*), and being free from all desires and free from all bondages, I have no anxiety or thought of liberation.

मोक्षो विषयवैरस्यं बन्धो वैषयिको रसः ।
एतावदेव विज्ञानं यथेच्छसि तथा कुरु ॥ 15.2 ॥

Non-attachment (lit. disgust or aversion) towards the objects of the world is liberation. Attachment (lit. taste or desire) towards sense objects is bondage. This is knowledge of the Truth. Now, knowing this, do as you please.

रागद्वेषौ मनोधर्मौ न मनस्ते कदाचन ।
निर्विकल्पोऽसि बोधात्मा निर्विकारः सुखं चर ॥ 15.5 ॥

Likes and dislikes (i.e., attachment and hatred) are characteristics of the mind and not yours. The mind is not yours at any point in time. You are the Sentient Self (Consciousness), free from variety (doubt, etc.) and free from change. Knowing this to be your real nature, be happy.

सर्वभूतेषु चात्मानं सर्वभूतानि चात्मनि ।
विज्ञाय निरहङ्कारो निर्ममस्त्वं सुखी भव ॥ 15.6 ॥

Having realized the Self in all beings, and seeing all the beings in the Self, being free from egoism and being free from mineness, be happy.

गुणैः संवेष्टितो देहस्तिष्ठत्यायाति याति च ।
आत्मा न गन्ता नागन्ता किमेनमनुशोचसि ॥ 15.9 ॥

This human body is enveloped by the *guṇas* of Nature. The body is born, exists and departs. But the Self, transcending the body, neither comes (is born) nor goes (dies). Why then do you grieve over the body?

त्वय्यनन्तमहाम्भोधौ विश्ववीचिः स्वभावतः ।
उदेतु वास्तमायातु न ते वृद्धिर्न वा क्षतिः ॥ 15.11 ॥

In you, the limitless mighty ocean, the waves, in the form of the universe, rise and subside spontaneously. As a result of this rising and subsiding, there is no increase or decrease (gain or loss) for you.

आचक्ष्व शृणु वा तात नानाशास्त्राण्यनेकशः ।
तथापि न तव स्वास्थ्यं सर्वविस्मरणादृते ॥ 16.1 ॥

Dear child! Even though you may repeatedly listen to (and study) and speak about numerous scriptures, you will not attain contentment (abidance in the Self) except by forgetting all that. [Merely book learning will not bring about realization.]

इदं कृतमिदं नेति द्वन्द्वैर्मुक्तं यदा मनः ।
धर्मार्थकाममोक्षेषु निरपेक्षं तदा भवेत् ॥ 16.5 ॥

"This ought to be done, and this ought not to be done"–when the mind is free from this and other such pairs of opposites, then it becomes desireless towards the four *purushārthas–dharma, artha* (prosperity, wealth), *kāma* (enjoyment of the objects of the world) and *moksha* (liberation).

विरक्तो विषयद्वेष्टा रागी विषयलोलुपः ।
ग्रहमोक्षविहीनस्तु न विरक्तो न रागवान् ॥ 16.6 ॥

The one who hates sense-objects of the world is unattached. The one who longs for and possesses sense-objects of the world is attached. But the one who neither longs for (or possesses) nor rejects (or renounces) is neither unattached nor attached. [The Self is beyond wanting, possessing and rejecting.].

प्रवृत्तौ जायते रागो निर्वृत्तौ द्वेष एव हि ।
निर्द्वन्द्वो बालवद्धीमान् एवमेव व्यवस्थितः ॥ 16.8 ॥

Attachment is born in activity; in the cessation of (or abstention from) activity, hatred (dislike) results. But the wise one (the one who has realized the Self), free from the pairs of opposites (attachment and aversion), is like a child and thus lives like one.

हातुमिच्छति संसारं रागी दुःखजिहासया ।
वीतरागो हि निर्दुःखस्तस्मिन्नपि न खिद्यति ॥ 16.9 ॥

The one who is attached to the world and its objects, wishes to renounce these to be free from suffering (resulting from attachment). The one who is free from attachments, is free from any suffering and is not disturbed or agitated even while living (interacting freely) in this world among the objects.

यस्याभिमानो मोक्षेऽपि देहेऽपि ममता तथा ।
न च ज्ञानी न वा योगी केवलं दुःखभागसौ ॥ 16.10 ॥

The one who is egoistic (high opinion of oneself) towards the idea of liberation and has identification with the body considering it 'mine', such a one only undergoes suffering on account of the identification (egoism). He is neither wise (knower of truth) nor a yogi (one who is attained oneness).

हरो यद्युपदेष्टा ते हरिः कमलजोऽपि वा ।
तथापि न तव स्वाथ्यं सर्वविस्मरणादृते ॥ 16.11 ॥

Even if Hara (Lord Siva), Hari (Lord Vishnu) and the Lotus-born (Lord Brahmā) were your instructors, unless you forget them all, you will not find abidance in the Self (you will not be established in the Truth).

यस्यान्तः स्यादहङ्कारो न करोति करोति सः ।
निरहङ्कारधीरेण न किञ्चिद्धि कृतं कृतम् ॥ 18.29 ॥

One who has egoism within him, acts (is active) even though he is physically inactive. Being free from egoism, the wise one is inactive, though physically active, for he has realized the actionless Self within.

अप्रयत्नात् प्रयत्नाद्वा मूढो नाप्नोति निर्वृतिम् ।
तत्त्वनिश्चयमात्रेण प्राज्ञो भवति निर्वृतः ॥ 18.34 ॥

By inaction (by giving up action) or by action, the unwise does not attain final beatitude (because he has not given up the desires). But the wise one attains final beatitude merely by realizing the Truth. [In the case of the wise one, it does not matter whether he is active or inactive.]

यदा यत्कर्तुमायाति तदा तत्कुरुते ऋजुः ।
शुभं वाप्यशुभं वापि तस्य चेष्टा हि बालवत् ॥ 18.49 ॥

The wise one does whatever presents itself to be done. Whatever thus comes (by chance) may be agreeable or disagreeable. The actions are not initiated by his own preferences. The actions of such a wise one are like those of a child.

सर्वारम्भेषु निष्कामो यश्चरेद्बालवन्मुनिः ।
न लेपस्तस्य शुद्धस्य क्रियमाणेऽपि कर्मणि ॥ 18.64 ॥

Being pure and without any expectation in all endeavours, the wise one who moves about like a child has no attachment to any actions being performed by him.

न स्वर्गो नैव नरको जीवन्मुक्तिर्न चैव हि ।
बहुनात्र किमुक्तेन योगदृष्ट्या न किञ्चन ॥ 18.80 ॥

In the vision of oneness (in the realisation of a yogi), there is no heaven, there is no hell and there is no *jīvan-mukti* (liberation while living). None of these notions are real for one who has realized the oneness. There is nothing much to be said in this regard.

निःस्नेहः पुत्रदारादौ निष्कामो विषयेषु च ।
निश्चिन्तः स्वशरीरेऽपि निराशः शोभते बुधः ॥ 18.84 ॥

With non-attachment towards one's son, wife and others, without any desires or expectations of sense-objects, and without any worries regarding one's own body, the wise one–without any expectations–lives with grace and splendour.

क्व धर्मः क्व च वा कामः क्व चार्थः क्व विवेकिता ।
क्व द्वैतं क्व च वाऽद्वैतं स्वमहिम्नि स्थितस्य मे ॥ 19.2 ॥

For me, who is established in the power and glory of the Self, (and thus being completely free from any sense of identification or attachment with the world), where is the question of *dharma*, *artha*, *kāma* or discrimination between real and unreal, and where is the question of duality and where is non-duality? [All these are mere notions and have no relevance for the one who is established in the Self.]

क्व मृत्युर्जीवितं वा क्व लोकाः क्वास्य क्व लौकिकम् ।
क्व लयः क्व समाधिर्वा स्वमहिम्नि स्थितस्य मे ॥ 19.7 ॥

For me, who is established in the power and glory of the Self, (and thus being completely free from any sense of identification or attachment with the world), where is the question of life and death, where are the worlds and people, and where is the idea of absorption or where is samadhi?

क्व लोकः क्व मुमुक्षुर्वा क्व योगी ज्ञानवान् क्व वा ।
क्व बद्धः क्व च वा मुक्तः स्वस्वरूपेऽहमद्वये ॥ 20.6 ॥

For me, who is of the nature of non-duality (who is one without a second), where is the question of the world, where is the notion of being an aspirant of liberation, where is the notion of being a yogi or where is the idea of knower, where is bondage and where is liberation?

क्व सृष्टिः क्व च संहारः क्व साध्यं क्व च साधनम् ।
क्व साधकः क्व सिद्धिर्वा स्वस्वरूपेऽहमद्वये ॥ 20.7 ॥

For me, who is of the nature of non-duality (who is one without a second), where is the question of creation, where is the question of destruction, where is the idea of something to be attained or the means to it, where is the question of a seeker, and where is the question of fulfilment?

क्वोपदेशः क्व वा शास्त्रं क्व शिष्यः क्व च वा गुरुः ।
क्व चास्ति पुरुषार्थो वा निरुपाधेः शिवस्य मे ॥ 20.13 ॥

For me, who is of the nature of Auspiciousness (Siva), and who is of the nature of Absolute (free from attributes; limitations), where is the question of instruction, where are the scriptures, where is the idea of disciple or guru, and where is the notion of *purushārtha* (*dharma, artha, kāma, moksha*)?

* * *

9

Avadhūta Gīta
(अवधूत गीता)

Abridged Avadhūta Gīta

This text was composed by Sage Dattātreya. Here are some selected verses:

येनेदं पूरितं सर्वमात्मनैवात्मनात्मनि ।
निराकारं कथं वन्दे ह्यभिन्नं शिवमव्ययम् ॥ 1.2 ॥

The Self with which everything in this phenomenal universe is verily filled, within the Self, and by the Self, in what manner should I worship that formless, indivisible and immutable Supreme Being?

आत्मैव केवलं सर्वं भेदाभेदो न विद्यते ।
अस्ति नास्ति कथं ब्रूयां विस्मयः प्रतिभाति मे ॥ 1.4 ॥

Everything is indeed the Self, and there is no differentiation or non-differentiation (for everything is but the One Self) in that. To proclaim, 'all this exists' or 'does not exist' is very perplexing.

वेदान्तसारसर्वस्वं ज्ञानं विज्ञानमेव च ।
अहमात्मा निराकारः सर्वव्यापी स्वभावतः ॥ 1.5 ॥

The entirety of the essence of Vedanta is knowledge and the realization of the Self alone. By my very nature, I am the formless and all-pervading Self.

यो वै सर्वात्मको देवो निष्कलो गगनोपमः ।
स्वभावनिर्मलः शुद्धः स एवायं न संशयः ॥ 1.6 ॥

I am that Self, which is all-pervading (the Universal Self), effulgent (divine), undivided (without parts) like the sky (space), blemishless by its very nature, and pure. There is no doubt regarding this.

न मानसं कर्म शुभाशुभं मे
न कायिकं कर्म शुभाशुभं मे ।
न वाचिकं कर्म शुभाशुभं मे
ज्ञानामृतं शुद्धमतीन्द्रियोऽहम् ॥ 1.8 ॥

For me, there is no mental action, good or bad; for me, there is no bodily action, good or bad; for me, there is no speech-based action, good or bad. I am the nectar of the form of knowledge (of the Self). I am pure and beyond the senses (I am not the subject of the senses).

मनो वै गगनाकारं मनो वै सर्वतोमुखम् ।
मनोऽतीतं मनः सर्वं न मनः परमार्थतः ॥ 1.9 ॥

The mind is indeed like the space. The mind, as if, faces all directions. The mind, as if, transcends everything. The mind, as if, is everything. From the position of the highest truth (Brahman), there is no mind.

आत्मानं सततं विद्धि सर्वत्रैकं निरन्तरम् ।
अहं ध्याता परं ध्येयमखण्डं खण्ड्यते कथम् ॥ 1.12 ॥

Know the Self to be always, perpetual (uninterrupted in its presence) and everywhere. If this is so, why do you divide the unfragmented One Absolute, saying, "I am the meditator", and "the Supreme is the undivided object of meditation"?

न जातो न मृतोऽसि त्वं न ते देहः कदाचन ।
सर्वं ब्रह्मेति विख्यातं ब्रवीति बहुधा श्रुतिः ॥ 1.13 ॥

You were never born, and you will never die. The body is never yours. "Everything is Brahman"–thus is the celebrated and repeatedly declared statement in the *shruti* (Upanishads).

जन्म मृत्युर्न ते चित्तं बन्धमोक्षौ शुभाशुभौ ।
कथं रोदिषि रे वत्स नामरूपं न ते न मे ॥ 1.17 ॥

You have neither birth, death, nor a mind for you; there is no bondage and liberation for you, and there is no good and evil (auspicious and inauspicious) for you. O dear! Why then do you weep? Neither you nor I have any name or form.

वदन्ति श्रुतयः सर्वाः निर्गुणं शुद्धमव्ययम् ।
अशरीरं समं तत्त्वं तन्मां विद्धि न संशयः ॥ 1.20 ॥

All Upanishads proclaim that Brahman is devoid of the three *guṇas* (*sattva, rajas* and *tamas*), is pure, immutable, bodiless and equally pervades everything. Know that I am That (Brahman). Be in no doubt.

साकारमनृतं विद्धि निराकारं निरन्तरम् ।
एतत्तत्त्वोपदेशेन न पुनर्भवसम्भवः ॥ 1.21 ॥

Know the formful to be unreal and the formless to be eternal (ever-present, perpetual). By means of the realisation of this truth, there is no rebirth ever again.

एकमेव समं तत्त्वं वदन्ति हि विपश्चितः ।
रागत्यागात्पुनश्चित्तमेकानेकं न विद्यते ॥ 1.22 ॥

The wise men (who have realised the Truth) say that Reality (Truth) is one. Having given up the attachment to objects of the world, the notions of one and many (manifoldness) cease to exist in the mind.

अनात्मरूपं च कथं समाधि-
रात्मस्वरूपं च कथं समाधिः ।
अस्तीति नास्तीति कथं समाधि-
र्मोक्षस्वरूपं यदि सर्वमेकम् ॥ 1.23 ॥

Where is the question of *samādhi* for one who thinks of himself as *anātmā* (non-Self)? Where is the question of *samādhi* for one who thinks of himself as *ātmā* (Self)? Where is the question of *samādhi* if there are notions of "is" and "is not" regarding the Self? If all is One (Brahman) and is of the nature of *moksha* (liberation), where is the need to discuss *samādhi*?

तत्त्वमस्यादिवाक्येन स्वात्मा हि प्रतिपादितः ।
नेति नेति श्रुतिर्ब्रूयादनृतं पाञ्चभौतिकम् ॥ 1.25 ॥

By means of statements like "*tattvamasi*" (You are That), etc., the Self alone is proved or established. That which is made up of the five elements (ether, fire, earth, water, air), i.e., the body, is unreal. In the context of the body, the Upanishads say '*neti-neti*' ("not this, not this").

आत्मन्येवात्मना सर्वं त्वया पूर्णं निरन्तरम् ।
ध्याता ध्यानं न ते चित्तं निर्लज्जं ध्यायते कथम् ॥ 1.26 ॥

The entire universe is entirely filled by you (the Self) in the Self. There is no meditator and meditation for you. Why then do you meditate without any shame?

शिवं न जानामि कथं वदामि
शिवं न जानामि कथं भजामि ।
अहं शिवश्चेत्परमार्थतत्त्वं
समस्वरूपं गगनोपमं च ॥ 1.27 ॥

I do not know Siva (the Auspicious One). How then can I speak of Him or describe Him? I do not know Siva (the Auspicious One). How then can I worship Him? If I am the Siva, who is of the nature of Supreme Truth, who is the Universal Self, equally present in all like space, how then can I speak of Him or worship Him?

घटे भिन्ने घटाकाशं सुलीनं भेदवर्जितम् ।
शिवेन मनसा शुद्धो न भेदः प्रतिभाति मे ॥ 1.31 ॥

When the pot is broken, the space within the pot becomes completely dissolved (merged) into the all-pervading space. When the mind becomes pure, it becomes one with the Universal Self, and there is no longer a differentiation perceived in me.

न घटो न घटाकाशो न जीवो जीवविग्रहः ।
केवलं ब्रह्म संविद्धि वेद्यवेदकवर्जितम् ॥ 1.32 ॥

There is no pot and there is no pot-space (space contained within the pot). Similarly, there is no *jīva* (individual Self), and there is no individual form (associated with the individual Self). Know very well the Absolute Brahman, which is neither the knowable (to be known) nor knower (that which knows).

सर्वत्र सर्वदा सर्वमात्मानं सततं ध्रुवम् ।
सर्वं शून्यमशून्यं च तन्मां विद्धि न संशयः ॥ 1.33 ॥

Know the Self as everything, existing everywhere and always. The Self is eternal, immovable (unchanging). Everything (in the world) is void (unreal), and everything is filled by the Self. I am that Self. There is no doubt regarding this.

परेण सहजात्मापि ह्यभिन्नः प्रतिभाति मे ।
व्योमाकारं तथैवैकं ध्याता ध्यानं कथं भवेत् ॥ 1.39 ॥

My true nature, the Self, appears to me to be the same as the Universal Self, like the one vast space. If this is so, where is the question of the notions of meditator and meditation?

यत्करोमि यदश्नामि यज्जुहोमि ददामि यत् ।
एतत्सर्वं न मे किंचिद्विशुद्धोऽहमजोऽव्ययः ॥ 1.40 ॥

Whatever I do, whatever I eat, whatever I offer (in worship or sacrifice) and whatever I give, none of these are for me (or belong to me). I am pure, unborn and unchanging.

सर्वं जगद्विद्धि निराकृतीदं
सर्वं जगद्विद्धि विकारहीनम् ।
सर्वं जगद्विद्धि विशुद्धदेहं
सर्वं जगद्विद्धि शिवैकरूपम् ॥ 1.41 ॥

Know this entire universe to be formless. Know this entire universe to be free from change. Know this entire universe to be the body of Pure Existence (Brahman). Know this entire universe to be of the nature of Siva (the One Auspiciousness).

षडङ्गयोगान्न तु नैव शुद्धं
मनोविनाशान्न तु नैव शुद्धम् ।
गुरूपदेशान्न तु नैव शुद्धं
स्वयं च तत्त्वं स्वयमेव शुद्धम् ॥ 1.48 ॥

The Self certainly cannot be purified by the practice of yoga consisting of six aspects (*āsana, prāṇāyāma, pratyāhāra, dhāraṇa, dhyāna and samādhi*). The Self cannot be purified by the destruction of the mind (*mano-nāsha*). The Self cannot be purified by the instruction of the preceptor. It is itself the Supreme Truth or Reality. It is pure by itself.

न हि पञ्चात्मको देहो विदेहो वर्तते न हि ।
आत्मैव केवलं सर्वं तुरीयं च त्रयं कथम् ॥ 1.49 ॥

There is no body made up of five gross elements (ether, fire, earth, water and air) associated with the Self, nor is the Self without a body. All this is verily the Self alone. If that is the case, then where is the question of three states (wakefulness, dream, sleep), and where is the question of the fourth (*Turīya*) in the context of the Self?

न गुरुर्नोपदेशश्च न चोपाधिर्न मे क्रिया ।
विदेहं गगनं विद्धि विशुद्धोऽहं स्वभावतः ॥ 1.54 ॥

There is neither a guru nor instruction, neither limiting adjuncts nor activity. Know that, by nature, I am like the sky, bodiless and pure.

कथं रोदिषि रे चित्त ह्यात्मैवात्मात्मना भव ।
पिब वत्स कलातीतमद्वैतं परमामृतम् ॥ 1.56 ॥

O Mind! Why are you weeping? You are indeed the Self. Be the Self, by means of the Self. Drink, my dear, the supreme nectar of non-duality, which is beyond all divisions of time.

ज्ञानं न तर्को न समाधियोगो
न देशकालौ न गुरूपदेशः ।
स्वभावसंवित्तरहं च तत्त्व-
माकाशकल्पं सहजं ध्रुवं च ॥ 1.58 ॥

Knowledge of the Self is not associated with reasoning (logic); it is not the practice of meditation (to attain *samādhi*); it is not anything associated with time or place; it is not an instruction of a guru. By nature, I am like the sky—I am Consciousness, the Truth, innate and eternal.

न जातोऽहं मृतो वापि न मे कर्म शुभाशुभम् ।
विशुद्धं निर्गुणं ब्रह्म बन्धो मुक्तिः कथं मम ॥ 1.59 ॥

I am not born; I will not die; I do not have any action–good or evil (auspicious or inauspicious). I am Brahman–pure and devoid of any attributes. Where is then the question of bondage or liberation?

नाहं कर्ता न भोक्ता च न मे कर्म पुराऽधुना ।
न मे देहो विदेहो वा निर्ममेति ममेति किम् ॥ 1.66 ॥

I am neither the doer of action nor the experiencer of the fruit of any action. Neither now nor earlier do I have any *karma*. Neither do I have a body, nor am I bodiless. Then where is the question of "mine" or "not mine"?

न मे रागादिको दोषो दुःखं देहादिकं न मे ।
आत्मानं विद्धि मामेकं विशालं गगनोपमम् ॥ 1.67 ॥

I am free from deficiencies like attachment, etc. I am free from any trouble or misery relating to the body, mind, etc. Know me to be the one Self, infinite (lit. vast) like the sky.

सतताऽभ्यासयुक्तस्तु निरालम्बो यदा भवेत् ।
तल्लयाल्लीयते चान्तर्गुणदोषविवर्जितः ॥ 2.16 ॥

When one is constantly engaged in the practice of yoga, one becomes independent (i.e., not attached to any objects of the world). Then, freed from the notions of good and evil, when the notion of objects is dissolved, there is dissolution (merger) into the Supreme.

भ्रान्तिज्ञानं स्थितं बाह्यं सम्यग्ज्ञानं च मध्यगम् ।
मध्यान्मध्यतरं ज्ञेयं नारिकेलफलाम्बुवत् ॥ 2.20 ॥

Knowledge of the outer world is false (mistaken) knowledge. True (right) knowledge is that which is within. That which is to be known is the knowledge which is inner to the innermost, like the (sweet) water within the kernel of the coconut.

रागद्वेषविनिर्मुक्तः सर्वभूतहिते रतः ।
दृढबोधश्च धीरश्च स गच्छेत्परमं पदम् ॥ 2.24 ॥

One who is free from attachment and aversion, devoted to the welfare of all beings, of steady understanding (established in right knowledge) and self-possessed, attains the Supreme Abode.

वेदो न दीक्षा न च मुण्डन क्रिया
गुरुर्न शिष्यो न च यन्त्रसम्पदः ।
मुद्रादिकं चापि न यत्र भासते
तमीशमात्मानमुपैति शाश्वतम् ॥ 2.32 ॥

The yogi attains that eternal Supreme Self, that neither all the Vedas nor the initiation into the spiritual path, nor the act of shaving the head, neither guru nor the disciple, nor mystical diagrams of occult powers, nor the positions of fingers in religious worship can bestow.

विधौ निरोधे परमात्मतां गते
न योगिनश्चेतसि भेदवर्जिते ।
शौचं न वाशौचमलिङ्गभावना
सर्वं विधेयं यदि वा निषिध्यते ॥ 2.39 ॥

Having attained the Supreme Self (*Paramātmā*), all injunctions and prohibitions are transcended. In the mind of the yogi, no differentiations arise, either in the form of purity or impurity and the mind is established in the Supreme without attributes. Having transcended all injunctions, things forbidden for others may be undertaken by the yogi.

गुणविगुणविभागो वर्तते नैव किञ्चित्
रतिविरतिविहीनं निर्मलं निष्प्रपञ्चम् ।
गुणविगुणविहीनं व्यापकं विश्वरूपं
कथमहमिह वन्दे व्योमरूपं शिवं वै ॥ 3.1 ॥

In Brahman, the idea of attributes or the absence of attributes does not exist. Brahman is free from delight (love) or the absence of delight (love); It is pure and is the real essence. How then do I worship that Siva (Auspicious one), who is all-pervading like space, in the form of this universe (omnipresent), and who is neither with nor without qualities?

निष्कामकाममिह नाम कथं वदामि
निःसङ्गसङ्गमिह नाम कथं वदामि ।
निःसारसाररहितं च कथं वदामि
ज्ञानामृतं समरसं गगनोपमोऽहम् ॥ 3.4 ॥

"There is desire or desirelessness here"–how can I speak thus in the context of Brahman? "There is attachment or non-attachment here"–how can I speak thus in the context of Brahman? "This is substance (real) or no substance (unreal)"–how can I speak thus in the context of Brahman? I am nectar in the form of Knowledge; like the sky, I am the homogeneous Existence.

निष्कर्मकर्मदहनो ज्वलनो भवामि
निर्दुःखदुःखदहनो ज्वलनो भवामि ।
निर्देहदेहदहनो ज्वलनो भवामि
ज्ञानामृतं समरसं गगनोपमोऽहम् ॥ 3.9 ॥

I am actionless; I am of the nature of the fire (of knowledge) that burns all *karma*. I am free from sorrow; I am of the nature of fire of knowledge that burns all sorrow. I am bodiless; I am of the nature of the fire of knowledge that burns the body-consciousness. I am nectar in the form of Knowledge; like the sky, I am the homogeneous Existence.

निष्पापपापदहनो हि हुताशनोऽहं
निर्धर्मधर्मदहनो हि हुताशनोऽहम् ।
निर्बन्धबन्धदहनो हि हुताशनोऽहं
ज्ञानामृतं समरसं गगनोपमोऽहम् ॥ 3.10 ॥

I am free from any sin; I am of the nature of the fire (of knowledge) that burns all sins. I am free from attributes; I am of the nature of the fire (of knowledge) that burns the notions of attributes. I am free from bondage; I am of the nature of the fire (of knowledge) that burns all bondages. I am nectar in the form of Knowledge; and like the sky, I am the homogeneous Existence.

निष्कम्पकम्पनिधनं न विकल्पकल्पं
स्वप्नप्रबोधनिधनं न हिताहितं हि ।
निःसारसारनिधनं न चराचरं हि
ज्ञानामृतं समरसं गगनोपमोऽहम् ॥ 3.16 ॥

I, Brahman, am neither motionless nor of the nature of vibration (motion); I am devoid of doubt and resolve. In me, there is dissolution of both the dream and wakeful states. The notions of favourable and unfavourable dissolve in me. In me, there is dissolution of the notions of unsubstantial and essential, as well as mobility and immobility. I am nectar in the form of Knowledge; and like the sky, I am the homogeneous Existence.

रागादिदोषरहितं त्वहमेव तत्त्वं
दैवादिदोषरहितं त्वहमेव तत्त्वम् ।
संसारशोकरहितं त्वहमेव तत्त्वं
ज्ञानामृतं समरसं गगनोपमोऽहम् ॥ 3.19 ॥

I am verily the Supreme Reality–free from deficiencies like attachment, etc. I am verily the Supreme Reality–free from any sufferings caused by divinities, etc. I am verily the Supreme Reality–free from grief caused by *samsāra* (worldly existence). I am nectar in the form of Knowledge; and like the sky, I am the homogeneous Existence.

मातापितादि तनयादि न मे कदाचित्
जातं मृतं न च मनो न च मे कदाचित् ।
निर्व्याकुलं स्थिरमिदं परमार्थतत्त्वं
ज्ञानामृतं समरसं गगनोपमोऽहम् ॥ 3.22 ॥

I never had a mother, father, etc., nor even children, etc. I never have birth or death. I never had or will ever have a mind. The Supreme Reality (Brahman) is never agitated and is ever-firm (settled). I am nectar in the form of Knowledge; and like the sky, I am the homogeneous Existence.

शुद्धं विशुद्धमविचारमनन्तरूपं
निर्लेपलेपमविचारमनन्तरूपम् ।
निष्खण्डखण्डमविचारमनन्तरूपं
ज्ञानामृतं समरसं गगनोपमोऽहम् ॥ 3.23 ॥

I am effulgent; I am absolutely pure. I am beyond reason (investigation), and I am of the nature of the infinite. Therefore, it is not possible to investigate my nature as tainted or untainted, and it is also not possible to investigate my nature as with parts (divided) or without parts (undivided). I am nectar in the form of Knowledge; and like the sky, I am the homogeneous Existence.

ब्रह्मादयः सुरगणाः कथमत्र सन्ति
स्वर्गादयो वसतयः कथमत्र सन्ति ।
यद्येकरूपममलं परमार्थतत्त्वं
ज्ञानामृतं समरसं गगनोपमोऽहम् ॥ 3.24 ॥

If the Supreme Reality (Brahman) is One, Absolute and pure, how can many gods like Brahmā be there? How can there be abodes (worlds) like heaven, etc.? I am nectar in the form of Knowledge; and like the sky, I am the homogeneous Existence.

निष्कर्मकर्मपरमं सततं करोमि
निःसङ्गसङ्गरहितं परमं विनोदम् ।
निर्देहदेहरहितं सततं विनोदं
ज्ञानामृतं समरसं गगनोपमोऽहम् ॥ 3.26 ॥

Though I am actionless by nature, I am constantly engaged in the highest activity. Though ever unattached, I greatly delight in the non-attachment. Though bodiless, I delight in the bodilessness. I am nectar in the form of Knowledge; and like the sky, I am the homogeneous Existence.

ध्याता न ते हि हृदये न च ते समाधि-
र्ध्यानं न ते हि हृदये न बहिः प्रदेशः ।
ध्येयं न चेति हृदये न हि वस्तु कालो
ज्ञानामृतं समरसं गगनोपमोऽहम् ॥ 3.41 ॥

In your heart (mind), there is neither meditator, meditation, nor is there any *samādhi*. In your heart, there is no object of meditation. In your heart, there is no space without, nor is there time or substance. I am nectar in the form of Knowledge; and like the sky, I am the homogeneous Existence.

मुञ्च मुञ्च हि संसारं त्यागं मुञ्च हि सर्वथा ।
त्यागात्यागविषं शुद्धममृतं सहजं ध्रुवम् ॥ 3.46 ॥

Renounce this *samsāra* (worldly existence); and then renounce this idea of renunciation altogether. Renounce the poison of renunciation and acceptance (non-renunciation). You are pure, immortal, innate (natural) and unchangeable.

नावाहनं नैव विसर्जनं वा
पुष्पाणि पत्राणि कथं भवन्ति ।
ध्यानानि मन्त्राणि कथं भवन्ति
समासमं चैव शिवार्चनं च ॥ 4.1 ॥

In the case of Brahman (the Supreme Reality), there is neither invocation nor ceremonial send-off. How can there be offerings of flowers and leaves? How can there be meditation and *mantras* for Brahman? How can there be worship for the Auspicious One (Siva), who is the unity and the diversity?

ननु आश्रमवर्णविहीनपरं
ननु कारणकर्तृविहीनपरम् ।
यदि चैकनिरन्तरसर्वशिव-
मविनष्टविनष्टमतिश्च कथम् ॥ 6.14 ॥

The Supreme (Brahman) is free from the idea of *āshrama* (stages of life, viz, *brahmacharya*, etc.) and caste (social classifications in society, viz, *brahmana,* etc.). The Supreme (Brahman) is indeed free from the idea of cause and agent. If the Supreme is One, Indivisible, Absolute and of the nature of Auspiciousness, then how can one apply the ideas of destruction and non-destruction to It?

आशापाशविबन्धनमुक्ताः
शौचाचारविवर्जितयुक्ताः ।
एवं सर्वविवर्जितशान्त-
स्तत्त्वं शुद्धनिरञ्जनवन्तः ॥ 7.3 ॥

The mendicant (*Avadhūta*) is free from the binding fetters of desires. He is established in the Supreme Truth, free from purificatory rites and established rules of conduct. Thus, tranquil and renouncing everything, he is one with Brahman, which is pure and blemishless.

योगवियोगै रहितो योगी
भोगविभोगै रहितो भोगी ।
एवं चरति हि मन्दं मन्दं
मनसा कल्पितसहजानन्दम् ॥ 7.9 ॥

He is a yogi (who has realized the Self and is established in the Self), though he may be given to the practice of yoga (spiritual practices) or abstain from them. He is an enjoyer, though he may have possessions (objects of enjoyment) or may be devoid of possessions. Thus, the *Avadhāta* wanders about slowly and indifferently while enjoying the natural bliss in his mind, which is pure.

इन्द्रजालमिदं सर्वं यथा मरुमरीचिका ।
अखण्डितमनाकारो वर्तते केवलः शिवः ॥ 7.13 ॥

All this (the entire universe) is an illusion, like a mirage (the illusory appearance of water in a desert). The Absolute, indivisible, formless, Siva (Auspiciousness, Supreme Beatitude, i.e., Brahman) alone exists.

त्वद्यात्रया व्यापकता हता ते
ध्यानेन चेतःपरता हता ते ।
स्तुत्या मया वाक्परता हता ते
क्षमस्व नित्यं त्रिविधापराधान् ॥ 8.1 ॥

By undertaking a pilgrimage to behold you somewhere, I destroyed the idea of Your all-pervading nature. By meditating upon You, I violated the idea of You transcending the mind. By eulogising You (and praising Your form), I have violated the truth that You are indescribable. Kindly forgive these three transgressions of mine, always.

* * *

10

Vivekacūḍāmaṇi (विवेकचूडामणि)

Abridged Vivekacūḍāmaṇi

This text was composed by Adi Shankarāchārya. Here are some selected verses:

वदन्तु शास्त्राणि यजन्तु देवान्
कुर्वन्तु कर्माणि भजन्तु देवताः ।
आत्मैक्यबोधेन विनापि मुक्तिः
न सिध्यति ब्रह्मशतान्तरेऽपि ॥ 6 ॥

One may study the scriptures, perform sacrifices (*yajña*) for different deities, perform different acts (including charity) and worship many deities. One may do all these, but without the knowledge of the oneness with the Self, there cannot be any liberation even in a hundred cosmic period of Brahmā.

अमृतत्त्वस्य नाशास्ति वित्तेनेत्येव हि श्रुतिः ।
ब्रवीति कर्मणो मुक्तेरहेतुत्वं स्फुटं यतः ॥ 7 ॥

By means of wealth, there is no hope of attaining immortality– thus say the *shrutis* (Vedas and Upanishads). Therefore, it is very clear that action can never be the means or cause of liberation.

चित्तस्य शुद्धये कर्म न तु वस्तूपलब्धये ।
वस्तुसिद्धिर्विचारेण न किञ्चित्कर्मकोटिभिः ॥ 11 ॥

Any work or action is meant for the purification of the mind alone, and not for realising the Supreme Reality (Truth,

Brahman). The realisation of the Supreme Reality is achieved by enquiry alone. Not even a little of that can be achieved by crores of actions.

अतो विचारः कर्तव्यो जिज्ञासोरात्मवस्तुनः ।
समासाद्य दयासिन्धुं गुरुं ब्रह्मविदुत्तमम् ॥ 15 ॥

Therefore, having approached a guru who is an excellent knower of Brahman and an ocean of compassion, a seeker of Truth (Reality) should enquire into the nature of the Self.

विवेकिनो विरक्तस्य शमादिगुणशालिनः ।
मुमुक्षोरेव हि ब्रह्मजिज्ञासायोग्यता मता ॥ 17 ॥

The one who has the faculty of *viveka* (discrimination between the real and unreal), who is unattached, who is endowed with qualities like mental restraint etc., and who yearns for *moksha* (liberation), such a one is indeed fit (has the necessary qualities) to enquire into the Supreme Reality (Brahman).

मोक्षकारणसामग्र्यां भक्तिरेव गरीयसी ।
स्वस्वरूपानुसन्धानं भक्तिरित्यभिधीयते ॥ 31 ॥

Out of all the means to attain *moksha* (liberation), devotion is the greatest one. Investigation (enquiry) into one's real nature is called devotion (*bhakti*).

स्वात्मतत्त्वानुसन्धानं भक्तिरित्यपरे जगुः ।
उक्तसाधनसम्पन्नस्तत्त्वजिज्ञासुरात्मनः ।
उपसीदेद्गुरुं प्राज्ञं यस्माद्बन्धविमोक्षणम् ॥ 32 ॥

"The investigation or enquiry into the real nature of the Self is devotion", say some others. The one endowed with the four qualities (viz., *viveka*, *vairāgya*, mental restraint, etc., and yearning for liberation), who yearns to realise the Self, should approach a guru. That opens the path to liberation from bondage.

वेदान्तार्थविचारेण जायते ज्ञानमुत्तमम् ।
तेनात्यन्तिकसंसारदुःखनाशो भवत्यनु ॥ 45 ॥

By contemplating the meaning and purport of Vedanta, knowledge arises and that results in the complete destruction of misery born of *samsāra*.

वस्तुस्वरूपं स्फुटबोधचक्षुषा
स्वेनैव वेद्यं न तु पण्डितेन ।
चन्द्रस्वरूपं निजचक्षुषैव
ज्ञातव्यमन्यैरवगम्यते किम् ॥ 54 ॥

Just as the form of the moon is seen only by one's own eyes and not by another's, in the same manner, the true nature of the Self is realised by means of the eye of awakened knowledge of one's own self, by oneself, and not by a wise one's (preceptor's).

न योगेन न साङ्ख्येन कर्मणा नो न विद्यया ।
ब्रह्मात्मैकत्वबोधेन मोक्षः सिध्यति नान्यथा ॥ 56 ॥

Liberation is not attained by following the path of yoga, not by the path of Sānkhya, not by the path of action (*karma*), and not by knowledge of the scriptures. It is attained only by realising the oneness of the Self with Brahman and not by any other means.

वाग्वैखरी शब्दझरी शास्त्रव्याख्यानकौशलम् ।
वैदुष्यं विदुषां तद्वद्भुक्तये न तु मुक्तये ॥ 58 ॥

Proficiency in a language, eloquence with speech, ability to expound, skill in explaining the scriptures and scholarliness–all these are merely means of enjoyment. They do not lead one to liberation.

मोक्षस्य हेतुः प्रथमो निगद्यते
वैराग्यमत्यन्तमनित्यवस्तुषु ।
ततः शमश्चापि दमस्तितिक्षा
न्यासः प्रसक्ताखिलकर्मणां भृशम् ॥ 69 ॥

Absolute *vairāgya* (non-attachment) towards the objects that are transient (perishable) in nature is the first means to *moksha* (liberation). After that follows tranquility, self-restraint, forbearance and complete renunciation of all actions aimed at fulfilling one's desires.

विषयाख्यग्रहो येन सुविरक्त्यसिना हतः ।
स गच्छति भवाम्भोधेः पारं प्रत्यूहवर्जितः ॥ 80 ॥

By the sword of intense non-attachment, one who destroys the sharks of desires for sense objects crosses the ocean of *samsāra*, overcoming all obstacles.

मोक्षस्य काङ्क्षा यदि वै तवास्ति
त्यजातिदूराद्विषयान्विषं यथा ।
पीयूषवत्तोषदयाक्षमार्जव-
प्रशान्तिदान्तीर्भज नित्यमादरात् ॥ 82 ॥

If your yearning is indeed for liberation alone, abandon, by a long way, desires for objects as if they are poison. And always adopt with great care, the virtues of contentment, compassion, forbearance, straightforwardness, calmness and self-restraint, as if they are nectar.

शरीरपोषणार्थी सन् य आत्मानं दिदृक्षति ।
ग्राहं दारुधिया धृत्वा नदीं तर्तुं स गच्छति ॥ 84 ॥

Being indulgent with regard to the body (and everything related to it), one who aspires to realise the Self is as if he wishes to cross the river by holding on to a crocodile, thinking it is a floating log of wood.

मोह एव महामृत्युर्मुमुक्षोर्वपुरादिषु ।
मोहो विनिर्जितो येन स मुक्तिपदमर्हति ॥ 85 ॥

Any delusion regarding the body, etc. is indeed a dire death for the seeker of liberation. One who conquers this delusion alone deserves the abode of liberation.

मोहं जहि महामृत्युं देहदारसुतादिषु ।
यं जित्वा मुनयो यान्ति तद्विष्णोः परमं पदम् ॥ 86 ॥

Win over the grave death of delusion over the body, wife, children, etc. Having won over this delusion, the wise ones attain the supreme abode of Lord Vishnu.

त्वङ्मांसरुधिरस्नायुमेदोमज्जास्थिसङ्कुलम् ।
पूर्णं मूत्रपुरीषाभ्यां स्थूलं निन्द्यमिदं वपुः ॥ 87 ॥

This gross form (body) is a mingled assembly of skin, flesh, blood, ligament, lymph, marrow and bones and is completely filled with urine and faeces, and this gross body is reprehensible.

सर्वोऽपि बाह्यसंसारः पुरुषस्य यदाश्रयः ।
विद्धि देहमिदं स्थूलं गृहवद्गृहमेधिनः ॥ 90 ॥

On the body of the human being rests all the transactions and interactions with the world of external phenomena. Know that this gross body is just like the house in the case of a householder.

अव्यक्तनाम्नी परमेशशक्तिः
अनाद्यविद्या त्रिगुणात्मिका परा ।
कार्यानुमेया सुधियैव माया
यया जगत्सर्वमिदं प्रसूयते ॥ 108 ॥

Māyā, also called 'unmanifested', is the power of the Lord. It is beginningless ignorance, made up of the three *guṇas* (*sattva, rajas, tamas*) and is the cause of the entire universe. This is to be deduced by the right understanding from its effect. [In other words, it is to be deduced by investigating the effect (the universe) using right understanding.]

कामः क्रोधो लोभदम्भाद्यसूया
अहङ्कारेर्ष्यामत्सराद्यास्तु घोराः ।
धर्मा एते राजसाः पुम्प्रवृत्ति-
र्यस्मादेषा तद्रजो बन्धहेतुः ॥ 112 ॥

Desire, anger, greed, hypocrisy, jealousy, egoism, envy, selfishness, etc., are all dreadful traits that are *rājasic* in nature, primarily causing action in human beings. This *rajas* is the cause of bondage.

न जायते नो म्रियते न वर्धते
न क्षीयते नो विकरोति नित्यः ।
विलीयमानेऽपि वपुष्यमुष्मि-
न्न लीयते कुम्भ इवाम्बरं स्वयम् ॥ 134 ॥

The Self is neither born nor does it die, nor does it grow, nor does it decay, nor does it ever undergo any change. Also, just as when the pitcher breaks, the space inside it does not get destroyed; in the same manner, when the body dies, the Self does not cease to exist.

अज्ञानमूलोऽयमनात्मबन्धो
नैसर्गिकोऽनादिरनन्त ईरितः ।
जन्माप्ययव्याधिजरादिदुःख-
प्रवाहपातं जनयत्यमुष्य ॥ 146 ॥

This bondage of the *anātmā* (non-Self, i.e., everything that is not the Self, including objects of the world, including the body) is rooted in ignorance, is naturally occurring, and is said to be beginningless and endless. It creates a series of miseries for the human being in the form of birth, death, disease, old age, etc.

नास्त्रैर्न शस्त्रैरनिलेन वह्निना
छेत्तुं न शक्यो न च कर्मकोटिभिः ।
विवेकविज्ञानमहासिना विना
धातुः प्रसादेन शितेन मञ्जुना ॥ 147 ॥

This bondage (as described above) is not destroyed by any weapons, invocations, wind, fire, ceremonies and rituals. Only with the sword of *viveka* (the faculty of discrimination between real and unreal) and realisation of knowledge of the Self, and with the purity of the mind, can this bondage be destroyed.

श्रुतिप्रमाणैकमतेः स्वधर्म-
निष्ठा तयैवात्मविशुद्धिरस्य ।
विशुद्धबुद्धेः परमात्मवेदनं
तेनैव संसारसमूलनाशः ॥ 148 ॥

Only through intellect and understanding, being devoted to the authority of the *Shrutis* (Upanishads), there is steadfastness in *svadharama* (one's duties that are aligned with one's nature and characteristics). And only through *svadharama* is there purity of the mind. Through this purity of the mind, one realises the Universal Self, and through that, there is the destruction of *samsāra*, along with its roots.

अत्रात्मबुद्धिं त्यज मूढबुद्धे
त्वङ्मांसमेदोऽस्थिपुरीषराशौ ।
सर्वात्मनि ब्रह्मणि निर्विकल्पे
कुरुष्व शान्तिं परमां भजस्व ॥ 161 ॥

O dull-witted one! Abandon the sense of identifying yourself with this heap of skin, flesh, fat (marrow), bone and excrement. (In other words, do not identify the Self with the body.) Instead, identify yourself with Brahman, the unchangeable Self of all. And then enjoy supreme peace.

देहेन्द्रियादावसति भ्रमोदितां
विद्वानहन्तां न जहाति यावत् ।
तावन्न तस्यास्ति विमुक्तिवार्ता-
प्यस्त्वेष वेदान्तनयान्तदर्शी ॥ 162 ॥

As long as a scholar (one who has the bookish knowledge alone of the scriptures) does not give up the idea of wrong identification (which is born out of delusion) with the body, sense organs, etc., which are all *asat* (unreal), till then there is no possibility of liberation, even if this person is very proficient in the philosophy of Vedanta.

स्वप्नेऽर्थशून्ये सृजति स्वशक्त्या
भोक्त्रादिविश्वं मन एव सर्वम् ।
तथैव जाग्रत्यपि नो विशेषः
तत्सर्वमेतन्मनसो विजृम्भणम् ॥ 170 ॥

By its own power, the mind creates an entire universe in the dream state, consisting of experiencer, experience, etc. The mind creates the dream universe without the foundation of objects. Likewise, the wakeful state is no different. Everything (the entire universe) is nothing but an expansion (projection) of the mind.

तन्मनःशोधनं कार्यं प्रयत्नेन मुमुक्षुणा ।
विशुद्धे सति चैतस्मिन्मुक्तिः करफलायते ॥ 181 ॥

Therefore, the aspirant of liberation (the seeker of Truth) must endeavour to purify the mind through diligent effort. And, when the mind is thus purified, *mukti* (liberation) will be as easy as a fruit placed in the palm of one's hand.

भ्रान्तिं विना त्वसङ्गस्य निष्क्रियस्य निराकृतेः ।
न घटेतार्थसम्बन्धो नभसो नीलतादिवत् ॥ 195 ॥

Only because of delusion is there an association of the Self with the world of visible phenomena. For the Self by itself is unattached, actionless and formless. This is the same as the case of the blue colour of the sky because the blue colour has no association with the sky.

यदि सत्यं भवेद्विश्वं सुषुप्तावुपलभ्यताम् ।
यन्नोपलभ्यते किञ्चिदतोऽसत्स्वप्नवन्मृषा ॥ 234 ॥

If the phenomenal universe is real, then let it also manifest itself in the state of deep sleep (devoid of dreams). Since the universe is not experienced in deep sleep, it is untrue (false), like the case of a dream.

लोकानुवर्तनं त्यक्त्वा त्यक्त्वा देहानुवर्तनम् ।
शास्त्रानुवर्तनं त्यक्त्वा स्वाध्यासापनयं कुरु ॥ 270 ॥

Giving up compliance with social formalities in the world (with the aim of enjoying the world), giving up gratification of the body, and giving up excessive indulgence in the scriptures, get rid of the false identification (or delusion) that has come upon you.

लोकवासनया जन्तोः शास्त्रवासनयापि च ।
देहवासनया ज्ञानं यथावन्नैव जायते ॥ 271 ॥

Desires regarding one's own name, fame, status, etc., in the society (and world), desires regarding knowledge of the scriptures and the desires regarding the body–from all these desires of the human being, true Self-knowledge never arises.

संसारकारागृहमोक्षमिच्छो-
रयोमयं पादनिबन्धशृङ्खलम् ।
वदन्ति तज्ज्ञाः पटु वासनात्रयं
योऽस्माद्विमुक्तः समुपैति मुक्तिम् ॥ 272 ॥

For the ones who seek freedom from the prison of *samsāra*, these three desires (regarding the world, knowledge of scriptures and body) are like strong iron chains binding the legs. So say the knowers of Truth. Those who become free from these three desires attain liberation.

अनात्मवासनाजालैस्तिरोभूतात्मवासना ।
नित्यात्मनिष्ठया तेषां नाशे भाति स्वयं स्फुटम् ॥ 275 ॥

The desire for the Self (Self-knowledge) is completely veiled by the web of desires for the non-Self-objects (objects other than the Self). When the web of desires (for objects of the world) is destroyed by the constant steadfastness in the Self, then that Self shines by itself.

यथा यथा प्रत्यगवस्थितं मनः
तथा तथा मुञ्चति बाह्यवासनाम् ।
निःशेषमोक्षे सति वासनानां
आत्मानुभूतिः प्रतिबन्धशून्या ॥ 276 ॥

To the extent the mind is turned inward (towards the Self), the mind is freed from the grip of desires (for the objects of the world). And when the desires are completely destroyed, then there is realisation of the Self without any obstruction.

घटाकाशं महाकाश इवात्मानं परात्मनि ।
विलाप्याखण्डभावेन तूष्णीं भव सदा मुने ॥ 288 ॥

When the clay pitcher breaks, the space enclosed by the pitcher merges into the infinite space. In the same manner, the Self merges with the *Paramātmā* (Universal Self) through meditation on the Universal Identity. Therefore, remain silent, O, Wise one!

चिदात्मनि सदानन्दे देहारूढामहन्धियम् ।
निवेश्य लिङ्गमुत्सृज्य केवलो भव सर्वदा ॥ 290 ॥

Having established the I-sense, which is currently with the body (i.e., the identification of the Self with the body), upon the ever-blissful Consciousness, and having discarded the identification with the subtle body also, be the ever-Absolute (non-dual) One.

यत्रैष जगदाभासो दर्पणान्तः पुरं यथा ।
तद्ब्रह्माहमिति ज्ञात्वा कृतकृत्यो भविष्यसि ॥ 291 ॥

Just as the city appears as a reflection in the mirror, in the same manner where the entire universe appears—that Brahman (the Supreme Reality) you are. Knowing (realizing) this, attain the goal of life, where there is nothing for you to do as a duty (or responsibility) in this world.

अतोऽभिमानं त्यज मांसपिण्डे
पिण्डाभिमानिन्यपि बुद्धिकल्पिते ।
कालत्रयाबाध्यमखण्डबोधं
ज्ञात्वा स्वमात्मानमुपैहि शान्तिम् ॥ 296 ॥

Give up the sense of identification with this body, which is the result of ignorance (delusion). Also, give up identification with the ego, which too has arisen out of ignorance of understanding. Realising the absolute unfragmented awareness of the nature of the Self, which is not opposed to (denied in) the three periods (of past, present and future), attain peace.

वासनावृद्धितः कार्यं कार्यवृद्ध्या च वासना ।
वर्धते सर्वथा पुंसः संसारो न निवर्तते ॥ 313 ॥

When there is an increase in the desires (regarding the objects of the world), there is an increase in the activities that are aimed at fulfilling those desires. And when the activities increase, there is again an increase in desires. For such a one, the grip of *samsāra* constantly increases and never ceases.

ताभ्यां प्रवर्धमाना सा सूते संसृतिमात्मनः ।
त्रयाणां च क्षयोपायः सर्वावस्थासु सर्वदा ॥ 315 ॥
सर्वत्र सर्वतः सर्वब्रह्ममात्रावलोकनैः ।
सद्भाववासनादार्ढ्यात्तत्त्रयं लयमश्नुते ॥ 316 ॥

Enhanced by these two (thought of sense objects and actions), the desires bring forth one's own bondage with *samsāra*. The following is the means to cause the destruction of these three (*vāsanās*, thought of objects and action): perceive everything as Brahman alone, in all states, always, everywhere and completely. By strengthening the steadfastness of the desire to be one with the Supreme Brahman, these three attain extinction.

क्रियानाशे भवेच्चिन्तानाशोऽस्माद्वासनाक्षयः ।
वासनाप्रक्षयो मोक्षः स जीवन्मुक्तिरिष्यते ॥ 317 ॥

When there is an elimination of actions (that are aimed at the fulfilment of desires), there is a cessation of constant thinking about the objects of the world. And from that, there is the destruction of desires. The complete destruction of desires is what is called *moksha* (liberation). And this is referred to as *jīvan-mukti* (liberation while living).

न प्रमादादनर्थोऽन्यो ज्ञानिनः स्वस्वरूपतः ।
ततो मोहस्ततोऽहन्धीस्ततो बन्धस्ततो व्यथा ॥ 322 ॥

For a wise one, there is no greater danger than negligence about one's true nature. This leads to delusion, then follows egotism, which is followed by bondage, and then comes misery or suffering.

लक्ष्यच्युतं चेद्यदि चित्तमीषद्
बहिर्मुखं सन्निपतेत्ततस्ततः ।
प्रमादतः प्रच्युतकेलिकन्दुकः
सोपानपङ्क्तौ पतितो यथा तथा ॥ 325 ॥

If the mind deviates from the goal of attaining the Supreme, even a little bit, and becomes outward-facing (i.e., it is drawn towards the objects of the world), then the mind goes down continuously (without control). This is like the case of a ball that falls from the hand and goes down a series of steps uncontrollably.

आवरणस्य निवृत्तिर्भवति हि सम्यक्पदार्थदर्शनतः ।
मिथ्याज्ञानविनाशस्तद्विक्षेपजनितदुःखनिवृत्तिः ॥ 347 ॥

Only with the realisation of the Supreme Truth, there is the destruction of the veil (that veils the Truth), and then there is the destruction of ignorance (in the form of delusion). From this follows the ending of suffering generated by delusion.

बहिस्तु विषयैः सङ्गं तथान्तरहमादिभिः ।
विरक्त एव शक्नोति त्यक्तुं ब्रह्मणि निष्ठितः ॥ 373 ॥

Only the one who is free from attachments and is firmly established in Brahman (the Supreme Reality) can give up attachments to external objects and also attachment to inner objects like the 'I-sense', etc.

वैराग्यबोधौ पुरुषस्य पक्षिवत्
पक्षौ विजानीहि विचक्षण त्वम् ।
विमुक्तिसौधाग्रलताधिरोहणं
ताभ्यां विना नान्यतरेण सिध्यति ॥ 374 ॥

O wise one! Non-attachment (*vairāgya*) and discrimination (*viveka*) are like the two wings of a bird. [Here, the bird is the seeker of Truth or the aspirant of liberation.] The climb to the uppermost storey of the mansion of *mukti* (liberation) is not possible without the presence of both these wings.

अत्यन्तवैराग्यवतः समाधिः
समाहितस्यैव दृढप्रबोधः ।
प्रबुद्धतत्त्वस्य हि बन्धमुक्तिः
मुक्तात्मनो नित्यसुखानुभूतिः ॥ 375 ॥

The one who is exceedingly and perpetually unattached (towards the objects of the world) attains *samādhi*. The one who is steadfast in *samādhi* attains unwavering and steady wisdom (i.e., knowledge of the Supreme Truth). The one with established wisdom alone is liberated from all bondages. And for the one free from bondages alone, there is experience of everlasting happiness.

आशां छिन्द्धि विषोपमेषु विषयेष्वेषैव मृत्योः कृति-
स्त्यक्त्वा जातिकुलाश्रमेष्वभिमतिं मुञ्चातिदूरात्क्रियाः ।
देहादावसति त्यजात्मधिषणां प्रज्ञां कुरुष्वात्मनि
त्वं द्रष्टास्यमनोऽसि निर्द्वयपरं ब्रह्मासि यद्वस्तुतः ॥ 377 ॥

Cut asunder the desires for the sense objects, which are like poison. The desires are of the nature of death. Giving up pride in caste, family, and the order of life one belongs to, abandon any actions being done for selfish motives. Also, give up any identification with the unreal, like the body, etc. Be steadfast in the knowledge of the Self. For, you are, by nature, the witness to everything and transcending the mind, you are the non-dual Brahman in essence.

लक्ष्ये ब्रह्मणि मानसं दृढतरं संस्थाप्य बाह्येन्द्रियं
स्वस्थाने विनिवेश्य निश्चलतनुश्चोपेक्ष्य देहस्थितिम् ।
ब्रह्मात्मैक्यमुपेत्य तन्मयतया चाखण्डवृत्त्याऽनिशं
ब्रह्मानन्दरसं पिबात्मनि मुदा शून्यैः किमन्यैर्भृशम् ॥ 378 ॥

Establishing the mind firmly in the goal, which is none other than the Supreme Brahman, resting the outward facing senses in their respective centres, keeping the body stable, giving up the body-identification, and attaining the oneness of Self with Brahman, become one with Brahman. In that oneness with Brahman, drink the nectar of the Supreme Bliss, in your own Self. What is the use of anything else which are all hollow?

घटकलशकुसूलसूचिमुख्यैः
गगनमुपाधिशतैर्विमुक्तमेकम् ।
भवति न विविधं तथैव शुद्धं
परमहमादिविमुक्तमेकमेव ॥ 385 ॥

The sky (space) is one and free from the hundreds of adjuncts (limitations) like jars, waterpot, granaries (store-room), needles, etc., and the sky is not manifold. In the same manner, the Pure-one (Brahman) is One and is free from limitations like egoism, etc.

स्वयं ब्रह्मा स्वयं विष्णुः स्वयमिन्द्रः स्वयं शिवः ।
स्वयं विश्वमिदं सर्वं स्वस्मादन्यन्न किञ्चन ॥ 388 ॥

The Self is Brahmā; the Self is Vishnu; the Self is Indra; the Self is Siva; the Self is this entire universe. There is nothing other than the Self.

आकाशवन्निर्मलनिर्विकल्पं
निःसीमनिःस्पन्दननिर्विकारम् ।
अन्तर्बहिःशून्यमनन्यमद्वयं
स्वयं परं ब्रह्म किमस्ति बोध्यम् ॥ 393 ॥

Brahman is like the sky—pure (unblemished), free from change (absolute), unbounded (limitless), motionless (unwavering), formless, devoid of the idea of inner and outer, One and non-dual (having no other, or without a second). That (Brahman) is verily one's own Self. What else is there to know?

स्वात्मन्यारोपिताशेषाभासवस्तुनिरासतः ।
स्वयमेव परं ब्रह्म पूर्णमद्वयमक्रियम् ॥ 397 ॥

Following the negation (or refutation) of the entire appearance (the entire visible phenomena) superimposed on the Self, the Supreme Brahman–the full, non-dual, actionless One–alone remains as Itself.

समाहितायां सति चित्तवृत्तौ
परात्मनि ब्रह्मणि निर्विकल्पे ।
न दृश्यते कश्चिदयं विकल्पः
प्रजल्पमात्रः परिशिष्यते यतः ॥ 398 ॥

When the functions (activities) of the mind are dissolved or merged (in *samādhi*) in the changeless absolute Brahman, the Universal Self, then this changeful (transient) universe is not at all seen. What remains becomes a mere idea (hollow words) and nothing else.

द्रष्टृदर्शनदृश्यादिभावशून्यैकवस्तुनि ।
निर्विकारे निराकारे निर्विशेषे भिदा कुतः ॥ 400 ॥

In the One, formless, changeless, attribute-less Supreme Brahman, which is free from the ideas of perceiver, perceiving and perceived, where is the scope for any kind of differentiation (or distinction)?

मायामात्रमिदं द्वैतमद्वैतं परमार्थतः ।
इति ब्रूते श्रुतिः साक्षात्सुषुप्तावनुभूयते ॥ 405 ॥

From the position of the Supreme Truth, this dualistic universe is merely illusory (*māyā*); only the non-dual Supreme is real. Thus say the *Shrutis* (Vedas, Upanishads). There is direct experience of this even in the sleep state.

चित्तमूलो विकल्पोऽयं चित्ताभावे न कश्चन ।
अतश्चित्तं समाधेहि प्रत्यग्रूपे परात्मनि ॥ 407 ॥

This ever-changing (transient) universe has its foundation (origin) in the mind, and in the absence (destruction) of the mind, it does not remain. Therefore, establish the mind (to merge or destroy it) in the inmost Universal (Supreme) Self.

अजरममरमस्ताभाववस्तुस्वरूपं
स्तिमितसलिलराशिप्रख्यमाख्याविहीनम् ।
शमितगुणविकारं शाश्वतं शान्तमेकं
हृदि कलयति विद्वान् ब्रह्म पूर्णं समाधौ ॥ 410 ॥

The wise one realises the full, absolute Supreme Brahman in his heart through *samādhi*. That Brahman is undecaying, immortal, is of the nature that has no possibility of non-existence (and devoid of negations), is like a calm ocean, is without a name (cannot be announced to be thus), is devoid of any merits or demerits, is eternal, is tranquil and is one.

सर्वोपाधिविनिर्मुक्तं सच्चिदानन्दमद्वयम् ।
भावयात्मानमात्मस्थं न भूयः कल्पसेऽध्वने ॥ 412 ॥

Meditate upon the Self that abides within you–the Self that is free from all adjuncts (limitations), which is Existence-Consciousness-Bliss (*sat-chit-ānanda*), and is non-dual. Then, you will no longer be subject to the recurring cycle of births and deaths. In other words, you shall attain *moksha*.

वैराग्यस्य फलं बोधो बोधस्योपरतिः फलम् ।
स्वानन्दानुभवाच्छान्तिरेषैवोपरतेः फलम् ॥ 419 ॥

The fruit of non-attachment (*vairāgya*) is knowledge (of the Self); the fruit of knowledge is withdrawal from pleasures of the senses (*uparati*), and the fruit of withdrawal from sense-enjoyments is the experience of the bliss of one's true nature (the Self), and that in turn leads to peace.

लीनधीरपि जागर्ति जाग्रद्धर्मविवर्जितः ।
बोधो निर्वासनो यस्य स जीवन्मुक्त इष्यते ॥ 429 ॥

One whose mind is established in the Supreme (is one with the Supreme), who is awake to the world around and is still free from the characteristics of the wakeful state (like egoism, likes, dislikes, desires, etc.) and whose awakening (realisation) is free from desires–such a one is said to be a *jīvan-mukta* (literally liberated while alive).

वर्तमानेऽपि देहेऽस्मिञ्छायावदनुवर्तिनि ।
अहन्ताममताऽभावो जीवन्मुक्तस्य लक्षणम् ॥ 431 ॥

While present in this body, which remains like a shadow and is free from the notions of 'I' and 'mine', is a characteristic of a *jīvan-mukta.*

अतीताननुसन्धानं भविष्यदविचारणम् ।
औदासीन्यमपि प्राप्तं जीवन्मुक्तस्य लक्षणम् ॥ 432 ॥

Not inquiring (investigating) into the past, not thinking about the future and being unattached to the present happenings (favourable or unfavourable) are the characteristics of a *jīvan-mukta.*

ज्ञानोदयात्पुरारब्धं कर्म ज्ञानान्न नश्यति ।
अदत्वा स्वफलं लक्ष्यमुद्दिश्योत्सृष्टबाणवत् ॥ 451 ॥

Just as an arrow that has been sent forth towards an object does not distinguish the nature of the object (at the time of striking it), in the same manner, even after the realisation of knowledge (of the Self), the effects of the past *karma* that have been set in motion (prior to the knowledge-realisation) are not destroyed without yielding their outcome. [This is a description of *prārabdha-karma.*]

व्याघ्रबुद्ध्या विनिर्मुक्तो बाणः पश्चात्तु गोमतौ ।
न तिष्ठति छिनत्येव लक्ष्यं वेगेन निर्भरम् ॥ 452 ॥

Thinking the target is a tiger, an arrow has been despatched towards it. Midway (after shooting the arrow), realising that the target is a cow, the arrow cannot be stopped. It will strike the target with all the force it was despatched with.

परिपूर्णमनाद्यन्तमप्रमेयमविक्रियम् ।
एकमेवाद्वयं ब्रह्म नेह नानास्ति किञ्चन ॥ 464 ॥

[Description of non-dual Brahman]: There is Brahman alone, which is complete, beginningless, eternal, unfathomable, unchangeable and one. There is no variety (duality) at all here.

असङ्गोऽहमनङ्गोऽहमलिङ्गोऽहमभङ्गुरः ।
प्रशान्तोऽहमनन्तोऽहममलोऽहं चिरन्तनः ॥ 489 ॥

I am unattached. I am devoid of the body (I have no identification with the body). I am free from the subtle body, also. I am unchangeable. I am tranquil. I am eternal. I am blemishless. I am eternal.

अकर्ताहमभोक्ताहमविकारोऽहमक्रियः ।
शुद्धबोधस्वरूपोऽहं केवलोऽहं सदाशिवः ॥ 490 ॥

I am a non-doer (free from the notion of doership). I am a non-experiencer (free from the notion of experiencer-ship). I am changeless. I transcend action and inaction. I am of the nature of pure knowledge. I am absolute (one). I am of the nature of everlasting auspiciousness.

मय्यखण्डसुखाम्भोधौ बहुधा विश्ववीचयः ।
उत्पद्यन्ते विलीयन्ते मायामारुतविभ्रमात् ॥ 496 ॥

In me, the mighty ocean of unbounded bliss, manifold waves in the form of the universe arise and subside, by the play of the wind called *māyā*.

आकाशवल्लेपविदूरगोऽहं
आदित्यवद्भास्यविलक्षणोऽहम् ।
अहार्यवन्नित्यविनिश्चलोऽहं
अम्भोधिवत्पारविवर्जितोऽहम् ॥ 499 ॥

Like the sky, I am beyond any contamination (blemish). Like the sun, I am different from any illuminating object. Like a mountain, I am ever-immovable. And like the ocean, I am beyond any limits (unbounded).

जले वापि स्थले वापि लुठत्वेष जडात्मकः ।
नाहं विलिप्ये तद्धर्मैर्घटधर्मैर्नभो यथा ॥ 509 ॥

This inert (insentient) body may roll down in water or on land. But I (the Self) am not tainted by these characteristics, just as the sky (space) inside the pitcher is untouched by the characteristics of the pitcher.

अयमात्मा नित्यसिद्धः प्रमाणे सति भासते ।
न देशं नापि कालं न शुद्धिं वाप्यपेक्षते ॥ 531 ॥

This ever-fulfilled Self shines when the right knowledge (of the Upanishads), nurtured by study, reflection and meditation, is present. This experience does not depend upon place, time and purificatory rites.

न खिद्यते नो विषयैः प्रमोदते
न सज्जते नापि विरज्यते च ।
स्वस्मिन्सदा क्रीडति नन्दति स्वयं
निरन्तरानन्दरसेन तृप्तः ॥ 536 ॥

The one who has realised the Self is not distressed and not elated by any sense object (thing or person) and neither clings to nor is averse to any sense object. But, content with everlasting bliss, such a wise one delights and sports in the Self by oneself.

चिन्ताशून्यमदैन्यभैक्षमशनं पानं सरिद्वारिषु
स्वातन्त्र्येण निरङ्कुशा स्थितिरभीर्निद्रा श्मशाने वने ।
वस्त्रं क्षालनशोषणादिरहितं दिग्वास्तु शय्या मही
सञ्चारो निगमान्तवीथिषु विदां क्रीडा परे ब्रह्मणि ॥ 538 ॥

The wise–without any anxiety and any sense of humiliation–have food obtained by begging. The drink for them is the water obtained from the streams or rivers. They live and move about freely and without any restraint and sleep in a forest or a cremation ground without fear. For clothing, they may use unwashed and undried clothes or just stay naked. They may use the bare ground as the bed. They wander in the path of the Vedas–they sport in the Supreme Brahman.

विमानमालम्ब्य शरीरमेतद्
भुनक्त्यशेषान्विषयानुपस्थितान् ।
परेच्छया बालवदात्मवेत्ता
योऽव्यक्तलिङ्गोऽननुषक्तबाह्यः ॥ 539 ॥

Without any insignia (marked features) or external attachments, the one who has realised the Self experiences all the sense-objects that come to him as if he were a child. He takes refuge in the body without any sense of identification with the body.

दिगम्बरो वापि च साम्बरो वा
त्वगम्बरो वापि चिदम्बरस्थः ।
उन्मत्तवद्वापि च बालवद्वा
पिशाचवद्वापि चरत्यवन्याम् ॥ 540 ॥

Established in the plane of Pure Consciousness, the wise one moves about on this earth sometimes naked (without any dress), sometimes with clothes, sometimes using skins of animals as dress, sometimes like a mad person, sometimes like a child or at other times like a devilish being.

जीवन्नेव सदा मुक्तः कृतार्थो ब्रह्मवित्तमः ।
उपाधिनाशाद्ब्रह्मैव सन् ब्रह्माप्येति निर्द्वयम् ॥ 554 ॥

The excellent knower of Brahman, even while living, is always liberated, having attained the object (liberation) of life. Because of the destruction of all limitations, being Brahman itself, such a one attains the non-dual Brahman.

शैलूषो वेषसद्भावाभावयोश्च यथा पुमान् ।
तथैव ब्रह्मविच्छ्रेष्ठः सदा ब्रह्मैव नापरः ॥ 555 ॥

An actor remains the same individual as he is, whether he puts on a costume for a particular role or is without the costume. In the same manner, a knower of Brahman is always Brahman and nothing else.

देहस्य मोक्षो नो मोक्षो न दण्डस्य कमण्डलोः ।
अविद्याहृदयग्रन्थिमोक्षो मोक्षो यतस्ततः ॥ 558 ॥

Death of the body is not *moksha* (liberation), nor is giving up the ceremonial staff and water bowl liberation. Complete destruction of the knots of ignorance (delusion) of the heart is real liberation.

पत्रस्य पुष्पस्य फलस्य नाशवद्-
देहेन्द्रियप्राणधियां विनाशः ।
नैवात्मनः स्वस्य सदात्मकस्या-
नन्दाकृतेर्वृक्षवदस्ति चैषः ॥ 560 ॥

Just as the leaf, flower and fruit fall from the tree and are destroyed, in the same manner, the body, the sense organs, the life forces and intellect are destroyed. There is no destruction of the Self. Just like the tree, one's real nature, which is of the nature of bliss, is never destroyed.

* * *

Section 4

This section presents the following six texts on Advaita Vedanta:

Tattvabodha

Ātmabodha

Amritabindu Upanishad

Dṛg-dṛśya-viveka

Upadesha Sāram

Sat-darshanam

11

Tattvabodhaḥ
(तत्त्वबोधः)

The Four-fold Means

साधन-चतुष्टय-संपन्नाधिकारिणां मोक्ष-साधन-भूतं तत्त्व-विवेक-प्रकारं वक्ष्यामः ।

For those who are endowed with the four-fold means–that are the means to accomplish the goal of liberation–we shall now expound the way to realise the Truth (Self-knowledge).

साधन-चतुष्टयं किम् ?

What are the four-fold means?

नित्यानित्य-वस्तु-विवेकः । इहामुत्रार्थ-फल-भोग-विरागः । शमादिषट्क-सम्पत्तिः । मुमुक्षुत्वं चेति ।

They are as follows: (1) The discrimination between the permanent and the impermanent; (2) Detachment or dispassion towards the enjoyment of fruits of one's own actions here and hereafter (in the other world); (3) Six virtues or excellences including mind control, etc.; and (4) Yearning for liberation.

नित्यानित्यवस्तुविवेकः कः ?

What is *viveka*, the discrimination between the permanent and the impermanent?

नित्यवस्त्वेकं ब्रह्म तद्व्यतिरिक्तं सर्वमनित्यम् । अयमेव नित्यानित्यवस्तुविवेकः ।

Brahman (the Supreme Reality) alone is eternal and permanent, and it is the only ONE; everything other than that is impermanent.

This faculty of discrimination between the permanent and the transient is *viveka*.

विरागः कः ?

What is detachment?

इह-स्वर्ग-भोगेषु इच्छा-राहित्यम् ।

Detachment (*virāga, vairāgya*) is being free from desires regarding pleasures or enjoyments here in this world (from objects, things, people, possessions, name, etc.) and from those related to heaven (i.e. otherworldly).

शमादिसाधनसम्पत्तिः का ?

What are control of the mind (*shama*) and other qualities or excellences that are the means to the spiritual goal?

शमो दम उपरमस्तितिक्षा श्रद्धा समाधानं च इति ।

They are: *shama, dama, uparama, titikshā, shraddhā and samādhāṇa.*

शमः कः ?

What is *shama*?

मनो निग्रहः ।

Restraining (mastering, controlling) the mind.

दमः कः ?

What is *dama*?

चक्षुरादि-बाह्येन्द्रिय-निग्रहः ।

Restraining (mastery over) the eye and the other external sense organs.

उपरमः कः ?

What is *uparama*?

स्वधर्मानुष्ठानमेव ।

Observance of one's own *svadharma*. [*svadharma*: literally 'own-dharma'. It means activities or functions that are based on one's own nature, traits, tendencies, etc. Loosely, it is translated as duty.]

तितिक्षा का ?

What is *titikshā*?

शीतोष्ण-सुखदुःखादि-सहिष्णुत्वम् ।

Forbearance or endurance of heat and cold, pleasure and pain, etc.

श्रद्धा कीदृशी ?

What is meant by *shraddhā*?

गुरुवेदान्तवाक्यादिषु विश्वासः श्रद्धा ।

Faith (belief, reliance) in the words of the guru and Vedanta (Upanishads) is *shraddhā*.

समाधानं किम् ?

What is *samādhāna*?

चित्तैकाग्रता ।

One-pointedness of the mind (towards the Self).

मुमुक्षुत्वं किम् ?

What is *mumukshutvam*?

मोक्षो मे भूयात् इति इच्छा ।

The intense yearning of "may I attain liberation" is called *mumukshutvam*.

एतत् साधन-चतुष्टयम् । ततः तत्त्वविवेकस्य अधिकारिणो भवन्ति ।

These are the four-fold means to attain the spiritual goal. Thereafter (i.e., acquiring these four-fold means), they become fit for true knowledge (tattva-viveka).

True Knowledge

तत्त्वविवेकः कः ?

What is true knowledge (*tattva-viveka*)?

आत्मा सत्यं तदन्यत् सर्वं मिथ्येति ।

The Self (*ātmā*) alone is real. Everything else other than the Self (*ātmā*) is unreal (*mithyā*)". This is true knowledge.

आत्मा कः ?

What is Self (*ātmā*)?

स्थूल-सूक्ष्म-कारण-शरीराद्व्यतिरिक्तः पञ्चकोशातीतः सन् अवस्थात्रयसाक्षी सच्चिदानन्द-स्वरूपः सन् यः तिष्ठति स आत्मा ।

That which is other than the gross, subtle and causal bodies, which is beyond the five sheaths (*kosha*), which is the witness of the three states and which is of the nature of Existence-Consciousness-Bliss (*sat-chit-ānanda*) is the Self (*ātmā*).

स्थूलशरीरं किम् ?

What is the gross body (*sthūla-sharira*)?

पञ्चीकृत-पञ्च-महाभूतैः कृतं, सत्कर्म-जन्यं, सुख-दुःखादि-भोगायतनं, शरीरम्, अस्ति, जायते, वर्धते, विपरिणमते, अपक्षीयते, विनश्यति इति षड्विकारवत् एतत् स्थूल-शरीरम् ।

It is the gross body, which is made up of the five gross elements (viz. space, fire, water, air and earth) through the process of *panchī-karaṇa* (making into five), which is born as a result of good actions (*sat-karma*) and is the seat of experiences like happiness, sorrow, etc. It is subject to six modifications (changes of form or nature)–is (exists), is born, grows, transforms (undergoes changes), declines (or decays) and perishes. This is the gross body (*sthūla-sharira*).

सूक्ष्मशरीरं किम् ?

What is the subtle body (*sūkshma-sharira*)?

अपञ्चीकृतपञ्चमहाभूतैः कृतं सत्कर्मजन्यं सुखदुःखादिभोगसाधनं पञ्चज्ञानेन्द्रियाणि पञ्चकर्मेन्द्रियाणि पञ्चप्राणादयः मनश्चैकं बुद्धिश्चैका एवं सप्तदशकलाभिः सह यत्तिष्ठति तत्सूक्ष्मशरीरम् ।

That which is composed of five elements prior to their undergoing the process of *panchī-karaṇa* is born as a result of good actions (*sat-karma*), is the means (or instrument) to experience pleasure, pain, etc., and that which exists with seventeen parts is the subtle body.

The seventeen parts are the five organs of perception or knowledge (*jñānendriyas*), the five organs of action (*karmendriyas*), the five vital airs (*prāṇa*, *apāna*, *udāna*, *samāna* and *vyāna*), the mind and intellect.

श्रोत्रं त्वक् चक्षुः रसना घ्राणम् इति पञ्च ज्ञानेन्द्रियाणि ।

Ear, skin, eyes, tongue and nose–these are the five organs of perception or knowledge.

श्रोत्रस्य दिग्देवता । त्वचो वायुः । चक्षुषः सूर्यः । रसनाया वरुणः । घ्राणस्य अश्विनौ । इति ज्ञानेन्द्रियदेवताः ।

The presiding deity of the ear is space (god of the directions). The presiding deity of the skin is the air (god of wind). The presiding deity of the eyes is the Sun. The presiding deity of the tongue is the water principle. The presiding deities of the nose are the Ashwin twins. Thus (the aforesaid) are the presiding deities of the organs of perception or knowledge.

श्रोत्रस्य विषयः शब्दग्रहणम् । त्वचो विषयः स्पर्शग्रहणम् । चक्षुषो विषयः रूपग्रहणम् । रसनाया विषयः रसग्रहणम् । घ्राणस्य विषयः गन्धग्रहणम् इति ।

The sphere of influence (or the function or department) for the ear is the reception of sound. The sphere of influence for the skin is the perceiving of touch. The sphere of influence for the eyes is the perception of forms. The sphere of influence for the tongue is the perception of taste. The sphere of influence for the nose is the perception of smell.

वाक्पाणिपादपायूपस्थानीति पञ्चकर्मेन्द्रियाणि ।

The mouth, hands, legs, anus (organ of excretion) and genitals (organ of procreation) are the five organs of action.

वाचो देवता वह्निः । हस्तयोरिन्द्रः । पादयोर्विष्णुः । पायोर्मृत्युः । उपस्थस्य प्रजापतिः । इति कर्मेन्द्रियदेवताः ।

The presiding deity of speech is fire. The presiding deity of the hands is Indra. The presiding deity of the feet is Vishnu. The presiding deity of the anus is *mrityu* (Yama). The presiding deity of the genitals is Prajāpati. Thus, these are the presiding deities for the organs of action.

वाचो विषयः भाषणम् । पाण्योर्विषयः वस्तुग्रहणम् । पादयोर्विषयः गमनम् । पायोर्विषयः मलत्यागः । उपस्थस्य विषयः आनन्द इति ।

The sphere of influence (or the function or department) of the organ of the speech is to speak. The function of the hands is to grasp things. The function of the legs is locomotion (or movement). The function of the anus (excretory organ) is the elimination (removal) of the waste. The function of the genitals is to have sensual pleasure.

कारणशरीरं किम् ?

What is the causal body (*kāraṇa-sharira*)?

अनिर्वाच्यानाद्यविद्यारूपं शरीरद्वयस्य कारणमात्रं स्वस्वरूपाज्ञानं निर्विकल्पकरूपं यदस्ति तत्कारणशरीरम् ।

That which is inexplicable, beginningless and is of the nature of ignorance, that which is the cause of the other two bodies (the subtle and the gross), that which is ignorant of its own real nature, and that which is free from any modifications (unlike the gross body), is the causal body.

The Three States

अवस्थात्रयं किम् ?

What are the three states of existence?

जाग्रत्स्वप्नसुषुप्त्यवस्थाः ।

The waking, dream, and sleep (sometimes referred to as deep sleep) states.

जाग्रदवस्था का ?

What is the waking state (*jāgrat avasthā*)?

श्रोत्रादिज्ञानेन्द्रियैः शब्दादिविषयैश्च ज्ञायते इति यत् सा जाग्रदावस्था ।

The state in which sound and other objects of the world are perceived (experienced) by the ears and other organs of knowledge, respectively, is the waking state.

स्थूलशरीराभिमानी आत्मा विश्व इत्युच्यते ।

The Self, identified with the gross body, is called *vishva*. [Vishva is the inner faculty which perceives the individuality underlying the gross body.]

स्वप्नावस्था केति चेत् जाग्रदवस्थायां यद्दृष्टं यद् श्रुतम् तज्जनितवासनया निद्रासमये यः प्रपञ्चः प्रतीयते सा स्वप्नावस्था ।

What is the dream state (*svapna avasthā)*?

From the mental impressions born out of whatever is seen or heard during the wakeful state, the appearance that manifests during sleep is the dream state.

सूक्ष्मशरीराभिमानी आत्मा तैजस इत्युच्यते ।

The Self, identified with the subtle body, is called *taijasa*.

अतः सुषुप्त्यवस्था का ?

So, what is the sleep (deep sleep) state (*sushupta avasthā*)?

अहं किमपि न जानामि सुखेन मया निद्राऽनुभूयत इति सुषुप्त्यवस्था ।

That state about which one says later "I didn't know anything. I slept happily", is the deep-sleep state.

कारणशरीराभिमानी आत्मा प्राज्ञ इत्युच्यते ।

The Self, identified with the causal body, is called *prājña*.

The Five Sheaths

पञ्च कोशाः के ?

What are the five sheaths (*kosha*, encasements)?

अन्नमयः प्राणमयः मनोमयः विज्ञानमयः आनन्दमयश्चेति ।

They are the food sheath, the vital air sheath, the mental sheath, the knowledge sheath and the bliss sheath.

अन्नमयः कः ?

What is the food sheath (*anna-maya kosha*)?

अन्नरसेनैव भूत्वा अन्नरसेनैव वृद्धिं प्राप्य अन्नरूपपृथिव्यां यद्विलीयते तदन्नमयः कोशः स्थूलशरीरम् ।

That which is born, caused by the essence of food, after achieving growth due to the essence of food, and that which merges completely with the earth, which is of the nature of food, that gross body is the food sheath.

प्राणमयः कः ?

What is the vital air sheath (*prāṇa-maya kosha*)?

प्राणाद्याः पञ्चवायवः वागादीन्द्रियपञ्चकं प्राणमयः कोशः ।

The five physiological functions such as *prāṇa,* etc. (*prāṇa*, *apāna*, *vyāna*, *udāna* and *samāna*), together with the five organs of action, namely speech etc., form the vital air sheath.

[The five life forces or vital airs are the functions of respiration (inhalation and exhalation), excretion/evacuation, circulation, reversing (e.g., vomiting), digestion and assimilation.]

मनोमयः कोशः कः ?

What is the mental sheath (*manomaya kosha*)?

मनश्च ज्ञानेन्द्रियपञ्चकं मिलित्वा यो भवति स मनोमयः कोशः ।

The mind together with the five organs of knowledge or perception (ear, skin, eyes, tongue and nose) forms the mental sheath.

विज्ञानमयः कः ?

What is the knowledge (intelligence) sheath (*vijñāna-maya kosha*)?

बुद्धिज्ञानेन्द्रियपञ्चकं मिलित्वा यो भवति स विज्ञानमयः कोशः ।

The intellect together with the five organs of knowledge or perception, forms the knowledge sheath.

आनन्दमयः कः ?

What is the bliss sheath (*ānandamaya kosha*)?

एवमेव कारणशरीरभूताविद्यास्थमलिनसत्त्वं प्रियादिवृत्तिसहितं सत् आनन्दमयः कोशः ।

That which is of the form of the causal body, is established in ignorance, is of impure nature, along with the modes like *priya*, etc., is the bliss sheath. [*priya* etc.: *priya* – dear, pleasant; *moda* – delight; *pramoda* – excessive joy]

एतत्कोशपञ्चकम् ।

These are the five sheaths.

मदीयं शरीरं मदीयाः प्राणाः मदीयं मनश्च मदीया बुद्धिर्मदीयं अज्ञानमिति स्वेनैव ज्ञायते तद्यथा मदीयत्वेन ज्ञातं कटककुण्डल गृहादिकं स्वस्माद्भिन्नं तथा पञ्चकोशादिकं स्वस्माद्भिन्नम् मदीयत्वेन ज्ञातमात्मा न भवति ॥

Though bangles, earrings, house, etc., are known by the notion of mineness (as my bangles, etc.), they do not become the Self. In the same manner, though we have similar notions like "my body, my vital airs (*prāṇa*, etc.), my mind, my intellect, and my ignorance, etc.", they do not become the Self. In the same manner, the five sheaths are different from the Self; though referred to with the idea of mine-ness, they do not become the Self.

The Self (*ātmā*)

आत्मा तर्हि कः ?

Then, what is Self (*ātmā*)?

सच्चिदानन्दस्वरूपः ।

It is of the nature of *sat-chit-ānanda* (Existence-Consciousness-Bliss).

सत्किम् ?

What is existence (*sat*)?

कालत्रयेऽपि तिष्ठतीति सत् ।

Existence (*sat*) is that which remains unchanged in all three periods of time (viz., past, present and future).

चित्किम् ?

What is consciousness (*chit*)?

ज्ञानस्वरूपः ।

It is of the nature of absolute knowledge.

आनन्दः कः ?

What is bliss (*ānanda*)?

सुखस्वरूपः ।

It is of the nature of absolute (independent of anything else) happiness.

एवं सच्चिदानन्दस्वरूपं स्वात्मानं विजानीयात् ।

Thus, one should know the Self to be of the nature of *sat-chit-ānanda* (Existence-Consciousness-Bliss).

The Universe

अथ चतुर्विंशति-तत्त्वोत्पत्ति-प्रकारं वक्ष्यामः ।

Now, we shall explain the production (origin) of the twenty-four principles (*tattva*).

ब्रह्माश्रया सत्त्वरजस्तमोगुणात्मिका माया अस्ति ।

That which is of the nature of the three modes (*guṇas,* namely *sattva*, *rajas* and *tamas*) and which is dependent on Brahman for its existence, is the illusory power (*māyā*).

ततः आकाशः सम्भूतः । आकाशाद् वायुः । वायोस्तेजः । तेजस आपः । अभ्दयः पृथिवी ।

From *māyā*, *ākāsha* (sky) is born; from sky, *vāyu* (air) is born; from air, *tejas* (fire) is born; from fire, *āpa* (water) is born; and from water, *pīthivī* (earth) is born.

एतेषां पञ्चतत्त्वानां मध्ये आकाशस्य सात्विकांशात् श्रोत्रेन्द्रियं सम्भूतम् । वायोः सात्विकांशात् त्वगिन्द्रियं सम्भूतम् । अग्नेः सात्विकांशात् चक्षुरिन्द्रियं सम्भूतम् । जलस्य सात्विकांशात् रसनेन्द्रियं सम्भूतम् । पृथिव्याः सात्विकांशात् घ्राणेन्द्रियं सम्भूतम् ।

From among these five elements (sky, air, fire, water and earth), out of the *sāttvic* aspect of the sky, evolved the ear, the organ of hearing. From the *sāttvic* aspect of air evolved the skin, the organ of touch. From the *sāttvic* aspect of fire evolved the eye, the organ of vision. From the *sāttvic* aspect of water evolved the organ of taste. From the *sāttvic* aspect of earth, evolved the organ of smell.

एतेषां पञ्चतत्त्वानां समष्टिसात्विकांशात् मनोबुद्ध्यहङ्कार चित्तान्तःकरणानि सम्भूतानि ।

From the aggregate *sāttvic* portion of these five elements, the inner faculties (or instruments), namely, the mind (*manas*), intellect (*buddhi*), ego (*ahankāra*) and memory (*chitta*), are formed.

सङ्कल्पविकल्पात्मकं मनः । निश्चयात्मिका बुद्धिः । अहङ्कर्ता अहङ्कारः । चिन्तनकर्तृ चित्तम् । मनसो देवता चन्द्रमाः । बुद्धे ब्रह्मा । अहङ्कारस्य रुद्रः । चित्तस्य वासुदेवः ।

That which is of the wavering nature of volition (decision) and indecision (doubt) is the mind (*manas*). That which is of the nature of conviction (resolve or decision) is intellect (*buddhi*).

The sense of "I am the doer" (or the sense of doership) is ego (*ahankāra*). The thinking faculty (or the faculty of recollections) is the memory (*chitta*). The presiding deity of the mind is the moon. The presiding deity of intellect is Brahmā. The presiding deity of ego is Rudra. The presiding deity of memory is Vāsudeva.

Creation of Organs of Action

एतेषां पञ्चतत्त्वानां मध्ये आकाशस्य राजसांशात् वागिन्द्रियं सम्भूतम् । वायोः राजसांशात् पाणीन्द्रियं सम्भूतम् । वन्हेः राजसांशात् पादेन्द्रियं सम्भूतम् । जलस्य राजसांशात् उपस्थेन्द्रियं सम्भूतम् । पृथिव्या राजसांशात् गुदेन्द्रियं सम्भूतम् । एतेषां समष्टिराजसांशात् पञ्चप्राणाः सम्भूताः ।

Of these five elements, from the *rajas* aspect of space, the organ of speech (mouth) is formed. From the *rajas* aspect of air, the organ of grasping (hand) is formed. From the *rajas* aspect of fire, the organ of movement (leg) is formed. From the *rajas* aspect of water, the organ of excretion (anus) is formed. From the *rajas* aspect of the earth, the organs of reproduction (genitals) are formed. From the collective *rajas* aspect of all these five elements, the five vital airs (*prāna*, *apāna*, *udāna*, *samāna* and *vyāna*) are born.

The Process of Creation

एतेषां पञ्चतत्त्वानां तामसांशात् पञ्चीकृतपञ्चतत्त्वानि भवन्ति ।

Out of the *tamas* aspect of the five fundamental elements, the grossified five elements are formed.

पञ्चीकरणं कथम् इति चेत् ।

If asked 'how this grossification takes place', then:

एतेषां पञ्चमहाभूतानां तामसांशस्वरूपम् एकमेकं भूतं द्विधा विभज्य एकमेकमर्धं पृथक् तूष्णीं व्यवस्थाप्य अपरमपरमर्धं चतुर्धा विभज्य स्वार्धमन्येषु अर्धेषु स्वभागचतुष्टयसंयोजनं कार्यम् । तदा पञ्चीकरणं भवति । एतेभ्यः पञ्चीकृतपञ्चमहाभूतेभ्यः स्थूलशरीरं भवति ।

The *tamas* aspect of each of the five elements is divided into two halves. One-half of each remains quiet. The other half gets divided into four equal parts. Then, to the intact half of one element, one one-eighth portion from each of the other four elements gets joined. Then *panchī-karaṇa* (the process by which the subtle elements become the gross elements) is complete. Thus, from these five elements (created by the above-described process of *panchī-karaṇa*), the gross body comes into existence.

एवं पिण्डब्रह्माण्डयोरैक्यं सम्भूतम् ।

Thus, there is an identity (oneness) between the microcosm and the macrocosm.

The Oneness of jīva and Īshvara

स्थूलशरीराभिमानि जीवनामकं ब्रह्मप्रतिबिम्बं भवति । स एव जीवः प्रकृत्या स्वस्मात् ईश्वरं भिन्नत्वेन जानाति ।

That which is identifying itself with the gross body is named *jīva*. It is a reflected image (mirror image) of Brahman (the Supreme Reality). That *jīva* thinks of itself as different (in its essence) from *Īshvara* (the Lord).

अविद्योपाधिः सन् आत्मा जीव इत्युच्यते ।

The Self (*ātmā*) conditioned (limited) by ignorance of its real nature is called *jīva*.

मायोपाधिः सन् ईश्वर इत्युच्यते ।

That which is conditioned (limited) by *māyā* is called *Īshvara*.

एवं उपाधिभेदात् जीवेश्वरभेददृष्टिः यावत्पर्यन्तं तिष्ठति तावत्पर्यन्तं जन्ममरणादिरूपसंसारो न निवर्तते ।

Thus, because of the conditioning (limiting nature), there is differentiation (differential vision) between *jīva* and *Īshvara* (the Lord). As long as this differential vision exists, the worldly existence (*samsāra*), in the form of a cycle of births and deaths, does not cease.

तस्मात्कारणान्न जीवेश्वरयोर्भेदबुद्धिः स्वीकार्या ।

Due to this reason, one should not give in to a differentiation between *jīva* and *Īshvara* (the Lord).

Thou Art That

ननु साहङ्कारस्य किञ्चिज्ज्ञस्य जीवस्य निरहङ्कारस्य सर्वज्ञस्य ईश्वरस्य तत्त्वमसीति महावाक्यात् कथमभेदबुद्धिः स्यादुभयोः विरुद्धधर्माक्रान्तत्वात् ।

Jīva is endowed with ego and limited knowledge, and *Īshvara* is free from ego and is endowed with omniscience. Thus, when they are endowed with opposing characteristics, how is it that, by the cardinal statement of the Upanishad (*mahāvākya*), "Thou art That" (*tattvamasi*), there is oneness?

इति चेत् । न स्थूलसूक्ष्मशरीराभिमानी त्वम्पदवाच्यार्थः । उपाधिविनिर्मुक्तं समाधिदशासम्पन्नं शुद्धं चैतन्यं त्वम्पदलक्ष्यार्थः ।

If this is the question, the answer is "No, it is not so". The 'literal' meaning of the word 'Thou' (in "Thou art That") is the one who identifies with the gross and subtle bodies, i.e., the *jīva*. The 'implied' meaning of the word 'Thou' (in "Thou art That") is the one which is free from any conditioning, is realised in the state of intense absorption in meditation (*samādhi*), and is pure Consciousness.

एवं सर्वज्ञत्वादिविशिष्ट ईश्वरः तत्पदवाच्यार्थः । उपाधिशून्यं शुद्धचैतन्यं तत्पदलक्ष्यार्थः ।

In the same manner, the 'literal' meaning of the word 'That' (in "Thou art That") is *Īshvara* (the Lord) characterised by omnipresence, etc. The 'implied' meaning of the word 'That' (in "Thou art That") is one which is Pure Consciousness, free from all conditioning.

एवं च जीवेश्वरयो चैतन्यरूपेणाऽभेदे बाधकाभावः ।

Thus, there is no contradiction regarding the identity (oneness) of *jīva* and *Īshvara* from the standpoint of Pure Consciousness.

एवं च वेदान्त-वाक्यैः सद्गुरूपदेशेन च सर्वेष्वपि भूतेषु येषां ब्रह्मबुद्धिरुत्पन्ना ते जीवन्मुक्ता इत्यर्थः ।

And thus, by the assertions (declarations) of Vedanta and by the instructions of a preceptor, those who have the realisation of Brahman (the Supreme Reality) in all beings, are liberated while living (*jīvan-mukta*).

ननु जीवन्मुक्तः कः ?

Then, who is *jīvan-mukta* (liberated while living)?

यथा देहोऽहं पुरुषोऽहं ब्राह्मणोऽहं शूद्रोऽहमस्मीति दृढनिश्चयस्तथा नाहं ब्राह्मणः न शूद्रः न पुरुषः किन्तु असङ्गः सच्चिदानन्दस्वरूपः प्रकाशरूपः सर्वान्तर्यामी चिदाकाशरूपोऽस्मीति दृढनिश्चयरूपोऽपरोक्षज्ञानवान् जीवन्मुक्तः ॥

Just as some have the firm conviction that "I am the body", "I am a man", "I am a *brāhmaṇa*", and "I am a *shūdra*", in the same manner, the one who has the direct realisation of transcendental knowledge, who has the conviction that "I am not a *brāhmaṇa*", "I am not a *shūdra*", and "I am not a man", but who is unattached, who is of the nature of Existence-Consciousness-Bliss (*sat-chit-ānanda*), who is of the nature of effulgence, who is the indweller (inner controller) of all, and who is the expanse (or sky) of Consciousness, is a *jīvan-mukta* (liberated while living).

ब्रह्मैवाहमस्मीत्यपरोक्षज्ञानेन निखिलकर्मबन्धविनिर्मुक्तः स्यात् ।

By the direct realisation of the imperceptible (transcendental) knowledge that "I am Brahman (the Supreme Reality)", one is freed of all the bondages of karma.

Types of Karma

कर्माणि कतिविधानि सन्तीति चेत् आगामिसञ्चितप्रारब्धभेदेन त्रिविधानि सन्ति ।

If asked, "How many kinds of karma are there?", the answer is: "There are three kinds of *karma,* namely: *āgāmi*, *sanchita* and *prārabdha*".

आगामि कर्म किम् ?

What is *āgāmi karma*?

ज्ञानोत्पत्त्यनन्तरं ज्ञानिदेहकृतं पुण्यपापरूपं कर्म यदस्ति तदागामीत्यभिधीयते ।

Following the awakening (realisation of the Self), the effects of all actions in the form of virtue and sin (merit and demerit), performed by the wise one, is referred to as *āgāmi*.

सञ्चितं कर्म किम् ?

What is *sanchita karma*?

अनन्तकोटिजन्मनां बीजभूतं सत् यत्कर्मजातं पूर्वार्जितं तिष्ठति तत् सञ्चितं ज्ञेयम् ।

The effects of actions gained by former actions (including those from previous births) that form the seed to many countless crores of births is called *sanchita karma*.

प्रारब्धं कर्म किमिति चेत् इदं शरीरमुत्पाद्य इह लोके एवं सुखदुःखादिप्रदं यत्कर्म तत्प्रारब्धं ।

If questioned, "What is *prārabdha karma?*", then the answer is: "Having given birth to this body, the actions which give results in this very world, in the form of happiness or misery, and which can be exhausted only by experiencing (enjoying or suffering) them, is called *prārabdha karma.*"

भोगेन नष्टं भवति प्रारब्धकर्मणां भोगादेव क्षय इति ।

By experience alone there is destruction of *karma*. Thus, effects of *prārabdha karma* are destroyed (exhausted) only by experiencing them.

सञ्चितं कर्म ब्रह्मैवाहमिति निश्चयात्मकज्ञानेन नश्यति ।

Sanchita karma is destroyed by the established knowledge of "I am Brahman".

आगामि कर्म अपि ज्ञानेन नश्यति किञ्च आगामि कर्मणां नलिनीदलगतजलवत् ज्ञानिनां सम्बन्धो नास्ति ।

The *āgāmi karma* (*karma* that will bear fruit in future) is also destroyed by Self-knowledge. Just as the lotus leaf is not affected by the water droplets on it, the wise ones are not affected by the *āgāmi karma.*

तथा चात्मवित्संसारं तीर्त्वा ब्रह्मानन्दमिहैव प्राप्नोति । तरति शोकमात्मवित् इति श्रुतेः ।

Thus, the one who has realised the Self, having transcended the worldly existence (being untouched by the world), attains the bliss of Brahman here, in this world itself. The Vedas declare: "The one who has realised the Self goes beyond all sorrows".

तनुं त्यजतु वा काश्यां श्वपचस्य गृहेऽथ वा । ज्ञानसम्प्राप्तिसमये मुक्तोऽसौ विगताशयः ।
इति स्मृतेश्च ।

Having attained liberation at the time of realisation of the Self and having become free from all desires, the wise one may drop the body in Kāshi (Vārānasi) or in the house of a lowly person. It is of no consequence to the wise one. So, assert the scriptures.

* * *

12

Ātmabodha (आत्मबोधः)

by Adi Shankarāchārya

तपोभिः क्षीणपापानां शान्तानां वीतरागिणाम् ।
मुमुक्षूणामपेक्ष्योऽयमात्मबोधो विधीयते ॥ 1 ॥

This text, Ātmabodha (Self-knowledge), is intended and has been composed for those whose sins have been destroyed by means of austerities (physical, oral and mental), who are tranquil, who are free from all forms of attachments and are aspirants of liberation.

बोधोऽन्यसाधनेभ्यो हि साक्षान्मोक्षैकसाधनम् ।
पाकस्य वह्निवज्ज्ञानं विना मोक्षो न सिध्यति ॥ 2 ॥

Knowledge of the Self alone is the direct means to moksha (liberation), nothing else (including *yajña*, charity and austerity). Just as fire is the direct means to cooking, in the same manner, without knowledge of the Self, liberation cannot be attained.

अविरोधितया कर्म नाविद्यां विनिवर्तयेत् ।
विद्याविद्यां निहन्त्येव तेजस्तिमिरसंघवत् ॥ 3 ॥

Since action is not opposed to ignorance (i.e., action is consistent with ignorance), it cannot destroy ignorance. Just as light removes intense darkness, knowledge of the Self alone removes ignorance.

अवच्छिन्न इवाज्ञानात्तन्नाशे सति केवलः ।
स्वयं प्रकाशते ह्यात्मा मेघापायेंऽशुमानिव ॥ 4 ॥

It is because of ignorance alone that the Self appears as if it is separate (finite). When that ignorance is destroyed, the one (non-dual) Self shines by itself, like the sun that shines when the clouds move away.

अज्ञानकलुषं जीवं ज्ञानाभ्यासाद्विनिर्मलम् ।
कृत्वा ज्ञानं स्वयं नश्येज्जलं कतकरेणुवत् ॥ 5 ॥

The *jīva* (the individual Self), which is rendered impure because of ignorance, is made extremely pure by means of constant practice of knowledge. [Practice of knowledge: The three-step process of *shravaṇa* (listening, study), *manana* (introspection, reflection), *nididhyāsana* (meditation)] Having purified the individual, the knowledge itself vanishes, just like the powder of the cleaning-nut disappears after having purified the water. [The knowledge is a mere means to realise the Truth. Ultimately, what remains is the Self alone.]

संसारः स्वप्नतुल्यो हि रागद्वेषादिसंकुलः ।
स्वकाले सत्यवद्भाति प्रबोधे सत्यसद्भवेत् ॥ 6 ॥

Samsāra (the worldly existence), which is abounding in likes and dislikes, attachment and hatred, and other such pairs of opposites, is like a dream. In its own time (when it lasts), it appears to be real, and when knowledge of the Self dawns, it becomes unreal.

तावत्सत्यं जगद्भाति शुक्तिकारजतं यथा ।
यावन्न ज्ञायते ब्रह्म सर्वाधिष्ठानमद्वयम् ॥ 7 ॥

The entire world appears to be real so long as the substratum of everything in the universe, the non-dual Brahman (the Supreme Reality), is not known or realised. This is just like the oyster shell or mother of pearl that appears to be silver (due to ignorance).

उपादानेऽखिलाधारे जगन्ति परमेश्वरे ।
सर्गस्थितिलयान्यान्ति बुद्बुदानीव वारिणि ॥ 8 ॥

Just as the bubbles rise, exist and dissolve in water, in the same way, all the worlds (the entire universe) go through creation, sustenance and dissolution in the Supreme, which is the material cause and substratum of everything.

सच्चिदात्मन्यनुस्यूते नित्ये विष्णौ प्रकल्पिताः ।
व्यक्तयो विविधास्सर्वा हाटके कटकादिवत् ॥ 9 ॥

All manifold names and forms are imagined appearances that are strung together in the all-pervading Brahman, which is of the nature of Existence-Intelligence (*sat* – Existence; *chidātman* – pure thought, intelligence) and is eternal, just as bracelet, ring, etc. are all names and forms of gold alone. [1. The term Vishnu used in the verse refers to the all-pervading Brahman; 2. Taittiriya Upanishad says, "Brahman is Existence, Intelligence, Eternal"]

यथाकाशो हृषीकेशो नानोपाधिगतो विभुः ।
तद्भेदाद्भिन्नवद्भाति तन्नाशे केवलो भवेत् ॥ 10 ॥

Space, on account of limiting adjuncts like pot, room, etc., appears different. In the same manner, on being subject to various limiting adjuncts, the all-pervading Brahman appears differently because of the differences in the limiting adjuncts. When the limiting adjuncts are destroyed. It (Brahman) reveals Itself as the one.

[According to Adi Shankarāchārya, the term *Hrishikesha* means the controller of all the senses or the Knower of the field of experiences, which is nothing but the Supreme, and *Vibhu* means one who becomes manifold or All-pervading.]

नानोपाधिवशादेव जातिवर्णाश्रमादयः ।
आत्मन्यारोपितास्तोये रसवर्णादिभेदवत् ॥ 11 ॥

The differences in taste, colour, form, etc., are all the result of superimpositions of limiting adjuncts like flavour, colour, etc., on water. (Water by itself is colourless.) In the same manner, distinctions like lineage, caste, race, colour, stage of life, etc., are indeed because of the superimpositions of the various limiting adjuncts on the Self.

पञ्चीकृतमहाभूतसम्भवं कर्मसञ्चितम् ।
शरीरं सुखदुःखानां भोगायतनमुच्यते ॥ 12 ॥

Produced by the coming together of the five elements (fire, air, earth, water and sky, after they have gone through the process of becoming gross) and resulting from past actions (on account of past karma), the gross body is said to be the seat of all experiences of pleasure and pain.

पञ्चप्राणमनोबुद्धिदशेन्द्रियसमन्वितम् ।
अपञ्चीकृतभूतोत्थं सूक्ष्माङ्गं भोगसाधनम् ॥ 13 ॥

Born out of the five elements before having become gross and consisting of five life forces, mind, intellect, five organs of knowledge (sense of hearing, touch, vision, taste and smell), and five organs of action (speech, hands, legs, anus and the genitals), the subtle body is the means (or the instrument) by which pleasure and pain are experienced.

[The five life forces or vital airs are: *prāṇa* – the function of respiration (inhalation and exhalation), *apāna* – the function of excretion/evacuation, *vyāna* – the function of circulation, *udāna* – the function of reversing (e.g., vomiting), *samāna* – the function of digestion/assimilation.]

अनाद्यविद्यानिर्वाच्या कारणोपाधिरुच्यते ।
उपाधित्रितयादन्यमात्मानमवधारयेत् ॥ 14 ॥

Ignorance (nescience), which is beginningless and indescribable, is said to be a limiting adjunct which is causal in nature. The Self should be ascertained to be other than the three limiting adjuncts (gross, subtle and causal bodies).

[The gross body, the subtle body and the causal body are three limiting adjuncts, superimposed by which the Self appears differently.]

पञ्चकोशादियोगेन तत्तन्मय इव स्थितः ।
शुद्धात्मा नीलवस्त्रादियोगेन स्फटिको यथा ॥ 15 ॥

The pure Self, by being subjected to the association with the five sheaths, appears to be one with them (or like them). This is similar to the case of a crystal appearing to be blue (or some other colour) by coming in contact with blue (or some other colour) cloth, etc.

[The five sheaths are the food sheath (the gross body, made of gross elements), the vital air sheath, the mental sheath, the intellectual sheath and the bliss sheath.]

वपुस्तुषादिभिः कोशैर्युक्तं युक्त्यवघाततः ।
आत्मानमन्तरं शुद्धं विविञ्च्यात्तण्डुलं यथा ॥ 16 ॥

Just as one separates the grain (rice), which is covered by the chaff, by skillfully threshing it, in the same manner, the seeker should separate the pure inmost Self, which appears to be covered by the five sheaths, by subjecting it to discrimination (investigation).

सदा सर्वगतोऽप्यात्मा न सर्वत्रावभासते ।
बुद्धावेवावभासेत स्वच्छेषु प्रतिबिम्बवत् ॥ 17 ॥

Though the Self is eternal and all-pervading, It does not shine (or appear) in everything (everywhere); It shines (manifests) in the intellect (buddhi) alone, like a reflection in clean surfaces (like water or a mirror).

देहेन्द्रियमनोबुद्धिप्रकृतिभ्यो विलक्षणम् ।
तद्वृत्तिसाक्षिणं विद्यादात्मानं राजवत्सदा ॥ 18 ॥

Realise the Self as distinct from the body, senses, mind, intellect and primordial matter, but know it to be the constant witness of their functions, like a king.

व्यापृतेष्विन्द्रियेष्वात्मा व्यापारीवाविवेकिनाम् ।
दृश्यतेऽभ्रेषु धावत्सु धावन्निव यथा शशी ॥ 19 ॥

For the ignorant ones (for those who do not discriminate between the Self and body, mind, senses, etc.), the Self appears to be active when it is the senses which are truly active. This is similar to the case where the moon appears to be moving when, in reality, it is the clouds which are moving.

आत्मचैतन्यमाश्रित्य देहेन्द्रियमनोधियः ।
स्वक्रियार्थेषु वर्तन्ते सूर्यालोकं यथा जनाः ॥ 20 ॥

Identifying with (taking refuge in) consciousness, which is the very nature of the Self, the body, senses, mind and intellect are engaged in their respective activities (functions), just as people perform their actions in the light from the sun.

देहेन्द्रियगुणान्कर्माण्यमले सच्चिदात्मनि ।
अध्यस्यन्त्यविवेकेन गगने नीलतादिवत् ॥ 21 ॥

Because of a lack of discrimination, the ignorant ones superimpose the characteristics and activities of the body and senses on the pure Self that is of the nature of Existence and Consciousness, just as people attribute qualities like blueness, etc., to the sky.

अज्ञानान्मानसोपाधेः कर्तृत्वादीनि चात्मनि ।
कल्प्यन्तेऽम्बुगते चन्द्रे चलनादि यथाम्भसः ॥ 22 ॥

Just as, due to ignorance, the movement and other characteristics of the water are attributed to the moon that is reflected in the water, in the same manner, due to ignorance, the limiting adjuncts of the mind, like doership, enjoyment, etc., are incorrectly superimposed on the Self.

रागेच्छासुखदुःखादि बुद्धौ सत्यां प्रवर्तते ।
सुषुप्तौ नास्ति तन्नाशे तस्माद्बुद्धेस्तु नात्मनः ॥ 23 ॥

Attachment, desires, pleasure, pain, etc., are perceived to be real only in the functioning of the mind; they are not perceived in the state of deep sleep when the mind ceases to function.

Therefore, they (attachment, etc.) all belong to the mind alone and not to the Self.

प्रकाशोऽर्कस्य तोयस्य शैत्यमग्नेर्यथोष्णता ।
स्वभावः सच्चिदानन्दनित्यनिर्मलतात्मनः ॥ 24 ॥

Just as light is the nature of the sun, coldness is the nature of water, and heat is the nature of fire, in the same manner, Existence, Consciousness, Bliss, Eternality and Purity are the nature of the Self.

आत्मनः सच्चिदंशश्च बुद्धेर्वृत्तिरिति द्वयम् ।
संयोज्य चाविवेकेन जानामीति प्रवर्तते ॥ 25 ॥

In the case of an ignorant person, the lack of discrimination causes the coming together of the two, viz., the function of the intellect and a portion of Existence and Consciousness of the Self, and thus comes into existence the idea of "I know".

आत्मनो विक्रिया नास्ति बुद्धेर्बोधो न जात्विति ।
जीवः सर्वमलं ज्ञात्वा ज्ञाता द्रष्टेति मुह्यति ॥ 26 ॥

There is never any change (or modification) of the Self. Also, there is never an awakening of the *buddhi* (intellect). [In other words, *buddhi* is never endowed with Consciousness.] But the individual self, incorrectly superimposing everything (mind, intellect, etc.) on the Self, becomes very deluded, thinking of himself as the knower and doer ("I am knower", "I am seer").

रज्जुसर्पवदात्मानं जीवं ज्ञात्वा भयं वहेत् ।
नाहं जीवः परात्मेति ज्ञातञ्चेन्निर्भयो भवेत् ॥ 27 ॥

Just like seeing a rope as a snake, the individual, regarding himself as the *jīva*, is overcome by fear. However, when the *jīva* realises that "I am the Universal Self", he becomes fearless.

आत्मावभासयत्येको बुद्ध्यादीनीन्द्रियाण्यपि ।
दीपो घटादिवत्स्वात्मा जडैस्तैर्नावभास्यते ॥ 28 ॥

The Self alone illumines the mind, intellect, senses, etc., just as a lamp illumines the pot, etc. But the Self cannot be illumined by these inert objects like mind, intellect and senses.

स्वबोधे नान्यबोधेच्छा बोधरूपतयात्मनः ।
न दीपस्यान्यदीपेच्छा यथा स्वात्मप्रकाशने ॥ 29 ॥

In the case of the Self, for its own illumination, there is no necessity for another source of illumination (another source for making it conscious) because it is of the nature of Consciousness. This is just as in the case of a lamp, which, for its source of light, does not need another lamp.

निषिध्य निखिलोपाधीन्नेति नेतीति वाक्यतः ।
विद्यादैक्यं महावाक्यैर्जीवात्मपरमात्मनोः ॥ 30 ॥

By warding off all limiting adjuncts (gross, subtle and causal bodies) by means of the assertion "not this, not this", realise the oneness of the individual Self and the Universal Self by means of the cardinal aphorisms of the Upanishads.

आविद्यकं शरीरादि दृश्यं बुद्बुदवत्क्षरम् ।
एतद्विलक्षणं विद्यादहं ब्रह्मेति निर्मलम् ॥ 31 ॥

Body, etc., are all visible objects (for they are an object to the Self, being perceived by the Self) and are the result of ignorance. They are transient and perishable like bubbles. Realise that you are different from these (the body, mind, etc.), and know that you are the pure (blemishless) Brahman.

देहान्यत्वान्न मे जन्मजराकार्श्यलयादयः ।
शब्दादिविषयैः सङ्गो निरिन्द्रियतया न च ॥ 32 ॥

By being distinct (separate) from the body, there is no birth, old age, emaciation, death, etc., for me. Also, being distinct (separate) from the senses, I have no attachment to the objects of senses like sound, taste, vision, etc. [In other words, I am unattached to the body and all objects of the world.]

अमनस्त्वान्न मे दुःखरागद्वेषभयादयः ।
अप्राणो ह्यमनाः शुभ्र इत्यादिश्रुतिशासनात् ॥ 33 ॥

Being other than the mind, I am free from sorrow, attachment, hatred, fear, etc. According to the instruction of the scriptures (Muṇḍaka Upanishad 2.1.2), "The Self is not the vital airs (the *prāṇas*), and is not the mind. It is pure".

निर्गुणो निष्क्रियो नित्यो निर्विकल्पो निरञ्जनः ।
निर्विकारो निराकारो नित्यमुक्तोऽस्मि निर्मलः ॥ 34 ॥

I am without any attributes (or the qualities or modes of *sattva*, *rajas* and *tamas*). I am devoid of action, free from doubt, free from blemish, changeless, formless, ever-free, eternal and pure.

अहमाकाशवत्सर्वं बहिरन्तर्गतोऽच्युतः ।
सदा सर्वसमस्सिद्धो निःसङ्गो निर्मलोऽचलः ॥ 35 ॥

I, like the sky, pervade everything, inside and outside. I am imperishable, always equally present in all, immutable (ever-full), unattached, pure and immovable.

नित्यशुद्धविमुक्तैकमखण्डानन्दमद्वयम् ।
सत्यं ज्ञानमनन्तं यत्परं ब्रह्माहमेव तत् ॥ 36 ॥

I am indeed that Supreme Brahman, which is the One, eternal, pure, free, undiminished bliss, non-dual, Truth (Reality), of the nature of knowledge and infinite (unbounded).

एवं निरन्तराभ्यस्ता ब्रह्मैवास्मीति वासना ।
हरत्यविद्याविक्षेपाद्रोगानिव रसायनम् ॥ 37 ॥

By means of uninterrupted practice (of listening, reflection and meditation), one realises (i.e., forms the impression) that "I am indeed Brahman, the Supreme". This realisation destroys the confusion (delusion, distraction) caused by ignorance, just as medicine destroys the disease.

विविक्तदेश आसीनो विरागो विजितेन्द्रियः ।
भावयेदेकमात्मानं तमनन्तमनन्यधीः ॥ 38 ॥

Seated in an isolated place (in solitude), freed from attachments, with complete mastery over the senses and with undivided attention (with one-pointedness), one should meditate on that infinite Self, that is One (without a second).

आत्मन्येवाखिलं दृश्यं प्रविलाप्य धिया सुधीः ।
भावयेदेकमात्मानं निर्मलाकाशवत्सदा ॥ 39 ॥

Having completely dissolved (merged) the entire visible phenomena (the universe of objects) in the Self, by means of the intelligence, the wise one should always meditate upon that Self alone, which is like the pure, untainted sky.

रूपवर्णादिकं सर्वं विहाय परमार्थवित् ।
परिपूर्णचिदानन्दस्वरूपेणावतिष्ठते ॥ 40 ॥

One who has realised Brahman (the Supreme Reality), having given up all names, forms, etc., is established in his own intrinsic nature, which is ever-full (infinite), consciousness and bliss.

ज्ञातृज्ञानज्ञेयभेदः परे नात्मनि विद्यते ।
चिदानन्दैकरूपत्वाद्दीप्यते स्वयमेव तत् ॥ 41 ॥

The distinction of the triad of knower, knowledge and knowable (the object of knowledge) does not exist in the Supreme Self. That (Self), being of the nature of One (Absolute), Consciousness and Bliss, verily shines by itself, alone.

एवमात्मारणौ ध्यानमथने सततं कृते ।
उदितावगतिर्ज्वाला सर्वाज्ञानेन्धनं दहेत् ॥ 42 ॥

By means of constant meditation on the Self, the flame of true Self-knowledge arises, which completely burns all the fuel in the form of ignorance. [Meditation is likened to the process of rubbing pieces of wood to kindle fire, and the Self is likened to the firewood used to kindle fire.]

अरुणेनेव बोधेन पूर्वं सन्तमसे हृते ।
तत आविर्भवेदात्मा स्वयमेवांशुमानिव ॥ 43 ॥

At first, when ignorance is destroyed by the dawn of knowledge, the Self reveals itself, just as the sun appears when the darkness is removed at dawn.

आत्मा तु सततं प्राप्तोऽप्यप्राप्तवदविद्यया ।
तन्नाशे प्राप्तवद्भाति स्वकण्ठाभरणं यथा ॥ 44 ॥

When wearing a necklace, though it is present all the time around the neck, on some occasions, one looks for it all around the house. In the same manner, though the Self is constantly present, it seems as if it is not to be found, due to ignorance. When that ignorance is destroyed, the Self shines and is attained.

स्थाणौ पुरुषवद्भ्रान्त्या कृता ब्रह्मणि जीवता ।
जीवस्य तात्त्विके रूपे तस्मिन्दृष्टे निवर्तते ॥ 45 ॥

Because of delusion, the individuality of the self is created (superimposed) on Brahman, just as the form of a man is seen (superimposed) on a trunk (or post, pillar). [When ignorance is realised, the form of man ceases to exist.] Similarly, when the true nature of the *jīva* (the individual Self) is seen, then the individuality of the being ceases.

तत्त्वस्वरूपानुभवादुत्पन्नं ज्ञानमञ्जसा ।
अहं ममेति चाज्ञानं बाधते दिग्भ्रमादिवत् ॥ 46 ॥

Just as the sun removes any confusion regarding the directions, in the same manner, the knowledge born out of the realisation of one's true nature (i.e., the Self) quickly removes the ignorance manifesting as ideas in the form of "I" and "mine".

सम्यग्विज्ञानवान्योगी स्वात्मन्येवाखिलं जगत् ।
एकं च सर्वमात्मानमीक्षते ज्ञानचक्षुषा ॥ 47 ॥

The yogi, who is enlightened, sees–by means of the eye of knowledge–the entire universe, verily in the Self, and sees everything as the Self alone. [A yogi is one who has realised the oneness of the Self and Brahman.]

आत्मैवेदं जगत्सर्वमात्मनोऽन्यन्न विद्यते ।
मृदो यद्वद्धटादीनि स्वात्मानं सर्वमीक्षते ॥ 48 ॥

This entire phenomenal universe is indeed the Self alone, and there is nothing else other than the Self. The wise see everything as his own Self, just as pots, pitchers, etc., are nothing but clay.

जीवन्मुक्तस्तु तद्विद्वान्पूर्वोपाधिगुणांस्त्यजेत् ।
सच्चिदानन्दरूपत्वात् भवेद्भ्रमरकीटवत् ॥ 49 ॥

A *jīvanmukta* (one who is liberated and completely free from all ignorance and bondage while living) gives up the characteristics and traits of the previous (prior to attaining the knowledge) limiting adjuncts (body, mind, senses). The insect, constantly thinking of the wasp (*bhramara-kīta*), takes the form of the wasp. In the same manner, the wise one, having constantly meditated on Brahman and having realised his true nature of *sat-chit-ānandā* (i.e., Existence, Consciousness, Bliss), becomes that Brahman.

[About the insect and wasp: An insect is lured into the dwelling of a wasp. Overcome by extreme fear and thus constantly thinking of the wasp, the insect attains the same form as the wasp, without discarding its original body. This is the natural phenomenon of mimicry among some insects.]

तीर्त्वा मोहार्णवं हत्वा रागद्वेषादिराक्षसान् ।
योगी शान्तिसमायुक्त आत्मारामो विराजते ॥ 50 ॥

The *yogi* (wise one), having crossed the ocean of delusion and having killed the daemons of attachment, hatred, etc., becomes one endowed with peace, and is firmly established in the Self, delighting in one's Self alone.

बाह्यानित्यसुखासक्तिं हित्वात्मसुखनिर्वृतः ।
घटस्थदीपवत्स्वस्थः स्वान्तरेव प्रकाशते ॥ 51 ॥

Giving up attachment to external and transient happiness (or pleasures derived from contact with sense objects), the one established in one's own Self, satisfied and tranquil in the bliss of the Self, verily shines within, like a lamp placed inside a pot.

उपाधिस्थोऽपि तद्धर्मैरलिप्तो व्योमवन्मुनिः ।
सर्वविन्मूढवत्तिष्ठेदसक्तो वायुवच्चरेत् ॥ 52 ॥

Though in contact with the limiting adjuncts, the wise one is untainted by their characteristics, like the sky. Though knowing everything, the wise one remains like a fool (ignorant person) and moves about like the wind, remaining unattached. [*Unattached like the wind*: The wind transports fragrance or odour, or any other smell, itself remaining unaffected by it.]

उपाधिविलयाद्विष्णौ निर्विशेषं विशेन्मुनिः ।
जले जलं वियद्व्योम्नि तेजस्तेजसि वा यथा ॥ 53 ॥

With the destruction of the limiting adjuncts, the wise one unites with the All-pervading Supreme, without any differentiation, just as water becomes one with water, ether with ether and light with light.

यल्लाभान्नापरो लाभो यत्सुखान्नापरं सुखम् ।
यज्ज्ञानान्नापरं ज्ञानं तद्ब्रह्मेत्यवधारयेत् ॥ 54 ॥

Realise that as Brahman, after the attainment of which there is no greater attainment, beyond the bliss of which there is no greater bliss, and beyond the knowledge of which there is no greater knowledge.

यद्दृष्ट्वा नापरं दृश्यं यद्भूत्वा न पुनर्भवः ।
यज्ज्ञात्वा नापरं ज्ञेयं तद्ब्रह्मेत्यवधारयेत् ॥ 55 ॥

Realise that as Brahman, after having seen which there is nothing more to be seen, having become which there is no being born again, having known which there is nothing more to be known.

तिर्यगूर्ध्वमधः पूर्णं सच्चिदानन्दमद्वयम् ।
अनन्तं नित्यमेकं यत्तद्ब्रह्मेत्यवधारयेत् ॥ 56 ॥

Realise that as Brahman, which fills everything above, below and in the middle, which is Existence, Consciousness (Knowledge), and Bliss, which is non-dual (without a second), infinite (unbounded), eternal and One.

अतद्व्यावृत्तिरूपेण वेदान्तैर्लक्ष्यतेऽद्वयम् ।
अखण्डानन्दमेकं यत्तद्ब्रह्मेत्यवधारयेत् ॥ 57 ॥

Realise that as Brahman, which is non-dual, undiminished bliss and indivisible, and is revealed by the Upanishads by the process of '*neti-neti*' (negation of everything saying not this not this, used in Vedantic enquiry).

अखण्डानन्दरूपस्य तस्यानन्दलवाश्रिताः ।
ब्रह्माद्यास्तारतम्येन भवन्त्यानन्दिनो लवाः ॥ 58 ॥

Even for a minute portion of their bliss, Brahmā (the Creator deity) and other gods depend on that Supreme Brahman, which is of the nature of unlimited (and unfragmented) bliss. It is by thus receiving bliss from Brahman in different degrees, in proportion to their status, that they 'appear' like blissful ones.

तद्युक्तमखिलं वस्तु व्यवहारस्तदन्वितः ।
तस्मात्सर्वगतं ब्रह्म क्षीरे सर्पिरिवाखिले ॥ 59 ॥

All objects (things) are imbued with that (Brahman). All actions and functions are endowed with that (Brahman). Therefore, Brahman pervades everything, like the butter, which pervades all of the milk.

अनण्वस्थूलमह्रस्वमदीर्घमजमव्ययम् ।
अरूपगुणवर्णाख्यं तद्ब्रह्मेत्यवधारयेत् ॥ 60 ॥

Realise that as Brahman, which is neither minute, nor gross, nor small (short), not long, is devoid of birth, is imperishable (changeless) and is without form, qualities, colour or name.

यद्भासा भास्यतेऽर्कादि भास्यैर्यत्तु न भास्यते ।
येन सर्वमिदं भाति तद्ब्रह्मेत्यवधारयेत् ॥ 61 ॥

Realise that as Brahman, by whose light, the sun and other heavenly bodies are illumined, but It (Brahman) is not illumined by the light of these heavenly bodies, and by which (Brahman) all this (the entire universe) is illumined.

स्वयमन्तर्बहिर्व्याप्य भासयन्नखिलं जगत् ।
ब्रह्म प्रकाशते वह्निप्रतप्तायसपिण्डवत् ॥ 62 ॥

A red-hot iron ball has been completely pervaded by fire (inside and outside) and appears to glow because of the fire. In the same manner, pervading the entire universe inside and outside, Brahman, illuminating the entire universe, also shines by itself.

जगद्विलक्षणं ब्रह्म ब्रह्मणोऽन्यन्न किञ्चन ।
ब्रह्मान्यद्भाति चेन्मिथ्या यथा मरुमरीचिका ॥ 63 ॥

Brahman is different from the universe, and there exists nothing other than Brahman. If there appears or manifests (lit. shines) something other than Brahman, then know it to be an illusion (unreal), just like the illusory appearance of water in a desert.

दृश्यते श्रूयते यद्यद्ब्रह्मणोऽन्यन्न तद्भवेत् ।
तत्त्वज्ञानाच्च तद्ब्रह्म सच्चिदानन्दमद्वयम् ॥ 64 ॥

Whatever is seen (perceived) or heard is Brahman and nothing other than Brahman. On realising the knowledge of the Supreme Reality, everything is seen as the non-dual (the one without a second) Brahman and *sat-chit-ānanda* (Existence-Consciousness-Bliss).

सर्वगं सच्चिदात्मानं ज्ञानचक्षुर्निरीक्षते ।
अज्ञानचक्षुर्नेक्षेत भास्वन्तं भानुमन्धवत् ॥ 65 ॥

The one with the eye of knowledge (of Reality) alone perceives the all-pervading Self, which is of the nature of Existence and Consciousness. The one whose sense of perception is shrouded by ignorance cannot perceive the luminous and splendid Self, just as the blind person cannot see the sun.

श्रवणादिभिरुद्दीप्तज्ञानाग्निपरितापितः ।
जीवः सर्वमलान्मुक्तः स्वर्णवद्द्योतते स्वयम् ॥ 66 ॥

The *jīva* (the individual self), freed from all impurities, having been heated (like in the case of gold) by the fire of knowledge that has been kindled, by means of the process of listening, contemplation and meditation, shines by itself, like the purified gold.

हृदाकाशोदितो ह्यात्मा बोधभानुस्तमोऽपहृत् ।
सर्वव्यापी सर्वधारी भाति भासयतेऽखिलम् ॥ 67 ॥

The Self, the Sun of knowledge, arising in the sky of the heart (purified mind), destroys the darkness of ignorance. The all-pervading and the sustainer of all, It shines itself and illuminates the entire universe. (i.e., everything in the universe shines as the Self itself.)

दिग्देशकालाद्यनपेक्ष्य सर्वगं
शीतादिहृन्नित्यसुखं निरञ्जनम् ।
यः स्वात्मतीर्थं भजते विनिष्क्रियः
स सर्ववित्सर्वगतोऽमृतो भवेत् ॥ 68 ॥

The one who is freed from (having given up) all actions and worships the pilgrimage of the Self, which is independent of directions, time and space, which is all-pervading, which destroys cold, heat, etc., which is eternally blissful (and bestower of bliss, always) and which is pure (blemishless), such a one becomes all-knowing, all-pervading and immortal.

* * *

13

Amritabindu Upanishad

(अमृतबिन्दु उपनिषद्)

मनो हि द्विविधं प्रोक्तं शुद्धं चाशुद्धमेव च ।
अशुद्धं कामसंकल्पं शुद्धं कामविवर्जितम् ॥ 1 ॥

The mind, indeed, is said to be of two kinds–pure and impure. The mind, which is filled with the definite thoughts of objects of desire, is said to be impure. And the mind which is free from desires is said to be pure.

मन एव मनुष्याणां कारणं बन्धमोक्षयोः ।
बन्धाय विषयासक्तं मुक्तं निर्विषयं स्मृतम् ॥ 2 ॥

Mind, indeed, is the cause of the bondage and liberation of human beings. Attachment to sense objects leads to bondage; being free from attachment to objects leads to liberation. So, it is said.

यतो निर्विषयस्यास्य मनसो मुक्तिरिष्यते ।
अतो निर्विषयं नित्यं मनः कार्यं मुमुक्षुणा ॥ 3 ॥

Since freedom (or liberation) is considered to be of the mind, which is free from attachment to objects, therefore, the mind should always be made free from attachment to sense objects.

निरस्तविषयासङ्गं संनिरुद्धं मनो हृदि ।
यदाऽऽयात्यात्मनो भावं तदा तत्परमं पदम् ॥ 4 ॥

When the mind, casting off the attachment to sense objects, withdraws (from the external world) within (in the Self, the seat of Pure Consciousness) and realises its own true nature, then that Supreme abode is reached. [Realising its own nature: oneness of the Individual and the Universal Self.]

तावदेव निरोद्धव्यं यावद्धृदि गतं क्षयम् ।
एतज्ज्ञानं च ध्यानं च शेषो न्यायश्च विस्तरः ॥ 5 ॥

Till that time, the mind should be restrained (controlled) until it dissolves completely in the heart (in the seat of thought and cognition). [This dissolution is nothing but the realisation of the Truth as "I am that Brahman".] This is *jñāna* (Self-knowledge), and this is *dhyāna* (meditation). Everything else is mere arguments and words and serves no purpose to the seeker.

नैव चिन्त्यं न चाचिन्त्यं न चिन्त्यं चिन्त्यमेव च ।
पक्षपातविनिर्मुक्तं ब्रह्म सम्पद्यते तदा ॥ 6 ॥

Brahman (the Supreme Reality) is neither something to be thought of as we think of other external objects of the world, nor is it something unworthy of being thought of (as in the case of unpleasant thoughts in mind), nor is it something to be thought of as a means of pleasure (in the form of sense-pleasure). But it alone should be thought of (contemplated upon) as the Ultimate Truth. Then, in that state, completely free from prejudice, Brahman is attained. ['Free from prejudice' implies one should perceive Brahman as equally present in all beings.]

स्वरेण संधयेद्योगमस्वरं भावयेत्परम् ।
अस्वरेणानुभावेन भावो वाऽभाव इष्यते ॥ 7 ॥

In the beginning, one should meditate on Om, as the sounds (*svara*) '*a*', '*u*' and '*m*' make up the Om (symbolising Brahman). Then, one should meditate on the non-sound, i.e., meditate on the Supreme, Om (Brahman as the Supreme Reality), transcending the individual sounds and focusing on what the sounds stand for. And thus, on the realisation of the Truth (the Oneness, i.e., "I am That"), the universe is realised as Brahman alone.

तदेव निष्कलं ब्रह्म निर्विकल्पं निरञ्जनम् ।
तद्ब्रह्माहमिति ज्ञात्वा ब्रह्म संपद्यते ध्रुवम् ॥ 8 ॥

That alone is Brahman, the undivided (without parts), undifferentiated and pure (without any blemish). Having realised that as "I am that Brahman", one certainly becomes that Brahman.

निर्विकल्पमनन्तं च हेतुदृष्टान्तवर्जितम् ।
अप्रमेयमनादिं च यज्ज्ञात्वा मुच्यते बुधः ॥ 9 ॥

Having realised that Brahman–which is free from change or differences (*), eternal, without any cause or comparison (**), unfathomable (immeasurable) and beginningless–a wise one becomes liberated.

[* *Free from change or difference*: free from difference of knower-known, and free from differentiation of qualifier-qualified]

[** *Without any cause or comparison*: To infer something, one needs experience that needs reference or comparison. And every experience has a cause. Brahman is devoid of these.]

न निरोधो न चोत्पत्तिर्न बद्धो न च साधकः ।
न मुमुक्षुर्न वै मुक्त इत्येषा परमार्थता ॥ 10 ॥

The highest Truth is–"there is no destruction", "there is no coming into existence", "I am not bound", "I am not a seeker", "I am not an aspirant of liberation", and "I am not liberated". [All these are mere notions, and for one who has realised the Truth, they are rendered void.]

एक एवाऽऽत्मा मन्तव्यो जाग्रत्स्वप्नसुषुप्तिषु ।
स्थानत्रयव्यतीतस्य पुनर्जन्म न विद्यते ॥ 11 ॥

The Self, indeed, should be regarded as the same one in the three states of wakefulness, dream and deep-sleep states. For one who has transcended these three states, there is no notion of rebirth or being born again. [Self is regarded as *turīya*, the fourth.]

एक एव हि भूतात्मा भूते भूते व्यवस्थितः ।
एकधा बहुधा चैव दृष्यते जलचन्द्रवत् ॥ 12 ॥

For it is the One Self that resides in each and every being. It is perceived as the 'one' and also as the 'manifold', just like the reflection of the moon in different water bodies.

घटसंवृतमाकाशं नीयमाने घटे यथा ।
घटो नीयेत नाऽकाशः तथा जीवो नभोपमः ॥ 13 ॥

When the pot (pitcher) is carried from one place to another, it is the pot alone that changes place, and not the ether (*ākāsha*, the all-pervading space) enclosed in the pot. The *jīva* (the Individual Self) is similar to the ether. [That is, the individual Self is all-pervading like ether.]

घटवद्विविधाकारं भिद्यमानं पुनः पुनः ।
तद्भेदे च न जानाति स जानाति च नित्यशः ॥ 14 ॥

[The ether (in verse 13) is not 'exactly' like the Individual Self.] When the manifold forms, in the case of the pot (pitcher), are broken again and again, the ether (*ākāsha,* the all-pervading space) does not know that breaking. But He (the Self) always knows. [Suggesting that the Self is always aware of the changes to the body, mind, senses, etc.]

शब्दमायावृतो नैव तमसा याति पुष्करे ।
भिन्ने तमसि चैकत्वमेक एवानुपश्यति ॥ 15 ॥

Veiled by *māyā*, which is nothing but mere sound or idea (and has no reality), because of ignorance, one does not attain the lotus (in the core of the heart), the Self. And when the darkness (ignorance) is destroyed, the one Self alone sees (realises) the oneness of the Individual Self and Universal Self (Supreme Reality).

शब्दाक्षरं परं ब्रह्म तस्मिन्क्षीणे यदक्षरम् ।
तद्विद्वानक्षरं ध्यायेद्यदीच्छेच्छान्तिमात्मनः ॥ 16 ॥

The sacred syllable Om is the Supreme Brahman. When the idea of the sacred syllable (*akshara,* which is Om, the symbol) has been eliminated, the wise one should meditate upon that *akshara* (Imperishable Brahman) if he/she desires tranquility for oneself.

द्वे विद्ये वेदितव्ये तु शब्दब्रह्म परं च यत् ।
शब्दब्रह्माणि निष्णातः परं ब्रह्माधिगच्छति ॥ 17 ॥

Two kinds of knowledge are to be known. One is *Shabda-Brahman* (including the Vedas, the auxiliary sciences, etc.), and the other is Supreme Brahman. One who is deeply versed in *Shabda-Brahman* attains the Supreme Brahman. [Two kinds of knowledge: (1) the higher that includes the knowledge of the Brahman; and (2) the lower knowledge that includes all other forms of knowledge.]

ग्रन्थमभ्यस्य मेधावी ज्ञानविज्ञानतत्परः ।
पलालमिव धान्यार्थी त्यजेद्ग्रन्थमशेषतः ॥ 18 ॥

Having studied the scriptures with diligence, the intelligent one–who has knowledge and realisation alone as the highest aim–should discard the scriptures completely, just as the one who is desirous of the grains completely discards the husk.

गवामनेकवर्णानां क्षीरस्याप्येकवर्णता ।
क्षीरवत्पश्यते ज्ञानं लिङ्गिनस्तु गवां यथा ॥ 19 ॥

The cows are of many colours, but the milk is of one colour alone. The wise one looks upon knowledge (the essence or Truth) like the milk and regards the forms or external appearances (the scriptures covering numerous philosophies by various authors) like the cows.

घृतमिव पयसि निगूढं भूते भूते वसति विज्ञानम् ।
सततं मनसि मन्थयितव्यं मनसा मन्थानभूतेन ॥ 20 ॥

The Self (Pure Consciousness) is concealed in every being (pervading the entire being), like butter concealed in milk. That ought to be churned out constantly in the mind, by the churning-stick of the mind. [Churning out the butter symbolises liberation.]

ज्ञाननेत्रं समादाय उद्धरेद्वह्निवत्परम् ।
निष्कलं निश्चलं शान्तं तद्ब्रह्माहमिति स्मृतम् ॥ 21 ॥

Apprehending the rope of knowledge (by which the churning stick is whirled around), one should draw out the Supreme like fire. I am That undivided (without parts), unchangeable (immutable) and tranquil Brahman. Thus, it is said (by the wise). [Here, 'churning' refers to the process of churning to kindle fire.]

सर्वभूताधिवासं यद्भूतेषु च वसत्यपि ।
सर्वानुग्राहकत्वेन तदस्म्यहं वासुदेवस्तदस्म्यहं वासुदेव इति ॥ 22 ॥

He is the abode or dwelling of all beings; also, being the bestower of grace to all, He resides in all the beings. I am That, Vāsudeva. I am That, Vāsudeva. [Vāsudeva is nothing but Brahman. Adi Shankara, in his commentary of the Vishnu-sahasranāma, says, "Being the Lord, He dwells in, infuses and covers everything. Thus, He is Vāsudeva."]

* * *

14

Dṛg-dṛśya-vivekaḥ
(दृग्दृश्यविवेकः)

रूपं दृश्यं लोचनं दृक् तद्दृश्यं दृक्तु मानसम् ।
दृश्या धीवृत्तयस्साक्षी दृगेव न तु दृश्यते ॥ 1 ॥

The form (any outward appearance or phenomenon) is the seen (perceived, known object); the eye (any organ of perception: eye, ear, nose, skin and tongue) is the seer (perceiver, knower). The senses are the seen, and the mind is the seer. The modifications of the mind (including thoughts and other activities) are the seen, and the witness (the Self) is the seer. But the witness (Self) itself is not ever seen (known or perceived) by anything or anyone else.

नीलपीतस्थूलसूक्ष्मह्रस्वदीर्घादि भेदतः ।
नानाविधानि रूपाणि पश्येल्लोचनमेकधा ॥ 2 ॥

The various forms (objects of the senses) we see are because of the distinctions like blue, yellow, gross, subtle, short, long, etc. But the eye (the seer) that sees all these distinctions is one and remains the same. [The seer remains unchanging.]

आन्ध्यमान्द्यपटुत्वेषु नेत्रधर्मेषु चैकधा ।
सङ्कल्पयेन्मनः श्रोत्रत्वगादौ योज्यतामिदम् ॥ 3 ॥

The mind, being one and the same, perceives the eye and the various characteristics of the eye, such as complete blindness, dullness of vision and sharp vision. This same analysis (investigation) may also be applied to the other sense organs–

ear, skin, nose and tongue. [The mind is the seer, and the senses and all their respective characteristics are the seen.]

कामः सङ्कल्पसन्देहौ श्रद्धाऽश्रद्धे धृतीतरे ।
ह्रीर्धीर्भीरित्येवमादीन् भासयत्येकधा चितिः ॥ 4 ॥

Consciousness, being one (and remaining the same), illumines (perceives) desire (passion), intention (or imagination, decision), doubt, *shraddhā*, absence of *shraddhā*, resolve, the absence of resolve, shame, understanding, fear and other such attributes of the mind.

नोदेति नास्तमेत्येषा न वृद्धिं याति न क्षयम् ।
स्वयं विभात्यथान्यानि भासयेत्साधनं विना ॥ 5 ॥

The Consciousness (Witness) does not rise (born or becomes existent) and does not set (nor does it die or become non-existent). It does not increase or undergo any decay. (Matter is subject to six changes of form or nature– is born, exists, grows, undergoes changes, declines, and perishes. Consciousness has none of these characteristics.) Moreover, Consciousness shines by itself (it is self-effulgent), and without any other means. It illumines all other things (sense objects of perception) in the universe.

चिच्छायाऽऽवेशतो बुद्धौ भानं धीस्तु द्विधा स्थिता ।
एकाहङ्कृतिरन्या स्यादन्तःकरणरूपिणी ॥ 6 ॥

With the infusion of the reflection of the Consciousness in it, the mind 'appears' to be conscious. [The term '*buddhi*' here refers to mind. The mind as if borrows consciousness from the Consciousness (Witness), for it is not conscious by itself. This is as in the case of the reflected light of the sun on the moon that illuminates the earth. The moon doesn't have light of its own. But we say, "the moon is illumining the earth at night"].

The mind is of two parts. One is the 'I-sense' (the individualness or selfness). The other is the mind-function (the *antah-karaṇa*), which includes the mind, intelligence and *chitta* (memory).

छायाऽहङ्कारयोरैक्यं तप्तायःपिण्डवन्मतम् ।
तदहङ्कारतादात्म्याद्देहश्चेतनतामगात् ॥ 7 ॥

The oneness of the reflection (the reflected-consciousness) and 'I-sense' (ego, individualness) is like the oneness of the fire and heated iron ball. This is the opinion of the wise. [We refer to this combination as the red-hot iron ball. The fire and the iron ball appear as one. The characteristics of both are 'as if' shared by each other].

In the same manner, the body (including the sense organs) identifying itself as the 'I-sense' (ego) appears to be a conscious entity. But remember, the 'I-sense' itself has borrowed consciousness from the Consciousness (the Witness), through reflection.

अहङ्कारस्य तादात्म्यं चिच्छायादेहसाक्षिभिः ।
सहजं कर्मजं भ्रान्तिजन्यं च त्रिविधं क्रमात् ॥ 8 ॥

The identity or the sameness of the 'I-sense' is with three entities– the reflection of the Consciousness, the body and the Witness-Consciousness. This identity experienced in the three cases is caused by the following: (1) The identity with the reflected-consciousness is natural (as in the case of the mirror, for it is the mirror's nature to reflect). (2) The identity with the body is born of *karma*. (3) The identity with the Witness-Consciousness is born of ignorance (delusion). In other words, there is no relationship between the 'I-sense' and the Witness-Consciousness.

सम्बन्धिनोः सतोर्नास्ति निवृत्तिः सहजस्य तु ।
कर्मक्षयात् प्रबोधाच्च निवर्तेते क्रमादुभे ॥ 9 ॥

[What happens to these three identifications discussed above?] (1) The identity of the 'I-sense' with the reflected consciousness is 'natural' and is there right from the time of birth and never ceases to exist. (As long as the mirror and face exist, the reflection will remain.) (2) The identity of the 'I-sense' with the body wears out when karma is exhausted (when the body dies). (3) The identity of the 'I-sense' with the Witness-Consciousness ends when there is an awakening of Self-knowledge. (In reality, the freedom from the 'I-sense' is the goal of the spiritual pursuit.)

अहङ्कारलये सुप्तौ भवेद्देहोऽप्यचेतनः ।
अहङ्कारविकासार्धः स्वप्नः सर्वस्तु जागरः ॥ 10 ॥

In the deep sleep state, the 'I-sense' (along with the mind) completely disappears, and the body (including the senses) also becomes completely unconscious. When there is a partial (half) manifestation of the 'I-sense', it is called the dream state. The full manifestation of the 'I-sense' and the mind is called the state of wakefulness. [These are the three states of the mind, and not of the Witness-Consciousness.]

अन्तःकरणवृत्तिश्च चितिच्छायैक्यमागता ।
वासनाः कल्पयेत् स्वप्ने बोधेऽक्षैर्विषयान् बहिः ॥ 11 ॥

In the dream state, the inner instrument (mind), which is nothing but a modification, produces (imagines) manifold mental images, identifying itself with the reflected Consciousness. [These images are created based on the impressions (*vāsana*) in the mind that are formed during the wakeful state, during the interaction with the world.] However, during the waking state, the mind creates images based on the interactions of the senses with the external sense objects.

मनोऽहङ्कृत्युपादानं लिङ्गमेकं जडात्मकम् ।
अवस्थात्रयमन्वेति जायते म्रियते तथा ॥ 12 ॥

The material cause of the mind and 'I-sense' is the same subtle body, and it is inert by nature. [The subtle body consists of seventeen parts: the five organs of perception or knowledge, the five organs of action, the five vital airs, the mind and intellect.]

The subtle body goes through three states of experience (wakefulness, dream and deep sleep), and it is born and also dies. [The birth of an individual is associated with the subtle body entering the gross body. What we call the death of the individual is when the subtle body exits the gross body.]

शक्तिद्वयं हि मायाया विक्षेपावृतिरूपकम् ।
विक्षेपशक्तिर्लिङ्गादि ब्रह्माण्डान्तं जगत् सृजेत् ॥ 13 ॥

There are two powers of *māyā* (the illusory power of Brahman). They are of the nature (or form) of the projecting power (*vikshepa*) and of the covering or veiling power (*āvarana* or *āvrti*). The projecting power of *māyā* projects (creates) everything from this subtle body to the entire gross universe and everything in between. [The projecting power is not the problem. The veiling power is the cause of our ignorance and prevents us from seeing the reality. In the dream state, too, this projecting power creates the dream, and the veiling power conceals the reality of the dream.]

सृष्टिर्नाम ब्रह्मरूपे सच्चिदानन्दवस्तुनि ।
अब्धौ फेनादिवत् सर्वनामरूपप्रसारणा ॥ 14 ॥

In Brahman, which is of the nature of *sat-chit-ānanda* (Existence-Consciousness-Bliss), the manifestation or projection of name and form (done by the projecting power of *māyā*) is called 'creation'. (Just as clay with a certain name and form is called a pot.) This is just like the foam or bubbles on the surface of the ocean (the manifestation of foam is caused by the wind). [Brahman is the one reality, and all this creation, which is unreal, is a result of the projecting power *māyā*.]

अन्तर्दृग्दृश्ययोर्भेदं बहिश्च ब्रह्मसर्गयोः ।
आवृणोत्यपरा शक्तिः सा संसारस्य कारणम् ॥ 15 ॥

The other power, i.e., the veiling or concealing power of *māyā*, on the one hand, conceals the distinction between the seer (the Self) and the seen (everything from the ego to the objects of the world) within the body. On the other hand, this power also conceals the distinction between Brahman (of the nature of Existence-Conscious-Bliss) and the created universe (visible phenomena of names and forms) outside the body. This veiling power is the cause of *samsāra*. [The ignorance of the distinction between the seer and the seen is the cause of suffering.]

साक्षिणः पुरतो भाति लिङ्गं देहेन संयुतम् ।
चितिच्छायासमावेशाज्जीवः स्याद्व्यावहारिकः ॥ 16 ॥

In the presence of the Witness Consciousness, the subtle body, together with the gross (physical) body, shines (exists). Since that Consciousness shines (reflected) in the subtle body, it becomes the individual Self. That individual *jīva* (the embodied one) is the one engaged in a life of action and interaction in the world of experiences.

अस्य जीवत्वमारोपात् साक्षिण्यप्यवभासते ।
आवृतौ तु विनष्टायां भेदे भातेऽपयाति तत् ॥ 17 ॥

Due to the superimposition of the status of being a *jīva*, the character of the *jīva* shines (appears) on the Witness Consciousness also. (Because of the ignorance of the real identity and the false identification with the mind and the body, we end up making false claims like 'I am agitated', 'I am ill', etc.) When the veiling power is destroyed, the distinction (between the Witness and the *jīva*, the seer and the seen) is clearly seen. And the superimposition disappears.

तथा सर्गब्रह्मणोश्च भेदमावृत्य तिष्ठति ।
या शक्तिस्तद्वशाद्ब्रह्म विकृतत्वेन भासते ॥ 18 ॥

In the same manner, under the influence of the veiling power of *māyā*, the distinction between Brahman and the creation (the phenomenal universe of names and forms) is veiled. Because of that (the veiling), Brahman (though changeless) appears as though endowed with modifications (changes). In other words, Brahman appears as this changeful universe. [Matter alone is subject to six modifications– is born, exists, grows, undergoes changes, declines and perishes.]

[Looking at the universe, we see only the universe, and Brahman is veiled. Just as in the case of a table, we talk about it as a table, and the wood is veiled. Like the table, the universe is just name and form.]

अत्राप्यावृतिनाशेन विभाति ब्रह्मसर्गयोः ।
भेदस्तयोर्विकारः स्यात् सर्गे न ब्रह्मणि क्वचित् ॥ 19 ॥

Here also (in the case of the Self), due to the destruction of the veiling power of *māyā*, the distinction between Brahman and the creation (the universe) shines or becomes clear. [This destruction of veiling, i.e., ignorance, can take place only by knowledge, the knowledge of Brahman.] Therefore, (because of this revelation), one comes to realise that any change is a characteristic of the universe alone and never in Brahman. [Note that the distinction between Brahman and the universe is not referring to the separation of Brahman from the universe. Brahman being Existence cannot be separated from the universe.]

अस्ति भाति प्रियं रूपं नाम चेत्यंशपञ्चकम् ।
आद्यत्रयं ब्रह्मरूपं जगद्रूपं ततो द्वयम् ॥ 20 ॥

All experiences in the universe have five aspects or components. They are–is (exists, am), shines (known, experienced), dearness, form (perceptible to the senses or mind, has property) and name. The first three are the nature of Brahman, and the next two are the nature of the universe. [This verse provides a way to discriminate between real and unreal. The 'is-ness' is associated with Existence (*sat*). The 'shines' is associated with knowledge, Consciousness (*chit*). Dearness is associated with Bliss (*ānanda*). Thus, Brahman is *sat-chit-ānanda* (Existence-Consciousness-Bliss).]

खवाय्वग्निजलोर्वीषु देवतिर्यङ्नरादिषु ।
अभिन्नाः सच्चिदानन्दाः भिद्यते रूपनामनी ॥ 21 ॥

Existence-Consciousness-Bliss (*sat-chit-ānanda*) is equally residing in all insentient things of the world made up of the five elements (ether, air, fire, water and earth), and also present in the sentient beings, viz. in gods, humans and life forms in between (including animals, birds). All entities appear different because of names and forms. [Existence-Consciousness-Bliss is real and permanent, and things of name and form are unreal and impermanent.]

उपेक्ष्य नामरूपे द्वे सच्चिदानन्दतत्परः ।
समाधिं सर्वदा कुर्याद्धृदये वाऽथवा बहिः ॥ 22 ॥

Giving up names and forms, being completely absorbed in Existence-Consciousness-Bliss (*sat-chit-ānanda,* Brahman), one should practise *samādhi* (*nididhyāsana*)–either in one's own heart (based on an internal thought or idea) or outside (meditating on the changeless aspect any external object).

[*Samādhi* is the constant, undivided abidance in the identity that "I am Brahman". Three types of inner meditations (*samādhi*) and three types of external meditations (*samādhi*) will be discussed in the following verses.

सविकल्पो निर्विकल्पः समाधिर्द्विविधो हृदि ।
दृश्यशब्दानुवेधेन सविकल्पः पुनर्द्विधा ॥ 23 ॥

Samādhi–to be practised within (in the heart), is of two types–*savikalpa* and *nirvikalpa*. *Savikalpa Samādhi* is again of two types. One is associated with an object, and the other is associated with sound (words) from the scriptures (Upanishads).

Savikalpa Samādhi and Nirvikalpa Samādhi:

Both these forms of *samādhi* are based on the presence or absence of distinctions (*vikalpa*). The distinctions are meditator (*dhyāta*), meditation (*dhyāna*) and meditated upon (*dhyeya*). When the notion of the distinction between meditator, meditation and meditated upon still persists, while being absorbed in Brahman, it is called *savikalpa samādhi*. When the notion of the distinction between the three is absent, it is called *nirvikalpa samādhi*. The goal in both cases is to be absorbed in Brahman.

कामाद्याश्चित्तगा दृश्यास्तत्साक्षित्वेन चेतनम् ।
ध्यायेद्दृश्यानुविद्धोऽयं समाधिः सविकल्पकः ॥ 24 ॥

Desires, etc. (including thoughts and emotions) are perceived objects (the seen) in the mind. Instead of focusing the attention on the object, one should meditate upon the Consciousness as the witness to these objects of the mind (i.e., as the illuminator of the objects of the mind). This is *savikalpa samādhi* associated with the seen (objects).

[When we see objects of the world, the desire for the object is in the mind alone. Instead of focusing the attention on the object, think of the Consciousness, which is the witness to that object.]

असङ्गः सच्चिदानन्दः स्वप्रभो द्वैतवर्जितः ।
अस्मीति शब्दविद्धोऽयं समाधिः सविकल्पकः ॥ 25 ॥

One should meditate upon "I am unattached", "I am *sat-chit-ānanda* (Existence-Consciousness-Bliss)", "I am self-effulgent (self-luminous)", "I am devoid of duality" and other such ideas or proclamations from the scriptures. [These are nothing but the way we describe the Consciousness (the witness) in the previous verse. In essence, these are other ways to express the same idea: "I am Brahman".] This is *savikalpa samādhi* associated with words of the scriptures (Upanishads, Bhagavad Gīta, etc.).

स्वानुभूतिरसावेशाद्दृश्यशब्दावुपेक्ष्य तु ।
निर्विकल्पः समाधिः स्यान्निवातस्थितदीपवत् ॥ 26 ॥

[In the previous two forms of meditation, there is a will and deliberateness of effort involved. Gradually, the deliberateness drops off. Then the distinction of 'meditator-meditation-meditated upon' disappears.]

When one is free from the objects and words (as described in the previous two verses), the complete absorption in the bliss of Self-experience (realisation of the Self) is called *nirvikalpa samādhi*. In this state, the mind is like the steady and unflickering flame of a lamp, kept in a place without any wind.

हृदीव बाह्यदेशेऽपि यस्मिन् कस्मिंश्च वस्तुनि ।
समाधिराद्यः सन्मात्रान्नामरूपपृथक्कृतिः ॥ 27 ॥

The first type of meditation done within the heart (*savikalpa samādhi* associated with an internal object, as discussed in verse 24) can also be practised with any objects whatsoever on the outside (in the world). In this *samādhi*, the practitioner should separate the name and form from the *sat* (Existence), i.e., Brahman. [The Existence or *sat* is the 'is-ness' of everything in this universe. The attention should be shifted from the name and form to the 'is-ness'. This is similar to the screen on which the movie is projected.] This is *savikalpa samādhi* associated with outer objects. [This is the foundational idea of equal-vision towards all.]

अखण्डैकरसं वस्तु सच्चिदानन्दलक्षणम् ।
इत्यविच्छिन्नचिन्तेयं समाधिर्मध्यमो भवेत् ॥ 28 ॥

On seeing anything in the outside world, the substance (entity), which is the very substratum of it all, is the absolute, undivided, unchanging and limitless (Brahman), which is of the nature of *sat-chit-ānanda* (Existence-Consciousness-Bliss). This unbroken meditation upon the undivided Existence (the substratum of all), being free from name and form, is called *savikalpa samādhi* associated with words of the scriptures (in the context of the outer world).

[In verses 24 and 25, the focus is on Consciousness; in verses 27 and 28, the focus is on Existence. Fundamentally, there is no difference between Existence and Consciousness.]

स्तब्धीभावो रसास्वादात्तृतीयः पूर्ववन्मतः ।
एतैः समाधिभिः षड्भिर्नयेत् कालं निरन्तरम् ॥ 29 ॥

As discussed earlier (in verse 26), the complete absorption of the mind in the words of the Upanishads (without any distraction by the world of names and forms) as a result of absorption in the bliss (of realisation of the Self) is referred to as the third kind of *samādhi* (of outer). This is *nirvikalpa samādhi*. The seeker should constantly practise these six kinds of *samādhi*.

देहाभिमाने गलिते विज्ञाते परमात्मनि ।
यत्र यत्र मनो याति तत्र तत्र समाधयः ॥ 30 ॥

When the identification of the Self with the body-mind has disappeared (i.e., one is free from notions like 'I am the body', 'I was born', 'I will die', 'I am sad', etc.), and when one has realised the Universal Self, then wherever the mind (wherever there is experience in this world), there is *samādhi* (inner or external).

भिद्यते हृदयग्रन्थिश्छिद्यन्ते सर्वसंशयाः ।
क्षीयन्ते चास्य कर्माणि तस्मिन् दृष्टे परावरे ॥ 31 ॥

When one sees (realises) the Supreme–that one Supreme Reality which is both the high (as the cause) and the low (as the effect)–then all knots of the heart (ideas caused by ignorance, e.g., thoughts such as 'I am this body, 'my house', 'I am sad') are disentangled (eliminated); all doubts (regarding what is to be known in the context of the world) are destroyed; and all effects of karma (all except the *prārabdha-karma*) are destroyed. [Also, all outcomes in the form of merit and demerit in the context of actions are also destroyed.]

[NOTE: In some versions, this text ends here, with the description of the benefits of this text.]

अवच्छिन्नश्चिदाभासस्तृतीयः स्वप्नकल्पितः ।
विज्ञेयस्त्रिविधो जीवस्तत्राद्यः पारमार्थिकः ॥ 32 ॥

There are three kinds of *jīva* (individual self): (1) The 'limited' (Witness Consciousness). Its existence does not depend on the body-mind; (2) Reflected Consciousness, which is manifested in the body-mind (*chidābhāsa*). This is the Consciousness that is used in all transactions in the world; (3) Reflected Consciousness imagined in the dream state. Among the three, the first is referred to as '*pāramārthika-jīva*'–the real nature of the *jīva*. [This is the true meaning of "I" in the idea "I am Brahman".]

अवच्छेदः कल्पितः स्यादवच्छेद्यं तु वास्तवम् ।
तस्मिन् जीवत्वमारोपाद्ब्रह्मत्वं तु स्वभावतः ॥ 33 ॥

[The nature of the *pāramārthika-jīva*] The limitedness (as discussed in verse 32) is imagined. That which is seemingly limited (by the body), in fact, is not limited; it is real. (While the space inside the pitcher seems limited by the shape of the pitcher, in reality, the space inside the pot is not limited.) The status as the individual self (*jīva*) has been bestowed because of the superimposition of attributes (or characteristics) of the body-mind upon the Self. In reality, it is nothing but Brahman.

अवच्छिन्नस्य जीवस्य पूर्णेन ब्रह्मणैकताम् ।
तत्त्वमस्यादिवाक्यानि जगुर्नेतरजीवयोः ॥ 34 ॥

The identity (or oneness) of the conditioned *jīva* (discussed above) and Brahman has been revealed in the cardinal statements of the Upanishads like "You are That (Brahman)", "I am Brahman", etc. But this identity is not agreeable in the case of the other two *jīvas* (discussed in verse 32).

ब्रह्मण्यवस्थिता माया विक्षेपावृतिरूपिणी ।
आवृत्यखण्डतां तस्मिन् जगज्जीवौ प्रकल्पयेत् ॥ 35 ॥

The illusory power of *māyā*, in Brahman, is two-fold: of the form of projection and of the form of veiling. Having veiled the indivisible (non-dual) nature of Brahman, it makes Brahman appear (in Brahman) as the universe and as the individual *jīva*. [This was discussed in verse 13]

जीवो धीस्थचिदाभासो भवेद्भोक्ता हि कर्मकृत् ।
भोग्यरूपमिदं सर्वं जगत् स्याद्भूतभौतिकम् ॥ 36 ॥

By the mere appearance (or reflection) of Consciousness in the mind [refer to point 2 in verse 32], and by being the doer of actions and the experiencer of the results, it is called *jīva*. [This *jīva* is the *vyāvahārika-jīva*, the one who acts, interacts, transacts, etc., in this universe.] All this (visible phenomena consisting of the sense objects) made from (and consisting of) the five elements, and which is of the nature of experience (in the form of pleasure and pain) is the universe or world (*jagat*).

अनादिकालमारभ्य मोक्षात् पूर्वमिदं द्वयम् ।
व्यवहारे स्थितं तस्मादुभयं व्यावहारिकम् ॥ 37 ॥

These two–the individual self (*jīva*) and the universe (discussed in verse 36)–starting from beginningless time (i.e., ever-existent), have transactional existence alone (for action, transaction, experience, etc.). And both (individual and the universe of experience) last until one attains *moksha* (liberation). They both are *vyāvahārika*, transactional (phenomenal existence) in nature.

चिदाभासस्थिता निद्रा विक्षेपावृतिरूपिणी ।
आवृत्य जीवजगती पूर्वे नूत्ने तु कल्पयेत् ॥ 38 ॥

Sleep is seated in the *chidābhāsa* (reflected consciousness that is manifested in the mind) and is of the nature of the projecting and veiling powers. First, it (sleep) veils the individual Self (*jīva*) and the universe (of the waking state), and then it creates an imaginary one afresh (in a dream).

प्रतीतिकाल एवैते स्थितत्वात् प्रातिभासिके ।
न हि स्वप्नप्रबुद्धस्य पुनः स्वप्ने स्थितिस्तयोः ॥ 39 ॥

Since both the dream-individual-self and the dream universe are present only during the dream experience, they are referred to as *prātibhāsika* (illusory or only in appearance). This is because, when one wakes up from the dream state, there is no continuity for the *dream-jīva* and dream universe when one moves into the dream state again. [Both *vyāvahārika* and *prātibhāsika* are treated as unreal. But there is only a slight difference in continuity.]

प्रातिभासिकजीवो यस्तज्जगत् प्रातिभासिकम् ।
वास्तवं मन्यतेऽन्यस्तु मिथ्येति व्यावहारिकः ॥ 40 ॥

In the dream state, for the *dream-jīva* (*prātibhāsika-jīva*), the dream world is real. But, on waking up, *vyāvahārika-jīva* (the *jīva* of the world of transactions and interactions) thinks of those as unreal (illusory).

व्यावहारिकजीवो यस्तज्जगद्व्यावहारिकम् ।
सत्यं प्रत्येति मिथ्येति मन्यते पारमार्थिकः ॥ 41 ॥

In the same manner, one who is a *vyāvahārika-jīva* (the *jīva* of the world of transactions and interactions) sees the *waking-state-jīva* and the waking-state-world as real. But the *pāramārthika-jīva* (*real-jīva*, the one who has realised one's true nature as the Witness Consciousness), which is beyond the three states (of wakefulness, dream and deep sleep), knows these to be unreal.

पारमार्थिकजीवस्तु ब्रह्मैक्यं पारमार्थिकम् ।
प्रत्येति वीक्षते नान्यद्वीक्षते त्वनृतात्मना ॥ 42 ॥

The *pāramārthika-jīva* (the *real-jīva*, the one who has realised one's true nature) knows its identity with Brahman (as "I am Brahman") as real. Having realised the Truth (regarding one's own nature), he does not see another (i.e., there exists nothing else other than Brahman). If at all he sees (for the purpose of transaction or interaction with the world), he knows it to be unreal.

माधुर्यद्रवशैत्यानि नीरधर्मास्तरङ्गके ।
अनुगम्याथ तन्निष्ठे फेनेऽप्यनुगता यथा ॥ 43 ॥

साक्षिस्थाः सच्चिदानन्दाः सम्बन्धाद्व्यावहारिके ।
तद्द्वारेणानुगच्छन्ति तथैव प्रातिभासिके ॥ 44 ॥

It is the characteristics of water, viz. beauty (or sweetness), fluidity and coldness, that also exist in the wave. In the same manner, these characteristics of the wave (acquired from water) are passed on by the wave to the foam (on top of the wave).

In the same manner, Existence-Consciousness-Bliss (*sat-chit-ānanda*), the characteristics (nature) of the *pāramārtika-jīva* appear to reside in the *vyāvahārika-jīva* (the *jīva* of the world of transactions and interactions), because of the relation with the Witness Consciousness; which in turn is passed on to the *prātibhāsika-jīva* (the dream state *jīva*). [It is the mind of the wakeful state that gives consciousness to the dream state body and mind.]

लये फेनस्य तद्धर्मा द्रवाद्याः स्युस्तरङ्गके ।
तस्यापि विलये नीरे तिष्ठन्त्येते यथा पुरा ॥ 45 ॥

[It is the wave that appears on the water and the foam that appears on the wave.] When the foam merges (disappears) on the wave, its characteristics, like fluidity, etc., merge (disappear) in the wave. And, when the wave merges back into the water, its characteristics abide in the water as before.

प्रातिभासिकजीवस्य लये स्युर्व्यावहारिके ।
तल्लये सच्चिदानन्दाः पर्यवस्यन्ति साक्षिणि ॥ 46 ॥

In the same manner (as in verse 45), when the *prātibhāsika-jīva* merges (in the *vyāvahārika-jīva*), its nature, Existence-Consciousness-Bliss (*sat-chit-ānanda*) merges in the *vyāvahārika-jīva*. And when that (*vyāvahārika-jīva*) disappears, these characteristics abide or merge into the Witness (Brahman).

* * *

15

Upadesha-sāram

(उपदेशसारम्)

कर्तुराज्ञया प्राप्यते फलम् ।
कर्म किं परं कर्म तज्जडम् ॥ 1 ॥

By the will of the Creator (the laws of nature), action bears fruit. Is action, then, supreme? No, it is inert, unconscious.

कृतिमहोदधौ पतनकारणम् ।
फलमशाश्वतं गतिनिरोधकम् ॥ 2 ॥

The fruit of action is transient and is the cause of the downfall into the great ocean of activity. It is also a hindrance to progress towards the ultimate goal of *moksha*.

ईश्वरार्पितं नेच्छया कृतम् ।
चित्तशोधकं मुक्तिसाधकम् ॥ 3 ॥

Action performed without desire and performed as an offering to the Lord purifies the mind and leads the seeker to liberation.

कायवाङ्मनः कार्यमुत्तमम् ।
पूजनं जपश्चिन्तनं क्रमात् ॥ 4 ॥

Worship, *japa* (repetition of names, *mantra*) and meditation are actions performed by the body, the speech and the mind, respectively, and they are excellent in that order.

जगत ईशधी-युक्त-सेवनम् ।
अष्टमूर्तिभृद्देवपूजनम् ॥ 5 ॥

To serve the world (all beings of the world), endowed with the attitude that "Lord alone is this world", is worshipping the Lord possessing eight forms (viz. earth, water, fire, air, ether, the sun, the moon and the individual soul).

उत्तमस्तवादुच्चमन्दतः ।
चित्तजं जपध्यानमुत्तमम् ॥ 6 ॥

As compared to the loud chanting or singing of prayers (or eulogies of the Lord), *japa* (repetition of a *mantra* or names of the Lord) uttered in a high voice or in low whispers is superior. Superior to that is *dhyāna* (meditation) in the mind. [The term *japa-dhyāna*–used in the verse–means *japa* done in the mind, which itself is *dhyāna* or meditation.]

आज्यधारया स्रोतसा समम् ।
सरलचिन्तनं विरलतः परम् ॥ 7 ॥

Like the flow of oil (or clarified butter) or like the flow of a river, constant (uninterrupted) meditation is superior to intermittently interrupted meditation.

भेदभावनात् सोऽहमित्यसौ ।
भावनाऽभिदा पावनी मता ॥ 8 ॥

Compared to meditation based on differentiation (duality) between the meditator (oneself) and the meditated upon (Lord or the object of meditation), meditation of the kind "I am That" (without any differentiation) is considered purifying.

भावशून्यसद्भावसुस्थितिः ।
भावनाबलाद्भक्तिरुत्तमा ॥ 9 ॥

By the power of meditation (free from differentiation between the meditator and meditated upon, by means of the notion "I am That"), devoid of any other thoughts whatsoever, one is established in one's true essence. This is the highest form of devotion.

हृत्स्थले मनः स्वस्थता क्रिया ।
भक्तियोगबोधाश्च निश्चितम् ॥ 10 ॥

To establish the mind in its own place (in its natural state) in the centre of the heart–the Self, is certainly the goal of devotion, yoga and knowledge.

वायुरोधनाल्लीयते मनः ।
जालपक्षिवद्रोधसाधनम् ॥ 11 ॥

By restraining the breath, the mind is subdued, just as a bird is restrained in the net (when caught by the hunter). This practice (of breath regulation) becomes a means to restrain the mind.

चित्तवायवश्चित्क्रियायुताः ।
शाखयोर्द्वयी शक्तिमूलका ॥ 12 ॥

The mind and the breath (vital air, *prāṇa*) are accompanied by Consciousness and action, respectively. They are both branches emanating from the same source, the Supreme power of the Lord. [Knowledge and action originate from the same source.]

लयविनाशने उभयरोधने ।
लयगतं पुनर्भवति नो मृतम् ॥ 13 ॥

There are two ways to restrain the mind–absorption of the mind (*laya*) and destruction of the mind (*nīsha*). [Absorption of the mind refers to the withdrawal of the mind from various functions and activities of the mind. Destruction refers to the destruction of the limited nature of the mind and realization of one's real nature as the Self.] In the case of absorption of the mind, the mind returns again, but not in the case of the mind, which is destroyed.

प्राणबन्धनाल्लीनमानसम् ।
एकचिन्तनान्नाशमेत्यदः ॥ 14 ॥

The mind that has been restrained (attaining *laya*, absorption) by means of control of breath (*prāṇa*, the vital air) can be led to destruction (*mano-nīsha*) by meditating upon the one thought. [The meditating on the one thought refers to single-pointed meditation on the real nature as the Self. In other words, the meditation on the oneness of the individual Self and the Universal Self.]

नष्टमानसोत्कृष्टयोगिनः ।
कृत्यमस्ति किं स्वस्थितिं यतः ॥ 15 ॥

Of the excellent yogi, whose mind has been destroyed (as discussed above), there is nothing more to be done or accomplished (as a duty, responsibility, injunction, etc.), for he is established in his own true nature, the Self.

दृश्यवारितं चित्तमात्मनः ।
चित्त्वदर्शनं तत्त्वदर्शनम् ॥ 16 ॥

When the mind is warded off (withdrawn) from the external visible phenomena and is established in the Self, i.e., when it realises its nature as that of Consciousness, then it perceives the vision of the Truth (Reality). [This is what is referred to as Self-realisation.]

मानसं तु किं मार्गणे कृते ।
नैव मानसं मार्ग आर्जवात् ॥ 17 ॥

But, when one enquires (investigates), "What is this mind?" it comes to light that there is no such thing as mind. This is the direct path (based on enquiry). [Even when one becomes a witness of the mind (i.e., its various functions or activities that we relate to the mind), we find that the idea of the mind ceases to exist. For the mind is nothing but an expression of the Self.]

वृत्तयस्त्वहं वृत्तिमाश्रिताः ।
वृत्तयो मनो विद्ध्यहं मनः ॥ 18 ॥

It is the thoughts that we call the mind. All activities of the mind (thoughts, etc.) depend on the "I-thought". [The "I-thought" is the root of all thoughts.] Therefore, know that "I-thought" to be the mind. [NOTE: There are two kinds of thoughts–"this-thought" and "I-thought". Only because of the "I-thought" are we able to have the "this-thought". This verse exposes us to the misconception that arises when we associate "I" with the body or mind. This false-identification or delusion is the cause of all suffering.]

अहमयं कुतो भवति चिन्वतः ।
अयि पतत्यहं निजविचारणम् ॥ 19 ॥

"Where from does the I-thought come?"–when you enquire (investigate) thus, the "I" notion falls (dissolves). This is Self-enquiry (*ātma-vichāra*).

अहमि नाशभाज्यहमहंतया ।
स्फुरति हृत्स्वयं परमपूर्णसत् ॥ 20 ॥

When the "I-thought" (the ego-sense) is destroyed, the Supreme-Fullness-Existence (the Infinite Existence) shines forth in the heart with the sense of "I", "I". [What is destroyed is the ego-sense in the mind, and the Self shines forth. The "I-I" is used to indicate the real "I" as its constant nature.]

इदमहं पदाऽभिख्यमन्वहम् ।
अहमिलीनकेऽप्यलयसत्तया ॥ 21 ॥

This constant "I-I" presence is the real "I". For, even when the "I" (ego-sense) is destroyed daily (in the deep-sleep state), the real "I" remains, because of its nature being that of Pure Consciousness which is imperishable.

विग्रहेन्द्रियप्राणधीतमः ।
नाहमेकसत्तज्जडं ह्यसत् ॥ 22 ॥

The real "I", of the nature of Reality, is not this form (body), not the senses, not the *prāṇa* (the vital air), not the intellect and not the ignorance. For, they are inert and verily insentient.

सत्त्वभासिका चित्क्ववेतरा ।
सत्तया हि चिच्चित्तया ह्यहम् ॥ 23 ॥

How is the Supreme Reality known (realised)? Is there another Supreme Reality that realises It? No, there is only one. For, it is that same One Entity that is the Supreme Reality, and that itself is the Consciousness at the individual level. [This is the core of Advaita Vedanta.]

ईशजीवयोर्वेषधीभिदा ।
सत्स्वभावतो वस्तु केवलम् ॥ 24 ॥

Thus, God (*Īshvara* or Creator) and the individual are one and the same Supreme Reality. In essence (in their true nature), both are the same. Any apparent differences between them are only in form and knowledge (perceptions). [In the final analysis, the differentiation as God, individual and world are just in perception. In essence, they are the same Supreme Reality.]

वेषहानतः स्वात्मदर्शनम् ।
ईशदर्शनं स्वात्मरूपतः ॥ 25 ॥

When the perceptions are abandoned, then one realises one's true nature (or there is a vision of one's true Self). The realisation of one's own Self is the vision of *Īshvara* (God), as it is the same Supreme Reality that manifests as the Self.

आत्मसंस्थितिः स्वात्मदर्शनम् ।
आत्मनिर्द्वयादात्मनिष्ठता ॥ 26 ॥

Being established in the Self is the true vision of the Self. The abidance in the Self is because of the non-dual nature of the Self. [The idea of the triad of knower, known and the knowing process is negated here.]

ज्ञानवर्जिताऽज्ञानहीनचित् ।
ज्ञानमस्ति किं ज्ञातुमन्तरम् ॥ 27 ॥

The True knowledge (realisation) of the Self is devoid of 'knowledge' and also 'ignorance'. In the context of non-duality, is there any difference that is to be known? [Earlier, we dispelled any difference between the knower and the object to be known. When one realises the absolute oneness, where is the question of 'knowledge' or 'ignorance'?]

किं स्वरूपमित्यात्मदर्शने ।
अव्ययाऽभवाऽऽपूर्णचित्सुखम् ॥ 28 ॥

When the Self is realised (*ātma-darshana*), if you enquire into "what is my real nature?", then the true nature is realized to be imperishable (*avyaya*), eternal (*abhāva*), full (*āpurna*), Consciousness (*chit*), bliss (*sukha*). [One realises the real identity to be beyond birth and death.]

बन्धमुक्त्यतीतं परं सुखम् ।
विन्दतीह जीवस्तु दैविकः ॥ 29 ॥

The individual Self (*jīva*) attains the status of the Divine (the Supreme) here (in this world), going beyond bondage (*bandhana*) and liberation (*mukti*), attaining Supreme Bliss.

अहमपेतकं निजविभानकम् ।
महदिदंतपो रमणवागियम् ॥ 30 ॥

Free from the 'I'-ness (which is the main cause of the origin of the mind), when the true nature shines forth, this is the great austerity (*tapas*). This is the word (utterance) of Ramaṇa. [This is the assurance of Ramaṇa.]

* * *

16

Sat-darshanam
(सद्दर्शनम्)

सत्प्रत्ययाः किं नु विहाय सन्तं
हृद्येष चिन्तारहितो हृदाख्यः ।
कथं स्मरामस्तममेयमेकं
तस्य स्मृतिस्तत्र दृढैव निष्ठा ॥ 1 ॥

Without the Existence principle (that which gives 'existence' to every object in this universe), can there be any notion of existence (i.e., the experience of any object in this universe)? (No, of course not.) This Existence principle, referred to as 'heart' and devoid of thought, is seated in the very core of the being. How then can we meditate upon (lit. remember) That (Existence) which is one, non-dual and infinite (immeasurable)? Meditation upon (lit. remembrance) that Existence is nothing but being firmly established in It (in That Supreme Brahman).

मृत्युञ्जयं मृत्युभियाश्रितानां
अहंमतिर्मृत्युमुपैति पूर्वम् ।
अथ स्वभावादमृतेषु तेषु
कथं पुनर्मृत्युधियोऽवकाशः ॥ 2 ॥

Driven by the fear of death, those who have taken refuge in the destroyer of death (Lord Siva), at first, their notion of "I" (*ahankāra*, the conception of one's individuality) is destroyed. [In other words, the duality of the individual and God, which is caused by the 'I-sense', is destroyed. In destruction of duality is the destruction of fear.] Thereafter (having freed from the notion of "I-ness"), in them who are immortal by the very nature, where is the scope for the notion of death?

सर्वैर्निदानं जगतोऽहमश्च
वाच्यः प्रभुः कश्चिदपारशक्तिः ।
चित्रेऽत्र लोक्यं च विलोकिता च
पटः प्रकाशोऽप्यभवत्स एकः ॥ 3 ॥

The cause of existence of the world and of the "I" is some Lord who is of limitless power. Thus, it is said by the wise. Here, in this picture (creation of names and forms), that One (Non-dual) alone manifests as the seen (the visible phenomena), as the seer (the sentient Self), as the canvas (the substratum of the world) and as the light (the means to perceive the world). [This verse essentially reinforces the statement "all this is indeed Brahman" from the Chāndogya Upanishad 3.14.1.]

आरभ्यते जीवजगत्परात्म-
तत्त्वाभिधानेन मतं समस्तम् ।
इदं त्रयं यावदहंमति स्यात्
सर्वोत्तमाऽहंमतिशून्यनिष्ठा ॥ 4 ॥

All doctrines or schools of philosophy commence with the declaration of the principles of the individual, world and the Supreme Self. These three (i.e., individual, world and Supreme) exist until the notion of 'I-sense' exists. [And this is the cause of all suffering.] Being firmly established in the freedom from the I-sense is the most excellent of all doctrines.

सत्यं मृषा वा चिदिदं जडं वा
दुःखं सुखं वेति मुधा विवादः ।
अदृष्टलोका निरहंप्रतीति-
र्निष्ठाऽविकल्पा परमाऽखिलेष्टा ॥ 5 ॥

Is this world real or unreal; is this sentient or inert; is this world happiness or sorrow? Such discussions are futile and vain. The state of complete apprehension (realization) of the freedom from the I-sense, in which the world is seen as unreal (lit., a state in which the world is not seen) and which is devoid of any divisions, is the most supreme state. Such a state is regarded as good by all followers of the Vedanta philosophy.

सरूपबुद्धिर्जगतीश्वरे च
सरूपधीरात्मनि यावदस्ति ।
अरूप आत्मा यदि कः प्रपश्येत्
सा दृष्टिरेकाऽनवधिर्हि पूर्णा ॥ 6 ॥

So long as there is a notion that the Self is with a form (i.e., there is identification of the Self with the body), until then, the notion of form will also apply to the world and God. If the Self is without form, then who sees? That vision will be a vision of oneness (of individual, God and world), eternality and fullness.

यत्पञ्चकोशात्मकमस्ति देहं
तदन्तरा किं भुवनं चकास्ति ।
देहं विना पञ्चविधं तदेतत्
पश्यन्ति के वा भुवनं भणन्तु ॥ 7 ॥

Different from this body, which is made up of five sheaths (i.e., without the perception that 'I am the body'), does the world ever shine (appear)? Without that body-consciousness (with the perception that "I am the body"), who will ever see this world? Let them speak. [The five sheaths are the food sheath, the vital air sheath, the mental sheath, the knowledge sheath and the bliss sheath.]

शब्दादिरूपं भुवनं समस्तं
शब्दादिसत्तेन्द्रियवृत्तिभास्या ।
सत्तेन्द्रियाणां मनसो वशे स्यात्
मनोमयं तद्भुवनं वदामः ॥ 8 ॥

The entire world is of the nature of the five-fold objects (of experience, viz. sound, sight, smell, taste and touch). The existence of the five-fold universe of objects is brought to light (perceived) by the activity (or function) of the five senses. The existence of the sense organs is under the control of the mind. Thus, we say that this world is made up of the mind.

धिया सहोदेति धियास्तमेति
लोकस्ततो धीप्रविभास्य एषः ।
धीलोकजन्मक्षयधाम पूर्णं
सद्वस्तु जन्मक्षयशून्यमेकम् ॥ 9 ॥

The world arises (comes into existence) along with the rise of the 'I-sense' (the source of all thoughts, also referred to as *ahankāra*, the conception of one's individuality) and sets with the setting of the 'I-sense'. Therefore, this world (the visible phenomena) is illumined by the 'I-sense' (the individuality). The substratum (abode) of the birth and decay of the 'I-sense' is the One (non-dual), real 'I' (the Existence principle), which is full (complete) and free from birth and decay.

भवन्तु सद्दर्शनसाधनानि
परस्य नामाकृतिभिः सपर्याः ।
सद्वस्तुनि प्राप्ततदात्मभावा
निष्ठैव सद्दर्शनमित्यवेहि ॥ 10 ॥

May the various forms of worship of the names and forms of the Supreme (Brahman) be the means to the attainment of the vision of the Truth. You should understand (or know) that being firmly established in the Supreme Reality with the realisation that "that Brahman am I" is the vision of Truth. [In other words, know that the worship of the names and forms is only a means to ultimately realise the Supreme as "I am That".]

द्वन्द्वानि सर्वाण्यखिलास्त्रिपुट्यः
किञ्चित्समाश्रित्य विभान्ति वस्तु ।
तन्मार्गणे स्याद्गलितं समस्तं
न पश्यतां सच्चलनं कदापि ॥ 11 ॥

All pairs of opposites (like self and non-self, inert and sentient, seer and seen, etc.) and all triads (viz., knower, knowledge, known) shine, having sought refuge in some substance (a fundamental, indescribable entity). When that substance is investigated, all differentiations in the form of pairs of opposites and triads perish. For those who have seen (known, realised) the Truth (that which remains when all pairs of opposites and triads have dropped off), there is no more any movement (for they are firmly established in the Truth).

विद्या कथं भाति न चेदविद्या
विद्यां विना किं प्रविभात्यविद्या ।
द्वयं च कस्येति विचार्य मूल-
स्वरूपनिष्ठा परमार्थविद्या ॥ 12 ॥

If there is no ignorance, how can knowledge shine? [How can we conceive of the idea of knowledge without the idea of ignorance?] Similarly, without knowledge, can one conceive of the idea of ignorance? [If the sun is always shining, will we ever understand the notion of darkness?] Having investigated the substratum of both knowledge and ignorance, then being firmly established in the innate nature (the substratum) is the real knowledge of the Truth (of Supreme Reality).

बोद्धारमात्मानमजानतो यो
बोधः स किं स्यात्परमार्थबोधः ।
बोधस्य बोध्यस्य च संश्रयं स्वं
विजानतस्तद्द्वितयं विनश्येत् ॥ 13 ॥

When the knower does not know oneself (the subject), then that knowledge which arises, can it ever be true knowledge (the knowledge of the Supreme Truth)? (No, it cannot be.) For the one who knows the Self, which is the substratum of both knowledge as well as the object of knowledge, then both these (i.e., the knowledge and the object of knowledge) disappear (and the Self alone remains).

निद्रा न विद्या ग्रहणं न विद्या
गृह्णाति किञ्चिन्न यथार्थबोधे ।
निद्रापदार्थग्रहणेतरा स्यात्
चिदेव विद्या विलसन्त्यशून्या ॥ 14 ॥

Sleep here refers to complete ignorance, a state where nothing is grasped, and there is a complete absence of perception and thought. We find that state, as in the case of sleep, to be blissful. Grasping refers to the perception of object knowledge (as in the case of all forms of object knowledge). Knowledge (*vidyā*) here refers to Self-knowledge.

Sleep is not knowledge. Grasping (perception through sense organs, the way we grasp object knowledge) is not knowledge (Self-knowledge). In the case of knowledge of Reality (Self-knowledge or *Brahma-vidyā*), the individual does not grasp (perceive) anything (object knowledge). Self-knowledge is different from both sleep and grasping. It is the Self-effulgent Consciousness, the very substratum of all, and not void.

सत्यश्चिदात्मा विविधाकृतिश्चित्
सिध्येत्पृथक्सत्यचितो न भिन्ना ।
भूषाविकाराः किमु सन्ति सत्यं
विना सुवर्णं पृथगत्र लोके ॥ 15 ॥

The Self, that is nothing but Consciousness, alone is real. The one Consciousness appears as different forms of knowledge. [Every knowledge is nothing but a different thought or cognition. It is the one Consciousness that appears as different thoughts or cognitions.] But they are not different from the one Consciousness, nor can they exist separately from Consciousness. Here, in this world, can the different modifications or forms of the ornament (i.e., in names and forms) truly exist separately without the existence of gold?

[Gold can exist without ornaments; the existence of the ornaments cannot be conceived of without gold. Here, gold is likened to Consciousness; and ornaments with knowledge.]

तद्युष्मदोरस्मदि सम्प्रतिष्ठा
तस्मिन् विनष्टेऽस्मदि मूलबोधात् ।
तद्युष्मदस्मन्मतिवर्जितैका
स्थितिर्ज्वलन्ती सहजात्मनः स्यात् ॥ 16 ॥

The notions of 'that, he or she' (third person) and 'you' (second person) are established on the notion of the finite 'I' (the first person). [When the notion of 'I' exists as egoism (which is the finite 'I'), the human being is subject to suffering.] From the knowledge of the substratum of these three (the triad of first person, second person, third person), the finite 'I' notion is destroyed. [Knowledge of the substratum means the realisation of "I am Brahman".] One is then free from the notions of that, you and I, and then, devoid of the differentiation (of the triad), the natural state of the Self shines forth.

भूतं भविष्यच्च भवत्स्वकाले
तद्वर्तमानस्य विहाय तत्त्वम् ।
हास्या न किं स्याद्गतभाविचर्चा
विनैकसंख्यां गणनेव लोके ॥ 17 ॥

The past and the future are nothing but 'present' in their own time of existence. Having ignored the true nature of that present, any deliberation regarding the past and the future, will it not be a laughable matter like the idea of counting without the numeral 'one' in this world? [The true nature of 'present' is 'I am'. It is the Self which is timeless.]

क्व भाति दिक्कालकथा विनाऽस्मान्
दिक्काललीलेह वपुर्वयं चेत् ।
न क्वापि भामो न कदापि भामो
वयं तु सर्वत्र सदा च भामः ॥ 18 ॥

Where is the question of a discussion regarding space (literally, direction) and time without the notion of 'I' (literally, us)? [In other words, only when 'I' comes into existence is there any notion of space and time.] If we identify the Self with the body (i.e., we believe that 'I am the body'), then there is the play of space and time. [The play includes past, future, old age, disease, death, suffering, etc.] We do not exist in one place. [Literally, it means we shine nowhere. It actually means we do not shine in any one place. We are not local to a place. 'We' has to be interpreted as 'the Self'.] We do not exist at one time. [Literally, it says, we shine at no time.] But we exist everywhere and at all times. [The Self is everywhere and transcends all three periods of time.]

देहात्मभावे ज्ञजडौ समानौ
एकस्य देहे हृदि दीप्त आत्मा ।
आक्रम्य देहं च जगच्च पूर्णः
परस्य मेयं तनुमात्रमात्मा ॥ 19 ॥

In the state of identification of the body with the Self (i.e., with regards to experiencing the characteristics of one's body, including pain), the wise person and the unintelligent are the same. [This does not mean 'I am the body'.] For the wise one, the Self is that which is (the Consciousness) shining in the body, in the heart (as the witness of everything). The Self is full, pervading (literally, eclipsing) the body and the entire universe. For the other (the unintelligent or ignorant one), the Self is comparable to the body alone.

अज्ञस्य विज्ञस्य च विश्वमस्ति
पूर्वस्य दृश्यं जगदेव सत्यम् ।
परस्य दृश्याश्रयभूतमेकं
सत्यं प्रपूर्णं प्रविभात्यरूपम् ॥ 20 ॥

Both the ignorant person and the wise perceive the world. To the former (the ignorant), the perceptible world of names and forms alone is real. To the latter (for the wise one), the One, non-dual Consciousness, which is the substratum of the entire visible phenomena (the universe), which is all-pervading, which is formless and which is the Truth, that alone shines (i.e., that alone is real).

विधेः प्रयत्नस्य च कोऽपि वाद-
स्तयोर्द्वयोर्मूलमजानतां स्यात् ।
विधेः प्रयत्नस्य च मूलवस्तु
सञ्जानतां नैव विधिर्न यत्नः ॥ 21 ॥

There is some debate or argument only among the ignorant, who do not know the origin of both fate (or destiny) and self-effort. [The source of both fate and effort is the 'I-sense', the individuality.] Knowing very well the true nature of the source of fate and effort, for the wise, there is no fate, and there is no effort. [That is when the 'I-sense' is destroyed, and one realises the Self, the idea of doer ceases, and the idea of experiencer ceases. And thus, there is no effort and there is no fate.]

यदीशितुर्वीक्षणमीक्षितारं
अवीक्ष्य तन्मानसिकेक्षणं स्यात् ।
न द्रष्टुरन्यः परमो हि तस्य
वीक्षा स्वमूले प्रविलीय निष्ठा ॥ 22 ॥

Ignoring (lit. not seeing) the Seer (the Self), whatever vision of the Lord is had, that is nothing but a mental vision (a mind projection) alone. Other than the Seer (the Self), there indeed is no Supreme (*Ishvara*). His (the Lord's) vision is nothing but being established in the source (the Self), being merged (absorbed) in the source (the Self).

आत्मानमीक्षेत परं प्रपश्येत्
इत्यागमोक्तेः सुलभो न भावः ।
नात्मैव दृश्यो यदि का कथेशे
स्वयं तदन्नीभवनं तदीक्षा ॥ 23 ॥

"One should realise the Self (i.e., one's own nature) in order to realise the Supreme (*Īshvara*)". It is not easy to understand the purport or meaning of such statements of the Upanishads. If the Self (one's true nature) itself is not realised, what to speak of the Lord (the Supreme Being)? Oneself becoming the food offering (to the Lord) is the true vision of Him (the Lord).

[Becoming the food offering: We are not able to realise our true nature because we identify the Self with the body and/or the mind (because of the 'I-sense', the individuality). To make oneself the offering to the Lord is to eliminate the individuality.]

धिये प्रकाशं परमो वितीर्य
स्वयं धियोऽन्तः प्रविभाति गुप्तः ।
धियं परावर्त्य धियोऽन्तरेऽत्र
संयोजनान्नेश्वरदृष्टिरन्या ॥ 24 ॥

The Supreme, having bestowed light (of Consciousness) to the mind (/intellect), shines (as the Consciousness), Itself staying concealed inside the mind (/intellect). Turning the mind inward (away from the world and all objects, including the body) and uniting (merging) the mind within, with the Consciousness, is the real vision of the Lord. There is no other vision of the Lord.

न वक्ति देहोऽहमिति प्रसुप्तौ
न कोऽपि नाभूवमिति प्रवक्ति ।
यत्रोदिते सर्वमुदेति तस्य
धियाऽहमः शोधय जन्मदेशम् ॥ 25 ॥

The body never says "I am". [This is because it is inert in nature.] Nobody says, "I was not (I was non-existent) in deep sleep". [The Self is ever-present; existent in all three states of wakefulness, dream and deep sleep.] When the 'I-sense' arises, everything arises (i.e., the worldly existence of interactions, transactions, suffering, challenges, etc. arises). By means of your intellect, investigate into the source of that 'I-sense'.

देहो न जानाति सतो न जन्म
देहप्रमाणोऽन्य उदेति मध्ये ।
अहंकृतिग्रन्थिविबन्धसूक्ष्म-
शरीरचेतोभवजीवनामा ॥ 26 ॥

The body (being inert) does not know. There is no birth (and death) for the *sat* (Existence). There is another entity which is between these two (i.e., body and the *sat;* or the non-self and the Self) and localised by the body (lit. of the size or of the measure of the body). This other entity is known by the following names: (1) ego (individuality of I am doer, I am experiencer); (2) knot (the identification of the Self with the body); (3) bondage (the obstruction to liberation); (4) subtle body; (5) the mind; (6) *samsāra*, the worldly existence; and (7) the individual (that which enlivens, associated with birth and death).

रूपोद्भवो रूपततिप्रतिष्ठो
रूपाशनो धूतगृहीतरूपः ।
स्वयं विरूपः स्वविचारकाले
धावत्यहङ्कारपिशाच एषः ॥ 27 ॥

The ego is born among forms (gross or subtle). It is firmly based or established in a crowd of forms. It feeds on the forms and depends on the forms for its sustenance (literally, it has forms as its food). It gives up and also takes on various forms. The ego, by itself, does not have a form of its own (i.e., it thrives on assumed characteristics or features). When one investigates the nature of this demon called ego, it vanishes (lit. runs away). [The term 'form' can also be interpreted as characteristics or features.]

भावेऽहमः सर्वमिदं विभाति
लयेऽहमो नैव विभाति किञ्चित् ।
तस्मादहंरूपमिदं समस्तं
तन्मार्गणं सर्वजयाय मार्गः ॥ 28 ॥

In the rise of the ego (I-sense), all this (the entire world) shines. In the disappearance (dissolution or extinction) of the ego (I-sense), nothing shines indeed. Therefore, all this (the entire world) is of the nature of ego (born of ego). The investigation (or enquiry) into the nature of that (ego) is the means (or path) to victory over everything (the ultimate victory, i.e., the victory over all attachments and bondages).

सत्या स्थितिर्नाहमुदेति यत्र
तच्चोदयस्थानगवेषणेन ।
विना न नश्येद्यदि तन्न नश्येत्
स्वात्मैक्यरूपा कथमस्तु निष्ठा ॥ 29 ॥

The state where the ego (*ahankāra*) does not arise at all is the state of being established in the Truth (or Reality). That (ego) does not get destroyed (permanently) without the enquiry into the place of origin of that ego. [Self-enquiry is the key to the destruction of the ego.] If the ego is not extinct, how can one attain the state of being established in the oneness with the Self?

कूपे यथा गाढजले तथान्त-
र्निमज्ज्य बुद्ध्या शितया नितान्तम् ।
प्राणं च वाचं च नियम्य चिन्वन्
विन्देन्निजाहंकृतिमूलरूपम् ॥ 30 ॥

Just as (a diver) dives into a well with deep waters (and retrieves the object that has been lost there), in the same manner, (the seeker of Truth) having controlled the breath and the speech, diving within and enquiring (into the Self) with a very sharp and refined intellect, he should attain (realise) the true nature of the root of one's ego.

मौनेन मज्जन्मनसा स्वमूल-
चर्चैव सत्यात्मविचारणं स्यात् ।
एषोऽहमेतन्न मम स्वरूप-
मिति प्रमा सत्यविचारणाङ्गम् ॥ 31 ॥

In complete silence (devoid of any distracting thoughts), immersing oneself within, the discussion into one's root (true nature) is indeed true Self-enquiry. [The term discussion can be interpreted as discussion with a guru or reflection.] 'This I am' ('This' here refers to the Self), and 'this is not my nature' (This implies everything that is not the Self is not my nature. This refers to the process of negation, i.e., *neti-neti*, 'not this, not this')–this knowledge is a part of enquiry into the Truth.

गवेषणात्प्राप्य हृदन्तरं तत्
पतेदहन्ता परिभुग्नशीर्षा ।
अथाहमन्यत्स्फुरति प्रकृष्टं
नाहंकृतिस्तत्परमेव पूर्णम् ॥ 32 ॥

By means of enquiry, having attained that (the source of ego) inside the heart, the ego (*ahankāra*) falls with its head broken. Thereafter, another I, which is pre-eminent (transcendental and pure), shines forth. That (I) is not the ego but is the Absolute Supreme alone.

अहंकृतिं यो लसति ग्रसित्वा
किं तस्य कार्यं परिशिष्टमस्ति ।
किञ्चिद्विजानाति स नात्मनोऽन्यत्
तस्य स्थितिं भावयितुं क्षमः कः ॥ 33 ॥

For the wise one (who has realised his real nature through Self-enquiry) who shines (excels) having swallowed (destroyed) the ego, what else remains to be done in this world? (For he is free from the sense of doership.) He (the realised one) knows nothing other than the Self. Who in this world is capable of imagining (or understanding) his state of realisation?

आह स्फुटं तत्त्वमसीति वेद-
स्तथाप्यसंप्राप्य परात्मनिष्ठाम् ।
भूयो विचारो मतिदुर्बलत्वं
तत्सर्वदा स्वात्मतया हि भाति ॥ 34 ॥

Vedas (Upanishads) clearly stated: "*tat-tvam-asi* (You are That Brahman)". In spite of that, not reaching the state of being established in the Supreme Self and again engaging in enquiry indicates weakness of the mind. That (Supreme Self) alone always shines as one's own nature (the Self).

न वेद्म्यहं मामुत वेद्म्यहं मां
इति प्रवादो मनुजस्य हास्यः ।
दृग्दृश्यभेदात् किमयं द्विधात्मा
स्वात्मैकतायां हि धियां न भेदाः ॥ 35 ॥

"I do not know myself" or "I know myself"–in this manner, any utterance of man is ridiculous. By division or separation in the form of the seer and the seen, does this Self become two-fold? (No.) Because of the oneness of the Self (i.e., the Self being only one), there certainly can be no divisions (as subject and object) in the knowledge of the Self.

हृत्प्राप्य सद्धाम निजस्वरूपे
स्वभावसिद्धेऽनुपलभ्य निष्ठाम् ।
मायाविलासः सदसत्सरूप-
विरूपनानैकमुखप्रवादाः ॥ 36 ॥

Diving deep within the heart and not attaining the abidance in one's own nature, which is the naturally evident abode of *sat* (Existence, Truth), mere talks about real or unreal, with form or without form, manifold or one, are all play of *māyā*.

सिद्धस्य वित्तिः सत एव सिद्धिः
स्वप्नोपमानाः खलु सिद्धयोऽन्याः ।
स्वप्नः प्रबुद्धस्य कथं नु सत्यः
सति स्थितः किं पुनरेति मायाम् ॥ 37 ॥

To realise and remain established in the ever-present Truth (or Reality) alone is the real attainment (*siddhi*). All other attainments are indeed like a dream (have no foundation). For one who has woken up from sleep, how can a dream be real? Being established in the Truth, does one enter the realm of *māyā* again? (No.)

सोऽहंविचारो वपुरात्मभावे
साहाय्यकारी परमार्गणस्य ।
स्वात्मैक्यसिद्धौ स पुनर्निरर्थो
यथा नरत्वप्रमितिर्नरस्य ॥ 38 ॥

In the state (of mind) where the body (gross or subtle) is identified with the Self, enquiry into 'I am That' is helpful in the investigation of the Supreme or the Truth (or in seeking liberation). But, in the state when one has attained the oneness of the Self, that enquiry (into "I am That") is useless (meaningless). Just as in the case of a man, the knowledge that "I am a man" is of no help.

द्वैतं विचारे परमार्थबोधे
त्वद्वैतमित्येष न साधुवादः ।
गवेषणात्प्राग्दशमे विनष्टे
पश्चाच्च लब्धे दशमत्वमेकम् ॥ 39 ॥

During the process of enquiry (and seeking the Truth), there is duality (of the seer and the seen, and of *jīva* and *Īshvara*), and when the Supreme Self is realised, there is non-duality–this kind of statement is incorrect. Before investigation into the loss of the tenth (not finding the tenth person), and later when the tenth person is found, the notion of the tenth (the tenth-ness, or the state of being the tenth) is one and the same. [Our true nature before enquiry and after enquiry remains the same.]

[**The story:** Ten boys crossed a river. Having reached the other bank, one of the boys decided to count if all ten had crossed the river. Counting all others, he counted only nine and thus was worried. He did not realise that he himself was the tenth. A wise passer-by clarified that he was the tenth, and the boy was very relieved. The tenth boy was present when the search was on and also when the search was concluded.]

करोमि कर्मेति नरो विजानन्
बाध्यो भवेत्कर्मफलं च भोक्तुम् ।
विचारधूता हृदि कर्तृता चेत्
कर्मत्रयं नश्यति सैव मुक्तिः ॥ 40 ॥

Thinking that 'I do work' (or 'I am the performer of action'), man becomes bound (or compelled) to experience the fruits of action performed. If the sense of doership is destroyed through enquiry, then all three types of karma (*āgāmi*, *sanchita* and *prārabdha*) are destroyed. That state (when the doership is destroyed) indeed is liberation.

बद्धत्वभावे सति मोक्षचिन्ता
बन्धस्तु कस्येति विचारणेन ।
सिद्धे स्वयं स्वात्मनि नित्यमुक्ते
क्व बन्धचिन्ता क्व च मोक्षचिन्ता ॥ 41 ॥

When there is a sense of bondage, there is anxiety or thought of liberation. But, by means of enquiry into "whose is the bondage?", for one who is established in the ever-full Self, which is ever-free from bondage (in all three states), where is the question of anxiety or thought of bondage, and where is the question of anxiety or thought of liberation?

रूपिण्यरूपिण्युभयात्मिका च
मुक्तिस्त्रिरूपेति विदो वदन्ति ।
इदं त्रयं या विविनक्त्यहन्धीः
तस्याः प्रणाशः परमार्थमुक्तिः ॥ 42 ॥

The wise scholars (of different schools of Vedanta) say that liberation is of three types: (1) with form (the *jīva* with the body); (2) without form (without the body); and (3) of the nature of both with and without form. It is the ego (I-notion) that differentiates or discriminates (classifies) between the three forms of liberation. The destruction of that ego (I-notion) is the highest form of liberation.

सद्दर्शनं द्राविडवाङ्निबद्धं
महर्षिणा श्रीरमणेन शुद्धम् ।
प्रबन्धमुत्कृष्टममर्त्यवाण्यां
अनूद्य वासिष्ठमुनिर्व्यतानीत् ॥ 43 ॥

Having translated into Sanskrit, the pre-eminent and pure composition in the Drāviḍa language (Tamil) by Śrī Ramaṇa Maharshi, Vāsiṣṭha Muni composed Saddarśana.

सतत्त्वसारं सरलं दधाना
मुमुक्षुलोकाय मुदं ददाना ।

अमानुषश्रीरमणीयवाणी-
मयूखभित्तिर्मुनिवाग्विभाति ॥ 44 ॥

The words of Muni (the author Vāsiṣṭha Muni) shine, as they are merely a wall of shining mirrors that reflect the divine words of Śrī Ramaṇa Maharshi, which are the essence of Truth, presented in a simple (honest) manner, and that bestow delight to the community of seekers of liberation.

* * *

Section 5

This section presents some smaller compositions of Adi Shankarāchārya, a saint and scholar in Advaita Vedanta.

17

Kāshī-panchakam
(काशी-पञ्चकम्)

The Glory of the Real Kāshi

मनोनिवृत्तिः परमोपशान्तिः
सा तीर्थवर्या मणिकर्णिका च ।
ज्ञानप्रवाहा विमलादिगङ्गा
सा काशिकाहं निजबोधरूपा ॥ 1 ॥

The cessation of all mental activities (thoughts, etc.) is supreme peace and quietude, and that is the Maṇikarṇikā Ghat in Kāshi. The continuous flow of knowledge (i.e., being in complete absorption, in that knowledge) is the pure primordial river Ganga. I am that Kāshi of the form of Self-knowledge.

(The holy city of Kāshi, one of the holiest pilgrimage centres, is also referred to as Vārānasi or Benaras. The term '*ghat*' refers to the steps or passage leading down to a river.)

यस्यामिदं कल्पितमिन्द्रजालं
चराचरं भाति मनोविलासम् ।
सच्चित्सुखैका परमात्मरूपा
सा काशिकाहं निजबोधरूपा ॥ 2 ॥

The One Existence-Consciousness-Bliss (*sat-chit-ānanda*) of the form of the Supreme Lord (*Paramātmā*), in which the magic (or illusion) of creation is conceived by the playful creation of the mind, in which shines the world of movable and immovable objects, I am that Kāshi of the form of Self-knowledge.

कोशेषु पञ्चस्वधिराजमाना
बुद्धिर्भवानी प्रतिदेहगेहम् ।
साक्षी शिवः सर्वगतोऽन्तरात्मा
सा काशिकाहं निजबोधरूपा ॥ 3 ॥

Residing in every human body, presiding over the five sheaths, where the intelligence (*buddhi*) is Goddess Pārvati (the consort of Lord Shiva), where the all-pervading Self, the witness, is none other than Lord Shiva, I am that Kāshi of the form of Self-knowledge.

काश्यां हि काश्यते काशी काशी सर्वप्रकाशिका ।
सा काशी विदिता येन तेन प्राप्ता हि काशिका ॥ 4 ॥

In Kāshi (the human body) shines Kāshi (the Self). And that Kāshi (the Self) illuminates everything. He who realises that Kāshi within (the Self, the Effulgent One), indeed attains Kāshi of the nature of Brahman (the Supreme Reality).

काशीक्षेत्रं शरीरं त्रिभुवन-जननी व्यापिनी ज्ञानगङ्गा
भक्तिः श्रद्धा गयेयं निजगुरु-चरणध्यानयोगः प्रयागः ।
विश्वेशोऽयं तुरीयः सकलजन-मनःसाक्षिभूतोऽन्तरात्मा
देहे सर्वं मदीये यदि वसति पुनस्तीर्थमन्यत्किमस्ति ॥ 5 ॥

This human body is the pilgrim centre of Kāshi; the flow of knowledge (of the Self) is the river Ganga, the mother of the three worlds. Devotion, together with *shraddhā*, is the holy Gayā. The meditation on the holy feet of the Guru is Prayāga. The inmost Self, being the Absolute (literally referred to as 'Fourth') and the witness of the mind in all beings, is the Lord of the universe. If all these reside in my own body, then what is the need for these various pilgrimage centres?

* * *

18

Upadesha-panchakam

(उपदेश-पञ्चकम्)

Instruction regarding the means to the Spiritual Goal

Also called Sādhana-panchakam or Sopāna-panchakam

वेदो नित्यमधीयतां तदुदितं कर्म स्वनुष्ठीयतां
तेनेशस्य विधीयतामपचितिः काम्ये मतिस्त्यज्यताम् ।
पापौघः परिधूयतां भवसुखे दोषोऽनुसन्धीयतां
आत्मेच्छा व्यवसीयतां निजगृहात्तूर्णं विनिर्गम्यताम् ॥ 1 ॥

Constantly study and dwell in the message of the Vedas and act in conformance to the disciplines proclaimed in them. Through every act, worship the Lord (i.e., let every act be an offering to the Lord). Renounce the thought of any actions performed for the fulfilment of selfish desires and thus wash away all accumulated sins. Investigate or enquire into the defects associated with the pleasures of the world. Be well-resolved in the aspiration for Self-knowledge. In order to realise the Self, immediately be free from attachment to your home.

सङ्गः सत्सु विधीयतां भगवतो भक्तिर्दृढाऽऽधीयतां
शान्त्यादिः परिचीयतां दृढतरं कर्माशु सन्त्यज्यताम् ।
सद्विद्वानुपसृप्यतां प्रतिदिनं तत्पादुका सेव्यतां
ब्रह्मैकाक्षरमर्थ्यतां श्रुतिशिरोवाक्यं समाकर्ण्यताम् ॥ 2 ॥

Be in the association of the noble and wise (that will strengthen the association with the Truth). Be resolute and firm in the devotion to the Supreme. Cultivate qualities like restraining the mind and the senses, forbearance, etc. Immediately abandon actions that are performed for the fulfilment of desires that cause bondage. With humility, approach a knower of the Supreme Truth. Daily, be of service to the teacher. Seek the One Imperishable Brahman. Listen to (and study) well the words of wisdom of the Upanishads.

वाक्यार्थश्च विचार्यतां श्रुतिशिरःपक्षः समाश्रीयतां
दुस्तर्कात्सुविरम्यतां श्रुतिमतस्तर्कोऽनुसन्धीयताम् ।
ब्रह्मास्मीति विभाव्यतामहरहर्गर्वः परित्यज्यतां
देहेऽहम्मतिरुज्झ्यतां बुधजनैर्वादः परित्यज्यताम् ॥ 3 ॥

Ruminate over the meaning and purport of the statements of the Upanishads. Always abide in the propositions of the Upanishads. Abstain from futile argumentation. Investigate and follow the reasoning that is in accordance with the position of the Upanishads. Always meditate upon the idea 'I am Brahman'. Abandon egoism and pride. Abandon the 'I'-feeling towards the body. Avoid argumentation with the wise.

क्षुद्व्याधिश्च चिकित्स्यतां प्रतिदिनं भिक्षौषधं भुज्यतां
स्वाद्वन्नं न तु याच्यतां विधिवशात् प्राप्तेन सन्तुष्यताम् ।
शीतोष्णादि विषह्यतां न तु वृथा वाक्यं समुच्चार्यतां
औदासीन्यमभीप्स्यतां जनकृपानैष्ठुर्यमुत्सृज्यताम् ॥ 4 ॥

Regard hunger as a disease and treat it. Daily treat that disease with the medicine of food obtained through begging. Do not seek or ask for delicious food for yourself. Be content and satisfied with whatever chance brings. Forbear the pairs of opposites like heat and cold, etc. Do not engage in frivolous or futile talk. Yearn to be neutral and indifferent in everything. Eschew the attitude of kindness towards some and harshness towards others that is influenced by preference and prejudice.

एकान्ते सुखमास्यतां परतरे चेतः समाधीयतां
पूर्णात्मा सुसमीक्ष्यतां जगदिदं तद्बाधितं दृश्यताम् ।
प्राक्कर्म प्रविलाप्यतां चितिबलान्नाप्युत्तरैः श्लिष्यतां
प्रारब्धं त्विह भुज्यतामथ परब्रह्मात्मना स्थीयताम् ॥ 5 ॥

Sit in peace, in solitude. Establish the outgoing mind in the Supreme Brahman. Investigate well into the ever-full Self. See the universe as annulled by That (the ever-full Self). Annihilate the effect of past actions by the power of Self-knowledge. Do not get attached to the fruits of actions to be performed. Experience the effects of past actions that have begun to bear fruit. (Do not lament or ponder over them unduly.) And then, abide in Brahman, the Supreme Reality.

***

19

Māyā-panchakam

(माया-पञ्चकम्)

The Power of Māyā

निरुपमनित्यनिरंशकेऽप्यखण्डे
मयि चिति सर्वविकल्पनादिशून्ये ।
घटयति जगदीशजीवभेदं
त्वघटितघटनापटीयसी माया ॥ 1 ॥

Māyā (the illusory power of the Supreme) is very skilled in connecting the unconnected (i.e., achieving the impossible). For, it brings about the differentiation or separation in the form of world, God (*Īshvara*) and individual, in the Consciousness, which is unfragmented, unequalled (incomparable), eternal, without parts and free from all distinctions and variations.

श्रुतिशतनिगमान्तशोधकान-
प्यहह धनादिनिदर्शनेन सद्यः ।
कलुषयति चतुष्पदाद्यभिन्ना-
नघटितघटनापटीयसी माया ॥ 2 ॥

Māyā (the illusory power of the Supreme) is very skilled in connecting the unconnected (i.e., achieving the impossible). Ah! By the sight of wealth, etc., it immediately deludes (contaminates) even those who have investigated into hundreds of scriptures (including Vedas and Upanishads), as if they are no different from the quadrupeds.

सुखचिदखण्डविबोधमद्वितीयं
वियदनलादिविनिर्मिते नियोज्य ।
भ्रमयति भवसागरे नितान्तं
त्वघटितघटनापटीयसी माया ॥ 3 ॥

Māyā (the illusory power of the Supreme) is very skilled in connecting the unconnected (i.e., achieving the impossible). For, by associating the Self–of the nature of awakening-bliss-consciousness, which is unfragmented and non-dual–with the body made of sky, wind, etc. (the gross elements), it makes it whirl around very much in the ocean of worldliness.

अपगतगुणवर्णजातिभेदे
सुखचिति विप्रविडाद्यहंकृतिं च ।
स्फुटयति सुतदारगेहमोहं
त्वघटितघटनापटीयसी माया ॥ 4 ॥

Māyā (the illusory power of the Supreme) is very skilled in connecting the unconnected (i.e., achieving the impossible). For, in the Self–that is of the nature of bliss-consciousness which is free from the distinctions of *guṇa*, *varṇa* and *jāti*–it gives rise to the ego of *brāhmaṇa*, cheat, etc. and also the delusion resulting from attachment to child, wife, house, etc.

विधिहरिहरविभेदमप्यखण्डे
बत विरचय्य बुधानपि प्रकामम् ।
भ्रमयति हरिहरभेदभावा-
नघटितघटनापटीयसी माया ॥ 5 ॥

Māyā (the illusory power of the Supreme) is very skilled in connecting the unconnected (i.e., achieving the impossible). Alas! Even in the unfragmented Supreme Brahman–having created the differentiation in the form of Brahmā, Vishnu and Siva–it very much bewilders (deludes) even the wise ones as having the differential notion between Hari (Vishnu) and Hara (Siva).

* * *

20

Prātaḥ-smaraṇa-stotram
(प्रातःस्मरण-स्तोत्रम्)

Contemplation upon one's True Nature at Dawn

प्रातः स्मरामि हृदि संस्फुरदात्मतत्त्वं
सच्चित्सुखं परमहंसगतिं तुरीयम् ।
यत्स्वप्नजागरसुषुप्तिमवैति नित्यं
तद्ब्रह्म निष्कलमहं न च भूतसङ्घः ॥ 1 ॥

At daybreak, I recall the true nature of the Self that is vibrating in the heart, the Existence-Consciousness-Bliss (*sat-chit-ānanda*), that which is the refuge of the liberated ones, the fourth (the transcendental state), that which impels (knows) the three states of dream, wakefulness, and sleep, and that which is eternal. That indivisible Brahman (the Supreme Reality) am I, and not this body–a collection or assemblage of elements (the five gross elements, viz. earth, air, fire, water and ether).

प्रातर्भजामि मनसो वचसामगम्यं
वाचो विभान्ति निखिला यदनुग्रहेण ।
यन्नेतिनेतिवचनैर्निगमा अवोचुः
तं देवदेवमजमच्युतमाहुरग्र्यम् ॥ 2 ॥

At daybreak, I worship him–who is inaccessible to mind and words, by whose kindness all speech manifests, of whom the Vedas (Upanishads) speak of by the statements 'not this', 'not this'–that God of gods they say is unborn, imperishable and the foremost.

प्रातर्नमामि तमसः परमर्कवर्णं
पूर्णं सनातनपदं पुरुषोत्तमाख्यम् ।
यस्मिन्निदं जगदशेषमशेषमूर्तौ
रज्ज्वां भुजङ्गम इव प्रतिभासितं वै ॥ 3 ॥

At daybreak, I offer my obeisance to the Complete One, who shining like the sun transcends darkness, who is the eternal abode, called *Purushottama* (the Supreme Being), and in which Perfect Being this entire universe indeed appears like the snake in the rope.

श्लोकत्रयमिदं पुण्यं लोकत्रयविभूषणम् ।
प्रातःकाले पठेद्यस्तु स गच्छेत्परमं पदम् ॥ 4 ॥

Early in the morning, the one who reads these three sacred verses, the ornament of the three worlds, attains the supreme abode.

* * *

21

Dhanyāṣṭakam

(धन्याष्टकम्)

The Glory of the ones who are 'Blessed'

तज्ज्ञानं प्रशमकरं यदिन्द्रियाणां
तज्ज्ञेयं यदुपनिषत्सु निश्चितार्थम् ।
ते धन्या भुवि परमार्थनिश्चितेहाः
शेषास्तु भ्रमनिलये परिभ्रमन्तः ॥ 1 ॥

That alone is Knowledge, which quietens the sense organs (brings one to a state of quiescence). That alone is to be known (or that which is worthy of knowing), which has been decisively ascertained in the Upanishads. They alone are blessed in the world who have resolved to realise the Supreme Truth. All the others are merely wandering about in a state of delusion.

आदौ विजित्य विषयान्मदमोहराग-
द्वेषादिशत्रुगणमाहृतयोगराज्याः ।
ज्ञात्वा मतं समनुभूय परात्मविद्या-
कान्तासुखं वनगृहे विचरन्ति धन्याः ॥ 2 ॥

Having at first won over the attractions of the sense objects, then having conquered a host of enemies like pride, delusion, attachment, dislikes, etc., then having conquered the kingdom of yoga, and realising the Truth (expounded in the Upanishads), blessed ones move about in a forest considering it to be their home, experiencing the joy of the company of the beloved in the form of Spiritual Knowledge.

त्यक्त्वा गृहे रतिमधोगतिहेतुभूता-
मात्मेच्छयोपनिषदर्थरसं पिबन्तः ।
वीतस्पृहा विषयभोगपदे विरक्ता
धन्याश्चरन्ति विजनेषु विरक्तसङ्गाः ॥ 3 ॥

Having renounced the sensory pleasures of their homes that are cause for downfall, full with the aspiration for realising the Self, drinking nectar of the essence of the Upanishads, and free from the desires for worldly enjoyments, blessed are they who move about in solitude and are completely free from attachment to sensory objects of the world.

त्यक्त्वा ममाहमिति बन्धकरे पदे द्वे
मानावमानसदृशाः समदर्शिनश्च ।
कर्तारमन्यमवगम्य तदर्पितानि
कुर्वन्ति कर्मपरिपाकफलानि धन्याः ॥ 4 ॥

Having given up the two binding notions of 'I' and 'mine', blessed are those who are equanimous (equable) towards honour and dishonour and who regard all things impartially and impersonally (i.e., who are of equal vision). Recognising that someone else is the doer (i.e., the Lord alone is the doer), blessed are the ones who perform all activities offering fruits of actions unto the Lord.

त्यक्त्वैषणात्रयमवेक्षितमोक्षमार्गा
भैक्षामृतेन परिकल्पितदेहयात्राः ।
ज्योतिः परात्परतरं परमात्मसंज्ञं
धन्या द्विजा रहसि हृद्यवलोकयन्ति ॥ 5 ॥

Having renounced the three kinds of desires (desire for offspring, desire for wealth, and the desire for the world that includes name, fame, etc.), and seeking the path of liberation, blessed are the twice-born who support the body's physical existence by means of the nectar of alms. Blessed are those who, in the privacy of their heart, realise the Supreme Effulgence, the greater than the greatest, known as the Supreme Self (*Paramātmā*).

नासन्न सन्न सदसन्न महन्न चाणु
न स्त्री पुमान्न च नपुंसकमेकबीजम् ।
यैर्ब्रह्म तत्समुपासितमेकचित्तै-
र्धन्या विरेजुरितरे भवपाशबद्धाः ॥ 6 ॥

"Brahman is neither non-existence nor existence; not a combination of existence and non-existence; not huge, not minute like an atom; neither a woman, nor a man, nor a eunuch; but it is the one source of all." Those who contemplate upon that Brahman as described above, with a one-pointed mind, shine as the blessed ones. Others (those who do not meditate on Brahman) are bound by the rope of worldly existence.

अज्ञानपङ्कपरिमग्नमपेतसारं
दुःखालयं मरणजन्मजरावसक्तम् ।
संसारबन्धनमनित्यमवेक्ष्य धन्या
ज्ञानासिना तदवशीर्य विनिश्चयन्ति ॥ 7 ॥

Having ascertained the ephemeral nature of life, the blessed are the ones who cut the fetters (described above) by means of the sword of Self-knowledge. They ascertained the transience of life by carefully investigating the fetters and bondages. Thus, they realised life to be an abode of sorrow that is fully immersed in the mire of ignorance, devoid of any value or meaning and associated with death, birth and old age.

शान्तैरनन्यमतिभिर्मधुरस्वभावै-
रेकत्वनिश्चितमनोभिरपेतमोहैः ।
साकं वनेषु विजितात्मपदस्वरुपं
तद्वस्तु सम्यगनिशं विमृशन्ति धन्याः ॥ 8 ॥

Blessed are those who introspect and enquire over the Supreme Reality very well and incessantly, in the forest (in solitude). They have a constant association with those who are tranquil, who have no other diversions in the mind (i.e., with those who are one-pointed), who are pleasant-natured, who have ascertained the Oneness of existence, who are free from delusion and who have realised their true nature.

सम्पूर्णं जगदेव नन्दनवनं सर्वेऽपि कल्पद्रुमाः
गाङ्गं वारि समस्तवारिनिवहाः पुण्याः समस्ताः क्रियाः ।
वाचः प्राकृतसंस्कृताः श्रुतिशिरो वाराणसी मेदिनी
सर्वावस्थितिरस्य वस्तुविषया दृष्टे परब्रह्मणि ॥ 9 ॥

For one who is established in Brahman (the Supreme Reality), the entire world is indeed like a divine grove; all objects are wish-fulfilling trees, all water bodies are the river Ganga; every action is holy, all unrefined or cultured speech are words of the Upanishads, the entire earth is a holy city of Vārānasi, and everything is a subject matter of Truth.

* * *

22

Ekaṣhlokī

(एकश्लोकी)

Our Real Identity

किं ज्योतिस्तव भानुमानहनि मे रात्रौ प्रदीपादिकं
स्यादेवं रविदीपदर्शनविधौ किं ज्योतिराख्याहि मे ।
चक्षुस्तस्य निमीलनादिसमये किं धीर्धियो दर्शने
किं तत्राहमतो भवान्परमकं ज्योतिस्तदस्मि प्रभो ॥

[*This is a one-verse composition, presented as a series of questions and answers.*]

What is your source of light (for seeing)?

During the day, it is the sun, and at night, it is lamp and other such things.

Yes, it is. Tell me, what light is the means of seeing the sun and the lamp?

It is the eye.

At the time of shutting the eyes, etc., what is the light?

It is intellect.

What is the source of light for the intellect?

It is "I", the Self.

Therefore, your own Self is the light of lights (or the Supreme light).

Yes, O Lord, I am That.

* * *

23

Jīvan-muktānanda-laharī (जीवन्मुक्तानन्दलहरी)

Waves of the Bliss of one who is Liberated

पुरे पौरान्पश्यन्नरयुवतिनामाकृतिमया-
न्सुवेषान्स्वर्णालंकरणकलितांश्चित्रसदृशान् ।
स्वयं साक्षाद्द्रष्टेत्यपि च कलयंस्तैः सह रम-
न्मुनिर्न व्यामोहं भजति गुरुदीक्षाक्षततमाः ॥ 1 ॥

Having received *deeksha* (spiritual initiation) from the guru, the wise one whose ignorance has been destroyed is not at all deluded seeing the denizens in the city, with the name and forms of man and woman dressed beautifully and well, and decked with gold ornaments. Being aware that he is just a witness of what one sees directly in front of the eyes, seeing them as if in the pictures, sporting and rejoicing with them, he is not deluded.

वने वृक्षान्पश्यन्दलफलभरान्नम्रसुशिखा-
न्घनच्छायाच्छन्नान्बहुलकलकूजद्द्विजगणान् ।
भजन्घस्रे रात्राववनितलतल्पैकशयनो
मुनिर्न व्यामोहं भजति गुरुदीक्षाक्षततमाः ॥ 2 ॥

In the forest, seeing the dense shady trees whose branches are bent low because of the weight of the leaves and fruits, with flocks of numerous birds cooing in their melodious tones, the wise one resorts to the shade during the day and during the night sleeps on the ground with the earth serving as a bed. The wise one, whose ignorance has been destroyed, having received *deeksha* (spiritual initiation) from the guru, is not at all deluded.

कदाचित्प्रासादे क्वचिदपि च सौधेषु धनिनां
कदा काले शैले क्वचिदपि च कूलेषु सरिताम् ।
कुटीरे दान्तानां मुनिजनवराणामपि वस-
न्मुनिर्न व्यामोहं भजति गुरुदीक्षाक्षततमाः ॥ 3 ॥

Sometimes he may stay in a palace and at other times in mansions of the rich, sometimes on the slopes of a rocky mountain, sometimes on the banks of rivers, and sometimes in the huts of sages and knowers who have attained self-seatedness. Even though living in different kinds of abodes according to the situation, he–whose ignorance has been destroyed, having received *deeksha* (spiritual initiation) from the guru–is not at all deluded.

क्वचिद्बालैः सार्धं करतलगतालैः सहसितः
क्वचित्तारुण्यालङ्कृतनरवधूभिः सह रमन् ।
क्वचिद्वृद्धैश्चिन्ताकुलितहृदयैश्चापि विलप-
न्मुनिर्न व्यामोहं भजति गुरुदीक्षाक्षततमाः ॥ 4 ॥

Sometimes he plays with innocent boys with laughter and clapping of hands; sometimes he is rejoicing with young men and women who are in their youth; sometimes he is lamenting with old men and women whose hearts are heavy with thoughts and agitation. Even though being in all these situations, he–whose ignorance has been destroyed, having received *deeksha* (spiritual initiation) from the guru–is not at all deluded.

कदाचिद्विद्वद्भिर्विविदिषुभिरत्यन्तनिरतैः
कदाचित्काव्यालङ्कृतिरसरसालैः कविवरैः ।
कदाचित्सत्तर्कैरनुमितिपरैस्तार्किकवरै-
र्मुनिर्न व्यामोहं भजति गुरुदीक्षाक्षततमाः ॥ 5 ॥

Sometimes he is with wise men, sometimes with earnest seekers who are deeply engaged in their pursuit, sometimes with the best of poets who rejoice in the essence and beauty of poetic compositions, and he is sometimes with the best of philosophers who, given to reason and inference, are engaged in discussions on systems of philosophy. Even though engaged in all these, the wise one whose ignorance has been destroyed, having received *deeksha* (spiritual initiation) from the guru, is not at all deluded.

कदा ध्यानाभ्यासैः क्वचिदपि सपर्यां विकसितैः
सुगन्धैः सत्पुष्पैः क्वचिदपि दलैरेव विमलैः ।
प्रकुर्वन्देवस्य प्रमुदितमनाः संनतिपरो
मुनिर्न व्यामोहं भजति गुरुदीक्षाक्षततमाः ॥ 6 ॥

Sometimes he is engaged in the practices of *dhyāna* (meditation), sometimes in a joyful state of mind with all humility engaged in deity worship with well-blossomed and beautiful fragrant flowers, and sometimes he worships with clean leaves and petals. Even though engaged in all these, the wise one whose ignorance has been destroyed, having received *deeksha* (spiritual initiation) from the guru, is not at all deluded.

शिवायाः शंभोर्वा क्वचिदपि च विष्णोरपि कदा
गणाध्यक्षस्यापि प्रकटितवरस्यापि च कदा ।
पठन्वै नामालिं नयनरचितानन्दसलिलो
मुनिर्न व्यामोहं भजति गुरुदीक्षाक्षततमाः ॥ 7 ॥

With tears of bliss flowing down his eyes, he sometimes is chanting the names of the consort of Lord Siva (Goddess Durga), sometimes of Lord Shambhu (Siva), sometimes of Lord Vishnu, at other times of Lord Ganesha and at times of the Sun God. Even though engaged in all these, the wise one whose ignorance has been destroyed, having received *deeksha* (spiritual initiation) from the guru, is not at all deluded.

कदा गङ्गाम्भोभिः क्वचिदपि च कूपोत्थसलिलैः
क्वचित्कासारोत्थैः क्वचिदपि सदुष्णैश्च शिशिरैः ।
भजन्स्नानं भूत्या क्वचिदपि च कर्पूरनिभया
मुनिर्न व्यामोहं भजति गुरुदीक्षाक्षततमाः ॥ 8 ॥

He sometimes bathes in the waters of the Ganges, sometimes with water springing from a well, at times with the waters from a pond, sometimes with cold or hot water, or sometimes simply smearing the body with ashes shining bright like camphor. Even though engaged in these, the wise one, whose ignorance has been destroyed, having received *deeksha* (spiritual initiation) from the guru, is not at all deluded.

कदाचिज्जागर्त्यां विषयकरणैः संव्यवहर-
न्कदाचित्स्वप्नस्थानपि च विषयानेव च भजन् ।
कदाचित्सौषुप्तं सुखमनुभवन्नेव सततं
मुनिर्न व्यामोहं भजति गुरुदीक्षाक्षततमाः ॥ 9 ॥

Sometimes in the wakeful state pursuing activities and interactions with the sense organs, sometimes in the dream state experiencing the 'dream' objects, and sometimes in deep sleep experiencing uninterrupted happiness, the wise one, whose ignorance has been destroyed having received *deeksha* from the guru, is not at all deluded.

कदाऽप्याशावासाः क्वचिदपि च दिव्याम्बरधरः
क्वचित्पञ्चास्योत्थां त्वचमपि दधानः कटितटे ।
मनस्वी निःसङ्गः सुजनहृदयानन्दजनको
मुनिर्न व्यामोहं भजति गुरुदीक्षाक्षततमाः ॥ 10 ॥

Sometimes having the sky's regions as a garment (i.e., being naked), sometimes wearing exquisite and wonderful garments, sometimes wearing the skin of the lion at the loins, the wise one–with a placid mind, free from any kind of attachment, and delightful to the hearts of the noble–is not at all deluded. For, his ignorance has been destroyed, having received *deeksha* from the guru.

कदाचित्सत्त्वस्थः क्वचिदपि रजोवृत्तिसुगत-
स्तमोवृत्तिः क्वापि त्रितयरहितः क्वापि च पुनः ।
कदाचित्संसारी श्रुतिपथविहारी क्वचिदहो
मुनिर्न व्यामोहं भजति गुरुदीक्षाक्षततमाः ॥ 11 ॥

Sometimes he is seated firm in *sattva-guṇa*, sometimes engaged in activities motivated by *rajo-guṇa*, sometimes engaged in actions under the influence of *tamas*, sometimes transcending the three *guṇas*, sometimes experiencing the world like a man of the world, and sometimes he is delighting in the Vedic path. O, what a wonder! The wise one, whose ignorance has been destroyed, having received *deeksha* from the guru, is not at all deluded.

कदाचिन्मौनस्थः क्वचिदपि च वाग्वादनिरतः
कदाचित्सानन्दं हसितरभसस्त्यक्तवचनः ।
कदाचिल्लोकानां व्यवहृतिसमालोकनपरो
मुनिर्न व्यामोहं भजति गुरुदीक्षाक्षततमाः ॥ 12 ॥

Sometimes immersed in silence, sometimes deeply engaged in talks and debates, sometimes giving up speaking, sometimes laughing with delight all of a sudden, and sometimes engrossed in observing activities of other people, the wise one, whose ignorance has been destroyed having received *deeksha* from the guru, is not at all deluded.

कदाचिच्छक्तीनां विकचमुखपद्मेषु कमलं
क्षिपंस्तासां क्वापि स्वयमपि च गृह्णन्स्वमुखतः ।
तदद्वैतं रूपं निजपरविहीनं प्रकटय-
न्मुनिर्न व्यामोहं भजति गुरुदीक्षाक्षततमाः ॥ 13 ॥

Sometimes he may throw a lotus flower on the radiant lotus-like faces of women, while at some other time, he may receive the lotus flower thrown at him. But on both these occasions, demonstrating the non-dual oneness, completely devoid of the distinction of one's own Self and another's Self, the wise one, whose ignorance has been destroyed having received *deeksha* from the guru, is not at all deluded.

क्वचिच्छैवैः सार्धं क्वचिदपि च शाक्तैः सह वस-
न्कदा विष्णोर्भक्तैः क्वचिदपि च सौरैः सह वसन् ।
कदा गाणाध्यक्षैर्गतसकलभेदोऽद्वयतया
मुनिर्न व्यामोहं भजति गुरुदीक्षाक्षततमाः ॥ 14 ॥

Sometimes he lives with the worshippers of Lord Siva, sometimes with the worshippers of Shakti, sometimes with the devotees of Lord Vishnu, sometimes with the worshippers of Sun God, and sometimes he stays with devotees of Lord Ganesha. Devoid of the sense of differentiation because of the non-dual knowledge, the wise one, whose ignorance has been destroyed, having received *deeksha* from the guru, is not at all deluded.

निराकारं क्वापि क्वचिदपि च साकारममलं
निजं शैवं रूपं विविधगुणभेदेन बहुधा ।
कदाऽऽश्चर्यं पश्यन्किमिदमिति हृष्यन्नपि कदा
मुनिर्न व्यामोहं भजति गुरुदीक्षाक्षततमाः ॥ 15 ॥

Sometimes contemplating upon the Supreme Reality (Brahman) devoid of any form; sometimes because of the association with the *guṇas*, visualising his own pure auspicious Self as having different forms, sometimes looking at in wonder as 'what is all this', and at times delighting, the wise one, whose ignorance has been destroyed having received *deeksha* from the guru, is not at all deluded.

कदाऽद्वैतं पश्यन्नखिलमपि सत्यं शिवमयं
महावाक्यार्थानामवगतिसमभ्यासवशतः ।
गतद्वैताभासः शिव शिव शिवेत्येव विलप-
न्मुनिर्न व्यामोहं भजति गुरुदीक्षाक्षततमाः ॥ 16 ॥

As a result of the practice of constant contemplation on the purport of the cardinal statements (*mahāvākyas*) of the Upanishads, seeing everything as the Supreme Reality, Auspiciousness, Non-dual, and uttering 'Siva Siva Siva', the wise one, whose ignorance has been destroyed having received *deeksha* from the guru, is not at all deluded.

इमां मुक्तावस्थां परमशिवसंस्थां गुरुकृपा-
सुधापाङ्गव्याप्यां सहजसुखवाप्यामनुदिनम् ।
मुहुर्मज्जन्मज्जन्भजति सुकृतैश्चेन्नरवरः
सदा त्यागी योगी कविरिति वदन्तीह कवयः ॥ 17 ॥

The excellent among humans, who daily immerses himself again and again in the stream of natural happiness (innate bliss, which is his true nature) owing to good deeds and virtues, and attains the state of liberation being well established in the Supreme Brahman, attainable through the nectar of guru's glance and grace, such a one according to the wise is a *sannyāsin (tyāgi)*, a *yogi*, or an enlightened one.

* * *

24
Kaupīna-panchakam
(कौपीन-पञ्चकम्)

The Glory of the Ascetic

Also called Yati-panchakam

वेदान्तवाक्येषु सदा रमन्तो
भिक्षान्नमात्रेण च तुष्टिमन्तः ।
विशोकमन्तःकरणे चरन्तः
कौपीनवन्तः खलु भाग्यवन्तः ॥ 1 ॥

Blessed indeed are those ascetics who are always reveling in the words of the Vedantic declarations (assertions of the Upanishads), are content with the food obtained merely from begging, are wandering about freely, and are completely free from any sorrow in the heart.

मूलं तरोः केवलमाश्रयन्तः
पाणिद्वयं भोक्तुममत्रयन्तः ।
कन्थामिव श्रीमपि कुत्सयन्तः
कौपीनवन्तः खलु भाग्यवन्तः ॥ 2 ॥

Blessed indeed are those ascetics who use the base of a tree as a shelter for rest, make the two hands into a cup and use it as a vessel for drinking and eating, and look upon wealth and riches as if they are mere rags and worthless.

देहादिभावं परिमार्जयन्तः
आत्मानमात्मन्यवलोकयन्तः ।
नान्तं न मध्यं न बहिः स्मरन्तः
कौपीनवन्तः खलु भाग्यवन्तः ॥ 3 ॥

Blessed indeed are those ascetics who are completely free from any sense of identification with the body and mind (i.e., free from the superimposition of the Self on the body, mind, etc.), who have realised the Universal Self within one's own Self, and completely disregard anything which is in the end, in the middle or in the outside (i.e., disregarding anything other than the Self).

स्वानन्दभावे परितुष्टिमन्तः
संशान्तसर्वेन्द्रियदृष्टिमन्तः ।
अहर्निशं ब्रह्मणि ये रमन्तः
कौपीनवन्तःखलु भाग्यवन्तः ॥ 4 ॥

Blessed indeed are those ascetics who are fully content in one's own blissful nature, who have attained complete mastery over the senses and the mind, and who revel in Brahman (the Supreme Reality) day and night.

पञ्चाक्षरं पावनमुच्चरन्तः
पतिं पशूनां हृदि भावयन्तः ।
भिक्षाशना दिक्षु परिभ्रमन्तः
कौपीनवन्तः खलु भाग्यवन्तः ॥ 5 ॥

Blessed indeed are those ascetics who utter the purificatory five-syllable mantra (*namah-sivāya*), who meditate upon the Lord of all living beings in their own heart, who eat what is obtained from begging and wander about freely in all directions.

* * *

25

Nirguṇa-mānasa-pūjā (निर्गुण-मानस-पूजा)

Mental Worship of Brahman (the one without any Attributes)

***Note*:** The process of formal worship involves a series of sixteen services. In this text, Adi Shankarāchārya describes how these sixteen services can be carried out in the mind when it comes to the impersonal, formless Brahman. In place of the physical materials we use in worship, he describes what the equivalent mental concepts are.

शिष्य उवाच ।
अखण्डे सच्चिदानन्दे निर्विकल्पैकरूपिणि ।
स्थितेऽद्वितीयभावेऽपि कथं पूजा विधीयते ॥ 1 ॥

Disciple said: In the case of the indivisible *sat-chit-ānanda*, that is by nature absolute, unconditioned, free from change and ever non-dual, how is worship prescribed?

पूर्णस्यावाहनं कुत्र सर्वाधारस्य चासनम् ।
स्वच्छस्य पाद्यमर्घ्यं च शुद्धस्याचमनं कुतः ॥ 2 ॥

What is the place in which to invoke the One who is full and complete (infinite)? What can be the seat for One who Himself is the support and substratum of all? Where is the question of water (for washing the feet) and other water offerings for One who is ever pure? How can we offer water for purification to One who is eternally pure?

निर्मलस्य कुतः स्नानं वासो विश्वोदरस्य च ।
अगोत्रस्य त्ववर्णस्य कुतस्तस्योपवीतकम् ॥ 3 ॥

Of what use is a bath for One who is ever blemishless (pure)? Of what use are garments (clothing) for One who holds the Universe in His womb? Of what use is a sacred thread for One who is without a lineage and for One who is without a caste (a place in the social order)?

निर्लेपस्य कुतो गन्धः पुष्पं निर्वासनस्य च ।
निर्विशेषस्य का भूषा कोऽलङ्कारो निराकृतेः ॥ 4 ॥

Of what use is perfume for One who is unattached to anything? Of what use are flowers for One who is without any desires or impressions? Of what use are ornaments for One who is without any distinguishing features? Where is the question of decoration for One who is formless?

निरञ्जनस्य किं धूपैर्दीपैर्वा सर्वसाक्षिणः ।
निजानन्दैकतृप्तस्य नैवेद्यं किं भवेदिह ॥ 5 ॥

Of what use is incense for the One who is untainted? Of what use is waving lamps in front of One who is the witness of all? Of what use are offerings of eatables to One who is ever contented in one's own bliss?

विश्वानन्दयितुस्तस्य किं ताम्बूलं प्रकल्प्यते ।
स्वयम्प्रकाशचिद्रूपो योऽसावर्कादिभासकः ॥ 6 ॥
गीयते श्रुतिभिस्तस्य नीराजनविधिः कुतः ।
प्रदक्षिणमनन्तस्य प्रणामोऽद्वयवस्तुनः ॥ 7 ॥

To the One who makes the entire universe happy, does it make sense to please him by presenting betel leaves? To the One who is self-effulgent being the nature of Consciousness, who is the illuminator of the sun and other such objects, and to One whose glory is sung by the Vedas, where is the sense in this ritual of waving lights or camphor? Where is the question of circumambulation of the One who is limitless? Where is the question of prostrations to the One non-dual Reality?

वेदवाचामवेद्यस्य किं वा स्तोत्रं विधीयते ।
अन्तर्बहिः संस्थितस्योद्वासनविधिः कुतः ॥ 8 ॥

For One who cannot be comprehended by the words of the Vedas, what hymns of praise can be prescribed? For One who is established both inside and outside, where is the question of a ritual for bidding farewell to the divinity (by performing a *visarjana).*

गुरुरुवाच ।
आराधयामि मणिसंनिभमात्मलिङ्गम्
मायापुरीहृदयपङ्कजसंनिविष्टम् ।
श्रद्धानदीविमलचित्तजलाभिषेकै-
र्नित्यं समाधिकुसुमैर्नपुनर्भवाय ॥ 9 ॥

The Guru said: I always worship the symbol in the form of the Self resembling a gem, abiding in the spectral city of the lotus of the heart, by offering a ceremonial bath which is a pure mind, with the waters of the river of *shraddhā*, and offering flowers of *samādhi*, for attaining immortality.

[*The sixteen steps involved in worship* (*pooja*) *are described in the following verses.*]

अयमेकोऽवशिष्टोऽस्मीत्येवमावाहयेच्छिवम् ।
आसनं कल्पयेत्पश्चात्स्वप्रतिष्ठात्मचिन्तनम् ॥ 10 ॥

"I am the One, the only One, and there is nothing other than the Self"; thus indeed one should invoke the Supreme, the Auspicious One. Then one should prepare the seat, which is nothing but an enquiry into the Self that abides within. (*1. āvāhanam: Invocation of the deity. 2. āsanam: Offering a seat.*)

पुण्यपापरजःसङ्गो मम नास्तीति वेदनम् ।
पाद्यं समर्पयेद्विद्वन्सर्वकल्मषनाशनम् ॥ 11 ॥

"I do not have any attachment with virtue and sin": this knowledge or proclamation, the wise one should offer as the water for washing of the feet. That, in reality, washes away all the impurities of the mind. (3. *pādyam: The water used for washing the feet.*)

अनादिकल्पविधृतमूलाज्ञानजलाञ्जलिम् ।
विसृजेदात्मलिङ्गस्य तदेवार्घ्यसमर्पणम् ॥ 12 ॥

One should pour forth the offering of a handful of water in the form of root-ignorance held since the beginning of time. That indeed is the water offering to the symbol of the Self. (4. *arghyam: Water offering at the respectful reception of a guest.*)

ब्रह्मानन्दाब्धिकल्लोलकणकोट्यंशलेशकम् ।
पिबन्तीन्द्रादय इति ध्यानमाचमनं मतम् ॥ 13 ॥

Indra and the others drink a tiny fraction of a drop of the many waves in the ocean of bliss of Brahman. Meditation is regarded as sipping water from the palm of the hand for purification. (5. *ācamanam: Sipping water for purification.*)

ब्रह्मानन्दजलेनैव लोकाः सर्वे परिप्लुताः ।
अच्छेद्योऽयमिति ध्यानमभिषेचनमात्मनः ॥ 14 ॥

All the worlds are as if bathed by the water of the ocean of bliss. "This Self is indivisible"–meditating thus is the act of sprinkling for purification of the Self. (6. *abhishechanam: Sprinkling of water for purification. Also referred to as snānam: The bath.*)

निरावरणचैतन्यं प्रकाशोऽस्मीति चिन्तनम् ।
आत्मलिङ्गस्य सद्वस्त्रमित्येवं चिन्तयेन्मुनिः ॥ 15 ॥

"I am the light, the unveiled Consciousness"–this reflection is the holy garment for the symbol of the Self. Thus, should the wise one think. (7. *vastram: A garment.*)

त्रिगुणात्माशेषलोकमालिकासूत्रमस्म्यहम् ।
इति निश्चयमेवात्र ह्युपवीतं परं मतम् ॥ 16 ॥

"I am the thread that goes through the garland of an entire world of the nature of three *guṇas*"–this conviction is indeed highly regarded as the sacred thread. (*8. upavītam: The sacred thread.*)

अनेकवासनामिश्रप्रपञ्चोऽयं धृतो मया ।
नान्येनेत्यनुसन्धानमात्मनश्चन्दनं भवेत् ॥ 17 ॥

"This manifold world with numerous mixed impressions is held by me (i.e., the Self is the substratum), not by another"–this form of enquiry is the sandal paste for the Self. (*9. gandham: Fragrance.*)

रजःसत्त्वतमोवृत्तित्यागरूपैस्तिलाक्षतैः ।
आत्मलिङ्गं यजेन्नित्यं जीवन्मुक्तिप्रसिद्धये ॥ 18 ॥

For attaining liberation, one should always worship the symbol of the Self, with the offering of sesame seeds and rice in the form of renunciation of the activities born of rajas, sattva and tamas. (*10. archanam: Offering.*)

ईश्वरो गुरुरात्मेति भेदत्रयविवर्जितैः ।
बिल्वपत्रैरद्वितीयैरात्मलिङ्गं यजेच्छिवम् ॥ 19 ॥

With *bilva* leaves in the form of the non-dual attitude (*bhāva*)–devoid of the triple division in the form of the Lord, the guru and the Self–one should worship the Self.

समस्तवासनात्यागं धूपं तस्य विचिन्तयेत् ।
ज्योतिर्मयात्मविज्ञानं दीपं सन्दर्शयेद्बुधः ॥ 20 ॥

The wise one should consider 'giving up all desires' as the incense. He should show the lamp, which is nothing but 'the radiance in the nature of Self-realisation'. (*11. dhūpam: Incense.; 12. dīpam: Lamp.*)

नैवेद्यमात्मलिङ्गस्य ब्रह्माण्डाख्यं महोदनम् ।
पिबानन्दरसं स्वादु मृत्युरस्योपसेचनम् ॥ 21 ॥

The great food called the 'universe', of the nature of the bliss (of Brahman), is the delicious 'food offering' to the Self. For this, 'death' is the ceremonial sprinkling of holy water to the food offering (*upasechanam*). (*13. naivedyam: Food offering.*)

अज्ञानोच्छिष्टकरस्य क्षालनं ज्ञानवारिणा ।
विशुद्धस्यात्मलिङ्गस्य हस्तप्रक्षालनं स्मरेत् ॥ 22 ॥

Cleansing the mind (lit. hands)–which has been rendered impure by ignorance–with the water of Self-knowledge, should be considered as washing hands in the context of worshipping the ever-pure self.

रागादिगुणशून्यस्य शिवस्य परमात्मनः ।
सरागविषयाभ्यासत्यागस्ताम्बूलचर्वणम् ॥ 23 ॥

Forsaking indulgence in the objects of desires should be regarded as the chewing of betel leaves in the context of the Auspicious, the Supreme Self, which is devoid of attributes like desires and passion. (*14. tāmbūlam: Betel leaves.*)

अज्ञानध्वान्तविध्वंसप्रचण्डमतिभास्करम् ।
आत्मनो ब्रह्मताज्ञानं नीराजनमिहात्मनः ॥ 24 ॥

The realisation of knowledge of our true nature as that of Brahman (the knowledge that "I am Brahman") is the great shining light greater than that of the sun and destroys the darkness or veil of ignorance. This realisation is the real waving of lights to the Self. (*15. nīrājanam: Waving of lights.*)

विविधब्रह्मसन्दृष्टिर्मालिकाभिरलङ्कृतम् ।
पूर्णानन्दात्मतादृष्टिं पुष्पाञ्जलिमनुस्मरेत् ॥ 25 ॥

One should regard the vision of the supreme blissful nature of the Self, decorated with the vision of the manifold Brahman, to be the offering of a handful of flowers. (*16. puṣpāñjali: Offering of flowers.*)

परिभ्रमन्ति ब्रह्माण्डसहस्राणि मयीश्वरे ।
कूटस्थाचलरूपोऽहमिति ध्यानं प्रदक्षिणम् ॥ 26 ॥

Thousands of universes revolve in me, the Supreme. "I am of the nature of the immovable and unchangeable": this contemplation is verily circumambulation of the Self.

विश्ववन्द्योऽहमेवास्मि नास्ति वन्द्यो मदन्यतः ।
इत्यालोचनमेवात्र स्वात्मलिङ्गस्य वन्दनम् ॥ 27 ॥

"I am indeed the One who is worshipable by the entire world; there is none other who is worshipable"–this reflection is the true worship of the symbol of the Self.

आत्मनः सत्क्रिया प्रोक्ता कर्तव्याभावभावना ।
नामरूपव्यतीतात्मचिन्तनं नामकीर्तनम् ॥ 28 ॥

It is said that the good deed for the Self is the attitude that "there is nothing to be done in the context of the Self". Contemplation on the Self, transcending name and form, is the act of repetition of the name of the Lord.

श्रवणं तस्य देवस्य श्रोतव्याभावचिन्तनम् ।
मननं त्वात्मलिङ्गस्य मन्तव्याभावचिन्तनम् ॥ 29 ॥

The knowledge that there is nothing to be known regarding the Self, by the process of listening (or by studying), is the real '*shravaṇa*' (listening or study). The knowledge that there is nothing to be contemplated upon regarding the Self is the real '*manana*' (contemplation).

ध्यातव्याभावविज्ञानं निदिध्यासनमात्मनः ।
समस्तभ्रान्तिविक्षेपराहित्येनात्मनिष्ठता ॥ 30 ॥
समाधिरात्मनो नाम नान्यच्चित्तस्य विभ्रमः ।
तत्रैव ब्रह्मणि सदा चित्तविश्रान्तिरिष्यते ॥ 31 ॥

The knowledge that there is nothing to be meditated upon regarding the Self is the real '*nididhyāsana*' (meditation).

Complete abidance in the Self with the absence of delusions and distractions is called *samādhi*. Considering anything else to be *samādhi* is a delusion of the mind. Thus, the mind always desires the constant abidance in Brahman (the Supreme Reality).

एवं वेदान्तकल्पोक्तस्वात्मलिङ्गप्रपूजनम् ।
कुर्वन्नामरणं वापि क्षणं वा सुसमाहितः ॥ 32 ॥
सर्वदुर्वासनाजालं पदपांसुमिव त्यजेत् ।
विधूयाज्ञानदुःखौघं मोक्षानन्दं समश्नुते ॥ 33 ॥

Thus, performing the worship of the Self as described in Vedanta until death or even for a moment, one who is well-established in the Self will be free from the web of bad tendencies, like shaking the dust of the feet. Having thus shaken off the impurities of ignorance and the resultant suffering, one attains the bliss of liberation.

***

26

Nirvāṇa-ṣaṭkam (निर्वाणषट्कम्)

Realization of one's real nature is Liberation

Also called Ātma-ṣaṭkam

मनोबुद्ध्यहंकारचित्तानि नाहं
न च श्रोत्रजिह्वे न च घ्राणनेत्रे ।
न च व्योम भूमिर्न तेजो न वायु-
श्चिदानन्दरूपः शिवोऽहं शिवोऽहम् ॥ 1 ॥

I am not the mind, the intellect, the ego or the thought. I am not the senses of perception (hearing, taste, smell and vision). I am not the gross elements (space, earth, fire and wind). I am of the nature of Consciousness-Bliss. I am the Supreme Being of the nature of Auspiciousness; I am the Supreme Being of the nature of Auspiciousness.

न च प्राणसंज्ञो न वै पञ्चवायु-
र्न वा सप्तधातुर्न वा पञ्चकोशः ।
न वाक्पाणिपादौ न चोपस्थपायू
चिदानन्दरूपः शिवोऽहं शिवोऽहम् ॥ 2 ॥

I am not that which is called *prāṇa*. I am not the five vital airs of the body (*prāṇa*, *apāna*, *vyāna*, *udāna*, *samāna*). I am not the seven primitive elements (viz. chyle, blood, flesh, fat, bone, marrow, and semen) of the body. I am not the five sheaths (food, vital air, mental, intellectual, bliss). I am not the five organs of action (speech, hands, legs, genitals and organs of excretion).

I am of the nature of Consciousness-Bliss. I am the Supreme Being of the nature of Auspiciousness; I am the Supreme Being of the nature of Auspiciousness.

[The five life forces or vital airs are: *prāṇa* – function of respiration (inhalation and exhalation), *apāna* – function of excretion/evacuation, *vyāna* – function of circulation, *udāna* – function of reversing (e.g., vomiting), *samāna* – function of digestion and assimilation.]

न मे द्वेषरागौ न मे लोभमोहौ
मदो नैव मे नैव मात्सर्यभावः ।
न धर्मो न चार्थो न कामो न मोक्ष-
श्चिदानन्दरूपः शिवोऽहं शिवोऽहम् ॥ 3 ॥

I have no aversion, attachment, greed, delusion, pride or jealousy (six enemies of the mind). I have no dharma, wealth, desires and liberation (four objects of human life). I am of the nature of Consciousness-Bliss. I am the Supreme Being of the nature of Auspiciousness; I am the Supreme Being of the nature of Auspiciousness.

न पुण्यं न पापं न सौख्यं न दुःखं
न मन्त्रो न तीर्थं न वेदा न यज्ञाः ।
अहं भोजनं नैव भोज्यं न भोक्ता
चिदानन्दरूपः शिवोऽहं शिवोऽहम् ॥ 4 ॥

I have neither virtue nor vice; I have neither happiness nor sorrow; I do not need a mantra, a pilgrimage, the Vedas or any sacrifices; I am not the enjoyer, the act of enjoying or what is enjoyed. I am of the nature of Consciousness-Bliss. I am the Supreme Being of the nature of Auspiciousness; I am the Supreme Being of the nature of Auspiciousness.

न मृत्युर्न शङ्का न मे जातिभेदः
पिता नैव मे नैव माता न जन्म ।
न बन्धुर्न मित्रं गुरुर्नैव शिष्य-
श्चिदानन्दरूपः शिवोऽहं शिवोऽहम् ॥ 5 ॥

I have no death. I have no doubts. I have no distinctions based on birth. I have no father, no mother and no birth. I have no relative, friend, teacher or disciple. I am of the nature of Consciousness-Bliss. I am the Supreme Being of the nature of Auspiciousness; I am the Supreme Being of the nature of Auspiciousness.

अहं निर्विकल्पो निराकाररूपो
विभुत्वाच्च सर्वत्र सर्वेन्द्रियाणाम् ।
न चासङ्गतं नैव मुक्तिर्न बन्ध-
श्चिदानन्दरूपः शिवोऽहं शिवोऽहम् ॥ 6 ॥

I am changeless, undifferentiated. I am of the nature of formlessness. Being all-pervading in every form, I am present everywhere in and through all objects of all sense perceptions. I am free from attachment everywhere. I am free from the notions of freedom and bondage. I am of the nature of Consciousness-Bliss. I am the Supreme Being of the nature of Auspiciousness; I am the Supreme Being of the nature of Auspiciousness.

* * *

27

Svarūpānusandhānāṣṭakam

(स्वरूपानुसंधानाष्टकम्)

Inquiry into one's own nature

तपोयज्ञदानादिभिः शुद्धबुद्धि-
विरक्तो नृपादेः पदे तुच्छबुद्ध्या ।
परित्यज्य सर्वं यदाप्नोति तत्त्वं
परं ब्रह्म नित्यं तदेवाहमस्मि ॥ 1 ॥

A pure mind is attained by means of austerity, sacrifice, charity, etc. The one with a pure mind, who has become completely free from attachment, who considers even the position of a king to be trifling and has abandoned everything, attains the Truth, the eternal Supreme Brahman. I am That Brahman alone.

दयालुं गुरुं ब्रह्मनिष्ठं प्रशान्तं
समाराध्य मत्या विचार्य स्वरूपम् ।
यदाप्नोति तत्त्वं निदिध्यास्य विद्वा-
न्परं ब्रह्म नित्यं तदेवाहमस्मि ॥ 2 ॥

Having approached a Guru who is compassionate, tranquil and established in the realisation of Brahman, the seeker of Truth should worship (serve) the Guru with devotion. Then, contemplating upon one's true nature and meditating upon the Reality (the Supreme Brahman), one attains that Reality, Brahman. I am That Brahman alone.

यदानन्दरूपं प्रकाशस्वरूपं
निरस्तप्रपञ्चं परिच्छेदहीनम् ।
अहंब्रह्मवृत्त्यैकगम्यं तुरीयं
परं ब्रह्म नित्यं तदेवाहमस्मि ॥ 3 ॥

The Supreme Brahman is of the nature of *ānanda* (bliss), is of the nature of effulgence, transcends the universe and its phenomena, is devoid of any kind of divisions, is knowable only by the mental disposition of "I am Brahman" and is referred to as the Fourth (beyond the three states, viz. wakeful, dream and sleep states). That Eternal Supreme Brahman am I.

यदज्ञानतो भाति विश्वं समस्तं
विनष्टं च सद्यो यदात्मप्रबोधे ।
मनोवागतीतं विशुद्धं विमुक्तं
परं ब्रह्म नित्यं तदेवाहमस्मि ॥ 4 ॥

Because of the ignorance regarding Brahman, the entire universe appears as real. And that ignorance regarding the universe is immediately destroyed with the dawn of Self-knowledge. That Brahman, which is pure and ever free, is beyond mind and speech (words). I am That eternal Supreme Brahman.

निषेधे कृते नेति नेतीति वाक्यैः
समाधिस्थितानां यदाभाति पूर्णम् ।
अवस्थात्रयातीतमद्वैतमेकं
परं ब्रह्म नित्यं तदेवाहमस्मि ॥ 5 ॥

That which shines for those who are in a state of *samādhi* (i.e., complete absorption with the Self), that which is obtained by denying everything in the phenomenal universe by means of the statements "not this, not this", that which is beyond the three states of experience (wakeful, dream and sleep), that non-dual, one (absolute) eternal Supreme Brahman am I.

यदानन्दलेशैः समानन्दि विश्वं
यदाभाति सत्त्वे तदाभाति सर्वम् ।

यदालोकने रूपमन्यत्समस्तं
परं ब्रह्म नित्यं तदेवाहमस्मि ॥ 6 ॥

By a small particle of *ānanda* (bliss) of Brahman, the whole universe is endowed with happiness. When Brahman shines, everything shines in the Consciousness, and in the light of That (Brahman), the whole world of forms is illumined (appears). That eternal Supreme Brahman am I.

अनन्तं विभुं निर्विकल्पं निरीहं
शिवं सङ्गहीनं यदोङ्कारगम्यम् ।
निराकारमत्युज्ज्वलं मृत्युहीनं
परं ब्रह्म नित्यं तदेवाहमस्मि ॥ 7 ॥

That which is boundless, all-pervading, unchanging, desireless, auspicious and free from all attachments, that which is attainable through the symbol Om, that which is formless, most luminous and is devoid of death, That eternal Supreme Brahman am I.

यदानन्दसिन्धौ निमग्नः पुमान्स्या-
दविद्याविलासः समस्तप्रपञ्चः ।
तदा न स्फुरत्यद्भुतं यन्निमित्तं
परं ब्रह्म नित्यं तदेवाहमस्मि ॥ 8 ॥

The entire phenomenal universe appears because of the ignorance regarding Brahman. And it is that wonder called Brahman, which is the cause of this universe. When a human being becomes immersed in the ocean of *ānanda* (bliss), which is Brahman, then the entire phenomenal universe does not manifest anymore. That eternal Supreme Brahman am I.

स्वरूपानुसंधानरूपां स्तुतिं यः
पठेदादराद्भक्तिभावो मनुष्यः ।
श्रृणोतीह वा नित्यमुद्युक्तचित्तो
भवेद्विष्णुरत्रैव वेदप्रमाणात् ॥ 9 ॥

The one who reads this eulogy (hymn of praise) called 'Svarūpānusandhānāṣṭakam' (an investigation into one's own true nature) with reverence (*shraddhā*) and devotion, or listens to it daily with diligence, such a one becomes Brahman, here (in this world) itself. This is according to the authority of the Vedas.

***

28

Brahmajñānāvalīmālā

(ब्रह्मज्ञानावलीमाला)

The garland of beads of the knowledge of Brahman

सकृच्छ्रवणमात्रेण ब्रह्मज्ञानं यतो भवेत् ।
ब्रह्मज्ञानावलीमाला सर्वेषां मोक्षसिद्धये ॥ 1 ॥

Just by listening to which, knowledge of the ultimate Truth will be attained, that Brahmajñānāvalīmālā is discussed here, for the attainment of liberation for all.

असङ्गोऽहमसङ्गोऽहमसङ्गोऽहं पुनः पुनः ।
सच्चिदानन्दरूपोऽहमहमेवाहमव्ययः ॥ 2 ॥

Unattached am I; unattached am I; unattached am I, always. I am of the nature of Existence-Consciousness-Bliss (*sat-chit-ānanda*). I alone am. Imperishable am I.

नित्यशुद्धविमुक्तोऽहं निराकारोऽहमव्ययः ।
भूमानन्दस्वरूपोऽहमहमेवाहमव्ययः ॥ 3 ॥

I am eternal, pure and free. I am formless and unchanging. I am of the nature of infinite bliss; I alone am; Imperishable am I.

नित्योऽहं निरवद्योऽहं निराकारोऽहमच्युतः ।
परमानन्दरूपोऽहमहमेवाहमव्ययः ॥ 4 ॥

Eternal am I, without any fault am I. Formless am I; Imperishable am I. I am of the nature of supreme happiness; I alone am; Imperishable am I.

शुद्धचैतन्यरूपोऽहमात्मारामोऽहमेव च ।
अखण्डानन्दरूपोऽहमहमेवाहमव्ययः ॥ 5 ॥

I am of the nature of Pure Consciousness. I delight in my own Self. I am of the nature of unbroken bliss; I alone am; Imperishable am I.

प्रत्यक्चैतन्यरूपोऽहं शान्तोऽहं प्रकृतेः परः ।
शाश्वतानन्दरूपोऽहमहमेवाहमव्ययः ॥ 6 ॥

I am of the nature of the innermost Consciousness. Tranquil am I; I transcend nature. I am of the nature of incessant bliss; I alone am; Imperishable am I.

तत्त्वातीतः परात्माहं मध्यातीतः परः शिवः ।
मायातीतः परंज्योतिरहमेवाहमव्ययः ॥ 7 ॥

Transcending all the tattvas, I am the Supreme Self. Beyond everything in the middle, I am the Supreme Auspicious One. Transcending *māyā*, I am the Supreme effulgence. I alone am; Imperishable am I.

नानारूपव्यतीतोऽहं चिदाकारोऽहमच्युतः ।
सुखरूपस्वरूपोऽहमहमेवाहमव्ययः ॥ 8 ॥

I am different from the manifold forms. I am of the nature of Consciousness. Imperishable am I. My true nature is of the nature of happiness; I alone am; Imperishable am I.

मायातत्कार्यदेहादि मम नास्त्येव सर्वदा ।
स्वप्रकाशैकरूपोऽहमहमेवाहमव्ययः ॥ 9 ॥

Māyā and its effects, like the body, etc., are never mine. I am of the nature of self-effulgence; I alone am; Imperishable am I.

गुणत्रयव्यतीतोऽहं ब्रह्मादीनां च साक्ष्यहम् ।
अनन्तानन्तरूपोऽहमहमेवाहमव्ययः ॥ 10 ॥

I transcend the three *guṇas*. I am the witness of Brahmā (the creator deity) and others. Infinitely boundless am I; I alone am; Imperishable am I.

अन्तर्यामिस्वरूपोऽहं कूटस्थः सर्वगोऽस्म्यहम् ।
परमात्मस्वरूपोऽहमहमेवाहमव्ययः ॥ 11 ॥

I am of the nature of the indwelling-regulator. I am immutable. I am all-pervading. I am the Supreme Self; I alone am; Imperishable am I.

निष्कलोऽहं निष्क्रियोऽहं सर्वात्माद्यः सनातनः ।
अपरोक्षस्वरूपोऽहमहमेवाहमव्ययः ॥ 12 ॥

I am indivisible and without parts. Actionless am I. I am the Universal Self. I am the first and unparalleled. I am eternal. I am of the nature of Self; I alone am; Imperishable am I.

द्वन्द्वादिसाक्षिरूपोऽहमचलोऽहं सनातनः ।
सर्वसाक्षिस्वरूपोऽहमहमेवाहमव्ययः ॥ 13 ॥

I am the witness to the pairs of opposites. I am immovable or unshakable. I am eternal. I am the witness to everything. I alone am; Imperishable am I.

प्रज्ञानघन एवाहं विज्ञानघन एव च ।
अकर्ताहमभोक्ताहमहमेवाहमव्ययः ॥ 14 ॥

I am nothing but the knowledge by which the Truth is known. I am nothing but Consciousness. I am not the doer of actions. I am not the experiencer. I alone am; Imperishable am I.

निराधारस्वरूपोऽहं सर्वाधारोऽहमेव च ।
आप्तकामस्वरूपोऽहमहमेवाहमव्ययः ॥ 15 ॥

I do not need any support or foundation. I am the substratum of everything in this universe. I am self-fulfilled. I alone am; Imperishable am I.

तापत्रयविनिर्मुक्तो देहत्रयविलक्षणः ।
अवस्थात्रयसाक्ष्यस्मि चाहमेवाहमव्ययः ॥ 16 ॥

I am completely free from the three kinds of afflictions. I transcend the three bodies–gross, subtle and causal. I am the witness to the three states of experience. I alone am; Imperishable am I.

दृग्दृश्यौ द्वौ पदार्थौ स्तः परस्परविलक्षणौ ।
दृग्ब्रह्म दृश्यं मायेति सर्ववेदान्तडिण्डिमः ॥ 17 ॥

The perceiver and the perceived–they are two things mutually opposed to each other. The perceiver is Brahman, and the perceived is *māyā*. This is the loud assertion of all of Vedanta.

अहं साक्षीति यो विद्याद्विविच्यैवं पुनः पुनः ।
स एव मुक्तः सो विद्वानिति वेदान्तडिण्डिमः ॥ 18 ॥

After the process of repeated discrimination, one who knows that "I am the witness", is indeed free and wise. This is the loud assertion of Vedanta.

घटकुड्यादिकं सर्वं मृत्तिकामात्रमेव च ।
तद्वद्ब्रह्म जगत्सर्वमिति वेदान्तडिण्डिमः ॥ 19 ॥

The earthen pot, wall, etc., are nothing but clay. In the same manner, the entire universe is nothing but Brahman. This is the loud assertion of Vedanta.

ब्रह्म सत्यं जगन्मिथ्या जीवो ब्रह्मैव नापरः ।
अनेन वेद्यं सच्छास्त्रमिति वेदान्तडिण्डिमः ॥ 20 ॥

Brahman alone is truth, and the entire universe is false. The individual Self is nothing but Brahman alone, nothing else. By this alone, the Truth of the scriptures is to be known. This is the loud assertion of Vedanta.

अन्तर्ज्योतिर्बहिर्ज्योतिः प्रत्यग्ज्योतिः परात्परः ।
ज्योतिर्ज्योतिः स्वयंज्योतिरात्मज्योतिः शिवोऽस्म्यहम् ॥ 21 ॥

I am the light within, the light outside, the indwelling Light, greater than the greatest, the effulgence of all Lights. I am self-luminous. I am the effulgence, that is the Self. I am the Auspicious One.

* * *

29

Advaita-pancha-ratnam

(अद्वैत-पञ्चरत्नम्)

Five Gems of Advaita

नाहं देहो नेन्द्रियाण्यन्तरङ्गो
नाहङ्कारः प्राणवर्गो न बुद्धिः ।
दारापत्यक्षेत्रवित्तादिदूरः
साक्षी नित्यः प्रत्यगात्मा शिवोऽहम् ॥ 1 ॥

I am not the body; I am not the sense organs; I am not the mind; I am not the ego; I am not the five different vital airs (*prāna*); and I am not the intellect. I am distant from (i.e., unattached to) wife, child, place, wealth, etc. I am none other than the witness, the eternal and the inmost Self, Siva (of the nature of Auspiciousness).

रज्ज्वज्ञानाद्भाति रज्जौ यथाहिः
स्वात्माज्ञानादात्मनो जीवभावः ।
आप्तोक्त्याऽहिभ्रान्तिनाशे स रज्जुः
जीवो नाहं देशिकोक्त्या शिवोऽहम् ॥ 2 ॥

Because of the ignorance of the presence of a rope, a snake is seen in place of the rope. In the same manner, because of the ignorance of the Self, there arises a sense of individuality. By listening to the words of a trusted person, there is destruction of the delusion regarding the snake, and one realises that it is just a rope. In the same manner, following the instructions of the guru, one realises that "I am not the individual *jīva* (having an individual identity), but I am Siva, of the nature of Auspiciousness".

आभातीदं विश्वमात्मन्यसत्यम्
सत्यज्ञानानन्दरूपे विमोहात् ।
निद्रामोहात्स्वप्नवत्तन्न सत्यम्
शुद्धः पूर्णो नित्य एकः शिवोऽहम् ॥ 3 ॥

A drcam (which is unreal) appears due to the delusion called sleep. In the same manner, because of delusion, this unreal world appears in the Self, which is of the nature of Self-knowledge and bliss. That world is not real. I am pure, complete, eternal, non-dual Siva, of the nature of Auspiciousness.

नाहं जातो न प्रवृद्धो न नष्टो
देहस्योक्ताः प्राकृताः सर्वधर्माः ।
कर्तृत्वादिश्चिन्मयस्यास्ति नाहं-
कारस्यैव ह्यात्मनो मे शिवोऽहम् ॥ 4 ॥

I am neither born nor do I age, nor do I die. All these characteristics are said to be derived from nature and are of the body (matter). The sense of doership, etc., belongs to *ahankāra* (ego) and not me, the Self, which is of the nature of Consciousness. I am of the nature of Siva (Auspiciousness).

मत्तो नान्यत्किञ्चिदत्रास्ति विश्वं
सत्यं बाह्यं वस्तु मायोपक्लृप्तम् ।
आदर्शान्तर्भासमानस्य तुल्यं
मय्यद्वैते भाति तस्माच्छिवोऽहम् ॥ 5 ॥

Here, different from me, there is no real world that exists. All external objects (of the world) created by *māyā* appear in me, the non-dual Self, like the things appearing in the mirror. Therefore, I am of the nature of Siva (Auspiciousness).

***

30

Dasha-shlokī

(दशश्लोकी)

The Essence of Vedanta

न भूमिर्न तोयं न तेजो न वायुः
न खं नेन्द्रियं वा न तेषां समूहः ।
अनेकान्तिकत्वात् सुषुप्त्येकसिद्धः
तदेकोऽवशिष्टः शिवः केवलोऽहम् ॥ 1 ॥

I am neither the earth nor the water, nor fire, nor air, nor the ether, nor any of the sense-organs individually, nor their aggregate (i.e., the body). Because of the multiplicity and transience in the wakeful and dream states, the Self exists as one and unchanging in the deep sleep state. I am that one which alone remains, the only One, the Auspicious one–the pure unconditioned Consciousness.

न वर्णा न वर्णाश्रमाचारधर्मा
न मे धारणाध्यानयोगादयोऽपि ।
अनात्माश्रयाहंममाध्यासहानात्
तदेकोऽवशिष्टः शिवः केवलोऽहम् ॥ 2 ॥

The idea of caste does not pertain to me; the orders and the codes related to the four stages of life also do not pertain to me. Concentration, meditation and other such yogic practices do not pertain to me. Because of the destruction of the superimposition of notions of "I" and "mine" on the non-self (body), I am that one which alone remains, the only One, the Auspicious one–the pure unconditioned Consciousness.

न माता पिता वा न देवा न लोका
न वेदा न यज्ञा न तीर्थं ब्रुवन्ति ।
सुषुप्तौ निरस्तातिशून्यात्मकत्वात्
तदेकोऽवशिष्टः शिवः केवलोऽहम् ॥ 3 ॥

They (the wise) say, in sleep, there is neither mother, nor father, nor the gods, nor the worlds, nor the Vedas, nor the *yajñas*, nor the pilgrim centres. Because even the idea of the void is rejected (in sleep), I am that which alone remains, the only One, the Auspicious one–the pure unconditioned Consciousness.

न साङ्ख्यं न शैवं न तत्पाञ्चरात्रं
न जैनं न मीमांसकादेर्मतं वा ।
विशिष्टानुभूत्या विशुद्धात्मकत्वात्
तदेकोऽवशिष्टः शिवः केवलोऽहम् ॥ 4 ॥

That (Supreme) is not the Sānkhya philosophy, not the Shaiva system, not the Vaishnava doctrine, not the Jaina system, and not the doctrine of the followers of Mimāmsa philosophy. By the direct experience (of the Supreme), because of the extremely pure nature of the Self, I am that which alone remains, the only One, the Auspicious one–the pure unconditioned Consciousness.

न चोर्ध्वं न चाधो न चान्तर्न बाह्यं
न मध्यं न तिर्यङ् न पूर्वापरा दिक् ।
वियद्व्यापकत्वादखण्डैकरूपः
तदेकोऽवशिष्टः शिवः केवलोऽहम् ॥ 5 ॥

The Supreme (Brahman) has no above, no concept of below, not inside, not outside, not middle, not across, not eastern or western direction, because of its all-pervading nature like ether. I am (Supreme) that which alone remains, the only One, the Auspicious one–the pure unconditioned Consciousness.

न शुक्लं न कृष्णं न रक्तं न पीतं
न कुब्जं न पीनं न ह्रस्वं न दीर्घम् ।
अरूपं तथा ज्योतिराकारकत्वात्
तदेकोऽवशिष्टः शिवः केवलोऽहम् ॥ 6 ॥

The Supreme (Brahman) is not white, not black, not red, not yellow, not small, not large, not short, not long, and being of the nature of effulgence, it is without form (not knowable by the physical characteristics). I am that (Supreme) which alone remains, the only One, the Auspicious one–the pure unconditioned Consciousness.

न शास्ता न शास्त्रं न शिष्यो न शिक्षा
न च त्वं न चाहं न चायं प्रपञ्चः ।
स्वरूपावबोधो विकल्पासहिष्णुः
तदेकोऽवशिष्टः शिवः केवलोऽहम् ॥ 7 ॥

There is neither the preceptor, nor the scripture, nor the disciple, nor the instruction, and there is neither you nor I and nor this universe. The knowledge (realisation) of one's real nature does not accept these different perceptions. I am that (Supreme) which alone remains, the only One, the Auspicious one–the pure unconditioned Consciousness.

न जाग्रन्न मे स्वप्नको वा सुषुप्तिः
न विश्वो न वा तैजसः प्राज्ञको वा ।
अविद्यात्मकत्वात्त्रयाणं तुरीयः
तदेकोऽवशिष्टः शिवः केवलोऽहम् ॥ 8 ॥

The three states of wakefulness, dream and deep sleep are not for me. *Vishva*, *taijasa* and *prājña* are also not for me. All these being states of ignorance, I am that 'Fourth' (beyond the three states). I am that (Supreme) which alone remains, the only One, the Auspicious one–the pure unconditioned Consciousness.

[The Self, identifying itself with the gross body, is called *vishva* (waker). The Self, identifying itself with the subtle body, is called *taijasa* (the dreamer). The Self, identifying itself with the causal body (in the deep sleep state), is called *prājña*.]

अपि व्यापकत्वाद्धितत्त्वप्रयोगात्
स्वतः सिद्धभावादनन्याश्रयत्वात् ।
जगत्तुच्छमेतत्समस्तं तदन्यत्
तदेकोऽवशिष्टः शिवः केवलोऽहम् ॥ 9 ॥

The Self is all-pervasive; It is the true ultimate goal (beatitude); It is self-existent and not dependent on anything else. But this entire universe, which is different from that (the Self), is trifling and empty (unreal). I am that which alone remains, the only One, the Auspicious one–the pure unconditioned Consciousness.

न चैकं तदन्यद्द्वितीयं कुतः स्यात्
न वा केवलत्वं न चाकेवलत्वम् ।
न शून्यं न चाशून्यमद्वैतकत्वात्
कथं सर्ववेदान्तसिद्धं ब्रवीमि ॥ 10 ॥

That (the Self) is not one. Then how can there be a second different from It (Self)? It is neither absoluteness (the state of being by itself) nor non-absoluteness. It is neither void nor non-void because it is non-dual (devoid of duality). How can I describe all that which is established by Vedanta (all the Upanishads)?

* * *

31

Manīṣā-panchakam
(मनीषापञ्चकम्)

The Conviction regarding Truth

The context: One day Adi Shankarāchārya was walking along with his disciples in Vārānasi. Just then, a person of a lower caste happened to approach him. Adi Shankarāchārya addressed him and said, "move away, move away". In response to this, that individual asked the Adi Shankarāchārya the following questions (in the first two verses below):

अन्नमयादन्नमयमथवा चैतन्यमेव चैतन्यात् ।
यतिवर दूरीकर्तुं वाञ्छसि किं ब्रूहि गच्छ गच्छेति ॥

O great ascetic! Please tell me. By saying "go away, go away", what is it you wish to make distant from yourself? Is this statement coming from one body (made of food and other material products) to another body? Or is it coming from one consciousness to another consciousness?

किं गङ्गाम्बुनि बिम्बितेऽम्बरमणौ चाण्डालवाटीपयः
पूरे वाऽन्तरमस्ति काञ्चनघटीमृत्कुम्भयोर्वाऽम्बरे ।
प्रत्यग्वस्तुनि निस्तरङ्गसहजानन्दावबोधाम्बुधौ
विप्रोऽयं श्वपचोऽयमित्यपि महान्कोऽयं विभेदभ्रमः ॥

Is there any difference between the reflection of the sun in the waters of the Ganges or a filthy body of water flowing through the slums? Or is there any difference in the reflection of the sun in the waters of a golden pot and a clay pot? What is this delusion of differentiation saying, "this is a *brāhmaṇa,* and this is a person of a lower caste"? Are they not simply reflections in the inmost Self, which is nothing but a natural wave-free ocean of knowledge-bliss?

The context (continued): *On hearing these questions from the individual, Adi Shankarāchārya realised that this person was no ordinary one and responded thus. The next five verses are his response.*

जाग्रत्स्वप्नसुषुप्तिषु स्फुटतरा या संविदुज्जृम्भते
या ब्रह्मादिपिपीलिकान्ततनुषु प्रोता जगत्साक्षिणी ।
सैवाहं न च दृश्यवस्त्विति दृढप्रज्ञापि यस्यास्ति चे-
च्चाण्डालोऽस्तु स तु द्विजोऽस्तु गुरुरित्येषा मनीषा मम ॥ 1 ॥

It is the Consciousness that shines distinctly in the three states of waking, dream and deep sleep, and it is the Consciousness which is the witness of the universe, pervading all the bodies of all creatures right from Brahmā (the creator) to an ant. If one has the established knowledge that he is that Consciousness and not an object of perception, then he is my guru, irrespective of whether he is an outcaste or a *brāhmaṇa*. This is my firm conviction.

ब्रह्मैवाहमिदं जगच्च सकलं चिन्मात्रविस्तारितं
सर्वं चैतदविद्यया त्रिगुणया शेषं मया कल्पितम् ।
इत्थं यस्य दृढा मतिः सुखतरे नित्ये परे निर्मले
चाण्डालोऽस्तु स तु द्विजोऽस्तु गुरुरित्येषा मनीषा मम ॥ 2 ॥

I am Brahman (the Supreme Reality) alone. It is consciousness alone that appears as this entire universe, fabricated by me because of the ignorance of the nature of the three *guṇas*. One who is thus firmly established in the blissful, eternal and pure Supreme, he is my guru, irrespective of whether he is a *chāndāla* (outcaste) or a *brāhmaṇa*. This is my firm conviction.

शश्वन्नश्वरमेव विश्वमखिलं निश्चित्य वाचा गुरो-
र्नित्यं ब्रह्म निरन्तरं विमृशता निर्व्याजशान्तात्मना ।
भूतं भावि च दुष्कृतं प्रदहता संविन्मये पावके
प्रारब्धाय समर्पितं स्ववपुरित्येषा मनीषा मम ॥ 3 ॥

Having established, by the instructions of the guru, that the entire universe is indeed forever perishable, one who meditates constantly upon the eternal Brahman with a pure and tranquil mind and who has completely destroyed the past and future sins in the fire of knowledge, such a one has handed over his/her body to *prārabdha-karma*. This is my firm conviction.

या तिर्यङ्नरदेवताभिरहमित्यन्तः स्फुटा गृह्यते
यद्भासा हृदयाक्षदेहविषया भान्ति स्वतोऽचेतनाः ।
तां भास्यैः पिहितार्कमण्डलनिभां स्फूर्तिं सदा भावय-
न्योगी निर्वृतमानसो हि गुरुरित्येषा मनीषा मम ॥ 4 ॥

It is the consciousness which is experienced clearly as "I" within, by the animals, humans and gods. It is in the effulgence of this consciousness that the insentient mind, senses and the body appear to be sentient. This Self is concealed by them (the mind, senses and body, which are illumined by the Self), just like the sun being hidden by the clouds. The tranquil-minded yogi who always meditates on this Self is indeed my guru. This is my firm conviction.

यत्सौख्याम्बुधिलेशलेशत इमे शक्रादयो निर्वृता
यच्चित्ते नितरां प्रशान्तकलने लब्ध्वा मुनिर्निर्वृतः ।
यस्मिन्नित्यसुखाम्बुधौ गलितधीर्ब्रह्मैव न ब्रह्मवि-
द्यः कश्चित्स सुरेन्द्रवन्दितपदो नूनं मनीषा मम ॥ 5 ॥

That ocean of bliss, attaining just a small fraction of which Indra and others attain fulfilment; having attained which, a sage with a tranquil mind attains fulfilment; in that ocean of eternal bliss, one whose mind has melted is Brahman indeed, not a knower of Brahman. Such a one, whosoever he may be, is one whose feet are fit to be worshipped by Lord Indra himself. This is certainly my firm conviction.

* * *

Section 6

This section presents selected verses from different texts that discuss some of the important ideas and concepts that form the foundation of Advaita Vedanta.

32

The Means to the Spiritual Goal

Note: The nine qualities described in this chapter are the means to attain the goal of liberation.

विवेकिनो विरक्तस्य शमादिगुणशालिनः ।
मुमुक्षोरेव हि ब्रह्मजिज्ञासायोग्यता मता ॥

One who possesses the faculty of discrimination between the real and the unreal (permanent and the impermanent), who is free from attachment, endowed with the qualities of equanimity, etc., and who is an aspirant of liberation, such a one is considered to be ready for inquiring into Brahman, the Supreme Reality. [VC 17]

ब्रह्म सत्यं जगन्मिथ्येत्येवंरूपो विनिश्चयः ।
सोऽयं नित्यानित्यवस्तुविवेकः समुदाहृतः ॥

A firm resolve of the nature of "Brahman alone is real, and the world is an illusion (unreal)" is called *viveka* or the faculty of discrimination between the Real and unreal. [VC 20]

तद्वैराग्यं जिहासा या दर्शनश्रवणादिभिः ।
देहादिब्रह्मपर्यन्ते ह्यनित्ये भोगवस्तुनि ॥

The indifference towards (or the desire to give up) all transient enjoyments from things heard, seen, etc.–ranging from the body up to the world of Brahmā (the creator)–is called *vairāgya* (detachment). [VC 21]

विरज्य विषयव्राताद्दोषदृष्ट्या मुहुर्मुहुः ।
स्वलक्ष्ये नियतावस्था मनसः शम उच्यते ॥

Constantly detaching the mind from the diverse variety of objects of the senses, having perceived their defects (the transient nature of the objects) and establishing the mind in one's goal (Brahman) is referred to as *shama* or control of the mind. [VC 22]

विषयेभ्यः परावर्त्य स्थापनं स्वस्वगोलके ।
उभयेषामिन्द्रियाणां स दमः परिकीर्तितः ।
बाह्यानालम्बनं वृत्तेरेषोपरतिरुत्तमा ॥

Withdrawing both the organs of perception (sense of hearing, touch, vision, taste and smell) and the organs of action (speech, hands, legs, anus and the genitals) from the sense objects of the world, and establishing them in their respective control centres is referred to as *dama* or self-control.

Restraining the mind-functions from depending on or seeking the external world of objects is referred to as *uparati* or desisting from seeking enjoyment from objects of the world. [VC 23]

सहनं सर्वदुःखानामप्रतीकारपूर्वकम् ।
चिन्ताविलापरहितं सा तितिक्षा निगद्यते ॥

Endurance of all afflictions without seeking any relief from them and at the same time without being tormented by the afflictions is referred to as *titikshā* or forbearance. [VC 24]

शास्त्रस्य गुरुवाक्यस्य सत्यबुद्ध्यवधारणम् ।
सा श्रद्धा कथिता सद्भिर्यया वस्तूपलभ्यते ॥

The faith and conviction in the ascertainment of the scriptures and of the guru's words as the truth is referred to as *shraddhā* by the wise, and it is that by which the spiritual goal (Brahman) is attained. [VC 25]

सर्वदा स्थापनं बुद्धेः शुद्धे ब्रह्मणि सर्वदा ।
तत्समाधानमित्युक्तं न तु चित्तस्य लालनम् ॥

The establishment of intelligence always in the pure Brahman (the Supreme Reality) is referred to as *samādhānā* or self-seatedness, and not indulgence of the mind and intelligence in other matters of the world. [VC 26]

अहङ्कारादिदेहान्तान् बन्धानज्ञानकल्पितान् ।
स्वस्वरूपावबोधेन मोक्तुमिच्छा मुमुक्षुता ॥

All bondages, right from the ego to (identification with) the body, are caused by ignorance (delusion or ignorance regarding one's true nature). The deep yearning to be free from all the bondages by realising the knowledge of one's true nature (i.e., Self) is called *mumukshutā* or 'yearning for liberation'. [VC 27]

* * *

33
Impermanence of the World

अनित्यं यौवनं बाल्यं शरीरं द्रव्यसंचयाः ।
भावाद्भावान्तरं यान्ति तरङ्गवदनारतम् ॥

Youth, childhood, the human body and the accumulation of material wealth are all transient. From one state of existence, they go to another state, like the waves continually changing states in an ocean. [YV 1.28.10]

पेलवं शरदीवाभ्रमस्नेह इव दीपकः ।
तरङ्गक इवालोलं गतमेवोपलक्ष्यते ॥

Life is tender and delicate, like a cloud in autumn. Life is like a lamp without oil. Life is unsteady, like the waves in the ocean. Like these, life appears to be passing by all the time and seen only as something gone. [YV 1.14.6]

बाल्यमल्पदिनैरेव यौवनश्रीस्ततो जरा ।
देहेऽपि नैकरूपत्वं कास्था बाह्येषु वस्तुषु ॥

Childhood is of a short duration. Thereafter the beauty and splendour of youth, too, is short-lived. Even the body does not have uniformity over time. Where is the question of any hope in the external objects of the world? [YV 1.28.37]

ऐश्वर्यं स्वप्नसंकाशं यौवनं कुसुमोपमम् ।
क्षणिकं जलमायुश्च तस्मात् जागृहि जागृहि ॥

Wealth is like a dream that vanishes on waking up. Youthfulness is like flowers, and it withers away. Life is unsteady like water, constantly flowing away. Therefore, Wake up! Wake up! [SUM]

रम्याश्चन्द्रमरीचयस्तृणवती रम्या वनान्तःस्थली
रम्यं साधुसमागमागतसुखं काव्येषु रम्याः कथाः ।
कोपोपाहितबाष्पबिन्दुतरलं रम्यं प्रियाया मुखं
सर्वं रम्यमनित्यतामुपगते चित्ते न किञ्चित्पुनः ॥

Cool rays of the moon are delightful; meadows in the inner regions of the forest are delightful; delightful is the joy from the gathering of wise persons; delightful are the fables in the poetic literature; and delightful are the glittering teardrops caused by passion on the face of the beloved. Everything is delightful. But, when there arises the realization of the transience of everything in the world, none of these is ever again delightful. [VS 79]

ब्रह्मेन्द्रादिमरुद्गणांस्तृणकणान्यत्र स्थितो मन्यते
यत्स्वादाद्विरसा भवन्ति विभवास्त्रैलोक्यराज्यादयः ।
भोगः कोऽपि स एक एव परमो नित्योदितो जृम्भते
भो साधो क्षणभङ्गुरे तदितरे भोगे रतिं मा कृथाः ॥

The realisation of the one Supreme ever-splendorous Brahman is the only experience that is permanent in this universe. Established in that Supreme, Brahmā, Indra and all other gods are rendered insignificant like a blade of grass. Also, established in that Supreme, the experience of all the glories and sovereignty of the kingship of the three worlds are insipid. O Noble one! Do not set your mind on the transient enjoyment of any other thing in this world. [VS 40]

* * *

34
The Mind

कामः सङ्कल्पो विचिकित्सा श्रद्धाऽश्रद्धा
धृतिरधृतिः ह्रीः धीः भीः इत्येतत्सर्वं मन एव ।

Desire, intention (purpose), doubt, *shraddhā*, *ashraddhā (non-shraddhā)*, resolve (steadiness), non-resolve, shame (modesty), thought and fear–all these are but the mind alone. [BU 1.5.3]

कामः क्रोधश्च लोभश्च मदो मोहश्च मत्सरः ।
न जिताः षडिमे येन तस्य शान्तिर्न सिध्यति ॥

Unless one conquers the six enemies of the mind in the form of desire, anger, greed, arrogance, delusion and jealousy, peace cannot be attained. [SVS 101]

नायं जनो मे सुखदुःखहेतुर्न देवतात्मा ग्रहकर्मकालाः ।
मनः परं कारणमामनन्ति संसारचक्रं परिवर्तयेद्यत् ॥

People are not the cause of my happiness and sorrow, nor are the gods, nor oneself, nor the planets, nor karma, and nor time. According to the wise: "the mind is the primary cause for the revolving wheel of *samsāra*". [SB 11.23.43]

मनो हि जगतां कर्तृ मनो हि पुरुषः परः ।
मनःकृतं कृतं लोके न शरीरकृतं कृतम् ॥

The mind indeed is the creator of the world. The mind indeed is the Supreme Being. That which is done by the mind is action and not that which is done by the body. [YV 3.89.1]

मनसैव कृतं पापं न शरीरकृतं कृतम् ।
येनैवालिङ्गिता कान्ता तेनैवालिङ्गिता सुता ॥

The sin committed by the mind is the real sin and not the act committed by the body. A man embraces his wife, and with the same body, he embraces his daughter, too. In both cases, it is the same body that performs the act of embracing. But still the two actions are different, for it is the mind which is performing the act. [SUM]

अहंकारवशादापदहंकाराद्दुराधयः ।
अहंकारवशादीहा त्वहंकारो ममामयः ॥

All misfortunes, calamities, anxieties and pains are the result of ego alone. It is under the control of the ego that we perform all activities. So, I consider ego to be a disease. [YV 1.15.3]

क्षणमानन्दितामेति क्षणमेति विषादिताम् ।
क्षणं सौम्यत्वमायाति सर्वस्मिन्नटवन्मनः ॥

One moment, the mind delights; then it becomes sorrowful (dejected) for a moment, and then again, it becomes gentle (benevolent) for a moment. In everything, the mind is like an actor (performing different roles). [YV 1.28.38]

पूर्णे मनसि सम्पूर्णं जगत्सर्वं सुधाद्रवैः ।
उपानद्गूढपादस्य ननु चर्मास्तृतैव भूः ॥

To the one who is wearing leather slippers, the entire earth feels as if a carpet has been spread over the earth. In the same manner, when the mind is content and full, the entire world appears nectarine. [YV 5.21.14]

समासक्तं यथा चित्तं जन्तोर्विषयगोचरे ।
यद्येवं ब्रह्मणि स्यात्तत्को न मुच्येत बन्धनात् ॥

The mind of the human being is completely dependent and attached to the objects of the senses. In the same manner, if the mind were committed and attached to Brahman, then that human can be free from any kind of bondage. [PD 11.115]

द्वैतभेदं चित्रभेदं जाग्रद्भेदं मनोमयम् ।
अहंभेदमिदंभेदमसदेव हि केवलम् ॥

Differences associated with duality, differences of manifoldness, and differences associated with the wakeful state are all of the mind alone. Differences associated with the notion of "I" and differences relating to what we refer to as "this" are all unreal. [RD 16.8]

* * *

35
The Self

पितृभुक्तान्नजात् वीर्याज्जातः अन्नेनैव वर्धते ।
देहः सोऽन्नमयो नात्मा प्राक् चोर्ध्वं तदभावतः ॥

The gross body, born of the food eaten by the parents, is born of virility. This body consists of food and also grows only by food. It is not the Self, for before birth and after death, this gross body does not exist. [PD 3.3]

नात्मा शरीरसम्बन्धी शरीरमपि नात्मनि ।
मिथो विलक्षणावेतौ प्रकाशतमसी यथा ॥

The Self has no relationship with the body. And there is no body in the Self. They are mutually distinct from each other, like light and darkness. [YV 6/1.6.6]

शब्दस्पर्शादयो वेद्या वैचित्र्याज्जागरे पृथक् ।
ततो विभक्ता तत्संविदैक्यरूप्यान्न भिद्यते ॥

The sense objects (associated with sound, touch, etc.) are perceived differently in the waking state because of their variety in characteristics. But the consciousness which is the witness to these is different from these objects and is one. [PD 1.3]

तथा स्वप्नेऽत्र वेद्यन्तु न स्थिरं जागरे स्थिरम् ।
तद्भेदोऽतस्तयोः संविदेकरूपा न भिद्यते ॥

In the same manner, in the case of the dream state, the objects that are experienced are transient, and in the waking state, they appear to be permanent. These two states seem to be different.

But the consciousness, that is but the same (one), does not change. [PD 1.4]

सुप्तोत्थितस्य सौषुप्ततमोबोधो भवेत्स्मृतिः ।
सा चावबुद्धविषयावबुद्धं तत्तदा ततः ॥

The one who wakes up from sleep remembers the ignorance (the absence of knowledge) during sleep. That remembrance indicates that the absence of knowledge is perceived. [PD 1.5]

स बोधो विषयाद्भिन्नो न बोधात्स्वप्नबोधवत् ।
एवं स्थानत्रयेऽप्येका संवित्तद्वद्दिनान्तरे ॥

That consciousness (in deep sleep) is different from ignorance (the absence of knowledge). But It is not different from the consciousness which is conscious of in the dream state. Thus, the consciousness is one and the same in all three states (waking, dream and sleep). It is the same on all the days. [PD 1.6]

मासाब्दायुगकल्पेषु गतागम्येष्वनेकधा ।
नोदेति नास्तमेत्येका संविदेषा स्वयम्प्रभा ॥

In the same manner, in the past and future, many months, years, ages (*yuga*) and *kalpa* (one thousand *yugas*), the consciousness does not get born and does not perish. It remains the same. It is of the nature of self-effulgence (self-luminous). [PD 1.7]

इयमात्मा परानन्दः परप्रेमास्पदं यतः ।
मा न भुवं हि भूयासमिति प्रेमात्मनीक्ष्यते ॥

This self-effulgent consciousness is nothing but the Self and is of the nature of supreme bliss. This is the object (or seat) of supreme love. This is the reason we experience feelings like "may I always be" and "may I never cease to exist". [PD 1.8]

तत्प्रेमात्मार्थमन्यत्र नैवमन्यार्थमात्मनि ।
अतस्तत्परमन्तेन परमानन्दतात्मनः ॥

All other objects of love (like the love of wealth, progeny, etc.) are also because of the love for the Self alone. But the love for the Self is not subordinate or dependent on the love for other objects. Therefore, the love for the Self is the greatest and is of the nature of supreme bliss. [PD 1.9]

यावत्सर्वं न संत्यक्तं तावदात्मा न लभ्यते ।
सर्ववस्तुपरित्यागे शेष आत्मेति कथ्यते ॥

Until everything is completely relinquished, the Self is not attained. When everything is renounced, what is left is called the Self. [YV 5.7.49]

शोकहर्षभयक्रोधलोभमोहस्पृहादयः ।
अहङ्कारस्य दृश्यन्ते जन्म मृत्युश्च नात्मनः ॥

Grief, joy, fear, anger, greed, delusion, desires, etc. and also birth and death are all experiences of *ahankāra* (ignorant sense of 'I'), and these do not belong to the Self. [SB 11.28.15]

अकार्यशेषमात्मानमक्रियात्मक्रियाफलम् ।
निर्ममं निरहंकारं यः पश्यति स पश्यति ॥

One truly sees, who sees the Self as actionless, with no association with either the action or the fruits of action, and as free from notions of 'me' and 'mine'. [US 14.22]

आत्मानमेव श्रोतव्यं आत्मानं श्रवणं भव ।
आत्मानं कामयेन्नित्यम् आत्मानं नित्यमर्चय ॥

The Self alone is worth hearing about. The Self alone should be heard (studied) and reflected upon. One should yearn for the Self always. Always worship the Self. [RG 13.33]

चित्तं नास्तीति चिन्ता स्यात् आत्ममात्रं प्रकाशते ।
चित्तमस्तीति चिन्ता चेत् चित्तत्वं स्वयमेव हि ॥

"There is no mind" – if one meditates thus, then the Self alone shines. "There is a mind". – if one thinks thus, then the Self itself becomes the mind-ness. [RG 18.16]

आत्मानं चेद्विजानीयादयमस्मीति पूरुषः ।
किमिच्छन्कस्य कामाय शरीरमनुसञ्ज्वरेत् ॥

If one realises the Self as "I am the Self", then desiring what or towards what aim will one be afflicted in the context of the body? [BU 4.4.12]

स होवाच न वा अरे पत्युः कामाय पतिः प्रियो भवत्यात्मनस्तु कामाय पतिः प्रियो भवति । ... न वा अरे देवानां कामाय देवाः प्रिया भवन्त्यात्मनस्तु कामाय देवाः प्रिया भवन्ति । ... आत्मा वा अरे द्रष्टव्यः श्रोतव्यो मन्तव्यो निदिध्यासितव्यो । मैत्रेय्यात्मनो वा अरे दर्शनेन श्रवणेन मत्या विज्ञानेनेदं सर्वं विदितम् ॥

He (Yājñavalkya) said: "It is not for the sake of the husband that he is dear (to the wife); it is for the sake of the Self that he is dear ... It is not for the sake of the gods that they are dear; it is for the sake of the Self that they are dear ... The Self should be heard of (from a preceptor); it should then be reflected upon and then should be meditated upon. By realising the Self through the process of listening, reflection and meditation, all this is known." [BU 2.4.5]

चिन्मात्रमेव शशिभृच्चिन्मात्रं गरुडेश्वरः ।
चिन्मात्रमेव तपनश्चिन्मात्रं कमलोद्भवः ॥

The one bearing the moon (Siva) is Consciousness alone; the Lord of Garuda (Vishnu) is Consciousness alone; the sun is Consciousness alone; and the one born of the lotus (Brahmā) is Consciousness alone. [YV 3.7.4]

* * *

36

Brahman (The Supreme Reality)

वदन्ति तत्तत्त्वविदस्तत्त्वं यज्ज्ञानमद्वयम् ।
ब्रह्मेति परमात्मेति भगवानिति शब्द्यते ॥

"That *tattvam* (Truth or Supreme Truth) is described by the Knowers of Truth as non-dual knowledge. It is also called Brahman, *Paramātmā* (the Universal Self) or Bhagavan (God)." [SB 1.2.11]

देहोऽहमिति यद्ज्ञानं तदेव नरकं स्मृतम् ।
कालत्रयेऽपि तन्नास्ति सर्वं ब्रह्मेति केवलम् ॥

The idea or understanding that "I am the body" is what is declared as 'hell'. In all three times (past, present and future), it is not so. Everything is Brahman alone. [RG 8.34]

नित्यानित्यवस्तुविवेकस्तावद् ब्रह्मैव नित्यं वस्तु
ततोऽन्यदखिलमनित्यमिति विवेचनम् ॥

Discrimination between the eternal and the transient consists of the investigation that Brahman alone is the eternal substance, and other than Brahman, the entire universe and its constituents are transient. [VSA 16]

देहबुद्ध्या तु दासोऽस्मि जीवबुद्ध्या त्वदंशकः ।
आत्मबुद्ध्या त्वमेवाहम् इति मे निश्चिता मतिः ॥

[Hanuman said to his Lord Rama] At the level of body-consciousness, I am your servant. At the level of consciousness as the *jīva*, I am a particle or fragment of you. And at the level of consciousness as the Self, I am you alone. This is my firm conviction. [SUM]

आत्मैकः सर्वभूतेषु तानि तस्मिंश्च खे यथा ।
पर्यगाद्व्योमवत् सर्वं शुक्रं दीप्तिमदिष्यते ॥

The one Self is in all beings. They (everything in this universe) are in That (Self), just as everything is in ether. Like in the case of ether, the Self, which is accepted to be pure and radiant, pervades everything in the universe. [US 15.9]

मातर्मेदिनि तात मारुत सखे तेजः सुबन्धो जल
भ्रातर्व्योम निबद्ध एव भवतामन्त्यः प्रणामाञ्जलिः ।
युष्मत्सङ्गवशोपजातसुकृतस्फारस्फुरन्निर्मल-
ज्ञानापास्तसमस्तमोहमहिमा लीये परब्रह्मणि ॥

O mother earth! O father wind! O friend fire! O good relative water! O brother sky! My respectful salutations with folded hands (palms together) to you for the last time. By means of the pure knowledge (of the Self) springing forth with abundant auspiciousness born out of the association with you all, I am free from all the delusion and vainglory. I now merge in the Supreme Brahman. [VS 100]

सर्वभूतेषु यः पश्येद्भगवद्भावमात्मनः ।
भूतानि भगवत्यात्मन्येष भागवतोत्तमः ॥

One who sees the Self in all the beings as the very nature of the Supreme and sees all the beings in the Supreme as the Self of all, such a one is the best among the devotees. [SB 11.2.45]

एको देवः सर्वभूतेषु गूढः
सर्वव्यापी सर्वभूतान्तरात्मा ।
कर्माध्यक्षः सर्वभूताधिवासः
साक्षी चेता केवलो निर्गुणश्च ॥

It is the one divinity that is abiding in all beings. He is all-pervading; He is the indwelling Self of all beings, the superintendent of all actions, the inhabitant in all beings. He is the witness, the Consciousness, the One Absolute, and devoid of the three *guṇas* (*sattva, rajas and tamas*). [SU 6.11]

दण्डन्यासः परं दानं कामत्यागस्तपः स्मृतम् ।
स्वभावविजयः शौर्यं सत्यं च समदर्शनम् ॥

The abandonment of punishment (power, control) of others (not harming others) is the greatest charity. The renunciation of sense enjoyments is considered the highest form of austerity. To win over one's own lower tendencies is true valour. And seeing the One Supreme in all beings is Truth. [SB 11.19.37]

***

37
Ignorance and Delusion

आत्मा प्रकाशकः स्वच्छो देहस्तामस उच्यते ।
तयोरैक्यं प्रपश्यन्ति किमज्ञानमतः परम् ॥

The Self is the illuminating one, and pure, whereas the body is affected by the quality of *tamas* (darkness, inertia and ignorance). Despite the distinct difference between the Self and the body, people see the two as one. If not this, what else is ignorance? [APR 20]

सर्पत्वेन यथा रज्जू रजतत्वेन शुक्तिका ।
विनिर्णीता विमूढेन देहत्वेन तथाऽऽत्मता ॥

Just as a piece of rope is mistakenly imagined to be a snake (in an ill-lit place), and an oyster shell is imagined to be silver, in the same manner, the Self is wrongly imagined to be the body by the ignorant one. [APR 70]

कनकं कुण्डलत्वेन तरङ्गत्वेन वै जलम् ।
विनिर्णीता विमूढेन देहत्वेन तथाऽऽत्मता ॥

Just as gold is imagined to be a ring or a bracelet, and water is imagined to be waves, in the same manner, the Self is wrongly imagined to be the body by the ignorant one. [APR 72]

मम माता मम पिता ममेयं गृहिणी गृहम् ।
एतदन्यं ममत्वं यत् स मोह इति कीर्त्तितः ॥

"My mother", "my father", "my house", "my wife"–this and such other forms of mine-ness are referred to as delusion. [PP]

देहापत्यकलत्रादिष्वात्मसैन्येष्वसत्स्वपि ।
तेषां प्रमत्तो निधनं पश्यन्नपि न पश्यति ॥

Even though one sees that everything around is transient and perishable, one fails to see their real perishable nature when faced with a situation. This is because of the delusion arising from attachment towards the body, children, spouse, oneself and other associations. [SB 2.1.4]

ते पराग्दर्शिनः प्रत्यक्तत्त्वबोधविवर्जिताः ।
कुर्वते कर्म भोगाय कर्म कर्तुं च भुञ्जते ॥

The ignorant see the external phenomenal world alone, for they are devoid of the knowledge of their own true nature (or identity). Therefore, they perform actions only aimed at the enjoyment of the fruits of their actions. [PD 1.29]

रज्जोस्तु तत्त्वमनवेक्ष्य गृहीतसर्प-
भावः पुमानयमहिर्वसतीति मोहात् ।
आक्रोशति प्रतिबिभेति च कम्पते त-
न्मिथ्यैव नात्र भुजगोऽस्ति विचार्यमाणे ॥

Not able to perceive the rope in an ill-lit place, one thinks, "there is a snake here". This is a result of delusion (or wrong perception). Thinking thus, he is scared, screams in a harsh language, and also trembles with fear. But when he does *vichāra* (investigation or enquiry), he realises that it is just a delusion and that there is no snake at all. [SVS 268]

तद्वत्त्वयाप्यात्मन उत्क्रमेत-
ज्जन्माप्ययव्याधिजराधिदुःखम् ।
मृषैव सर्वं भ्रमकल्पितं ते
सम्यग्विचार्यात्मनि मुञ्च भीतिम् ॥

You say that birth, death, disease, old age and grief all belong to you. But, in reality, they are all arising out of delusion alone and are your imaginations. Enquiring into the reality of it all, give up the fear of death. [SVS 269]

यदा तु सर्वभूतेषु दारुष्वग्निमिव स्थितम् ।
प्रतिचक्षीत मां लोको जह्यात्तर्ह्येव कश्मलम् ॥

When the seeker of liberation sees Me (the Supreme) as residing in all beings, like the fire that is abiding in wood, that very moment, the seeker will be free from delusion. [SB 3.9.32]

* * *

38

Samsāra (Worldly Existence)

का बुद्धिः कोऽयमाभासः को वात्मात्र जगत्कथम् ।
इत्यनिर्णयतो मोहः सोऽयं संसार इष्यते ॥

What is the nature of intellect? What is this reflected-consciousness? What is this Self? How did this world come about here? Because of the uncertainty regarding these questions, there is delusion (or wrong perception). This delusion is called *samsāra*. [PD 8.53]

इयं संसाररचना विचारोज्झितचेतसाम् ।
बालकाख्यायिकेवेत्थमवस्थितिमुपागता ॥

This fabrication of *samsāra* seems real for those whose intellect is devoid of contemplation (*vichāra*) on the Self, like in the case of a child who believes a narration to be real. [PD 13.27]

मनसो विजयान्नान्या गतिरस्ति भवार्णवे ।
महानरकसाम्राज्ये मत्तदुष्कृतवारणाः ।
आशाशरशलाकाढ्या दुर्जया हीन्द्रियारयः ॥

From this ocean of *samsāra*, there is no other way out except by conquering the mind. In this mighty dominion of hell, difficult to conquer are the following enemies–wicked deeds that are the mad elephants, sharp arrows of desires and enemies in the form of sense organs. [MAU 5.76]

विवेकं परमाश्रित्य बुद्ध्या सत्यमवेक्ष्य च ।
इन्द्रियारीनलं छित्त्वा तीर्णो भव भवार्णवात् ॥

Taking recourse to *viveka* (the faculty of discrimination between the real and unreal), perceiving the Supreme Truth by means of the intellect, and completely overcoming the enemies in the form of the sense organs, cross the ocean of *samsāra*. [MAU 5.84]

आयुः कल्लोललोलं कतिपयदिवसस्थायिनी यौवनश्री-
रर्थाः संकल्पकल्पा घनसमयतडिद्विभ्रमा भोगपूगाः ।
कण्ठाश्लेषोपगूढं तदपि च न चिरं यत्प्रियाभिः प्रणीतं
ब्रह्मण्यासक्तचित्ता भवत भवभयाम्बोधिपारं तरीतुम् ॥

Life is very unsteady like the waves in the ocean; beauty or glory of youth lasts only for some days; wealth, property and other such things are very transient like thought; the multitude of enjoyments are unsteady like the flashes of lightning during the rainy season; and even the intimate embrace around the neck offered by dear ones is not lasting. Therefore, in order to cross this ocean of worldly existence, become one whose mind is established in Brahman (the Supreme Reality). [VS 36]

यदि ते नेन्द्रियार्थश्रीः स्पन्दते हृदि वै द्विज ।
तदा विज्ञातविज्ञेया समुत्तीर्णो भवार्णवात् ॥

O wise one, if the glamour and attraction of the objects of the senses are not pulsating in (or charming) your heart, then having realised that which ought to be known (Self-knowledge), you will cross the ocean of *samsāra*. [MAU 5.174]

कुशला ब्रह्मवार्तायां वृत्तिहीनाः सुरागिणः ।
तेऽप्यज्ञानतया नूनं पुनरायान्ति यान्ति च ॥

Those who are skillful in scholarly discussions regarding Brahman and are passionately attached to the pleasures of the world but are devoid of direct realization of Brahman–they, because of their ignorance, are forever in *samsāra* (and are born again and again). [APR 133]

* * *

39

Māyā (Illusory Nature of the World)

स्पष्टं भाति जगच्चेदमशक्यं तन्निरूपणम् ।
मायामयं जगत्तस्मादीक्षस्वापक्षपाततः ॥

This world shines (is seen) very clearly, but it is impossible to define its nature. Therefore, being free from any bias, regard this entire world to be illusory (endowed with *māyā*). [PD 6.142]

मृगतृष्णां यथा बाला मन्यन्त उदकाशयम् ।
एवं वैकारिकीं मायामयुक्ता वस्तु चक्षते ॥

Just as children consider the mirage to be a place of water, in the same manner, the ignorant ones see permanence in the transitory (changeful) phenomena of the world. [SB 10.73.11]

अनुभूतोऽप्ययं लोको व्यवहारक्षमोऽपि सन् ।
असद्रूपो यथा स्वप्न उत्तरक्षणबाधतः ॥

Even though this phenomenal world is experienced by us and favourable for transactions and interactions, the entire phenomenon is unreal in nature. It is like a dream, as it is contradicted or proved fallacious the very next moment. [APR 56]

आपदः संपदः सर्वाः सुखं दुःखाय केवलम् ।
जीवितं मरणायैव बत मायाविजृम्भितम् ॥

All wealth and riches are calamities (misfortune); all pleasures are only for suffering; life is only for experiencing death. Alas! All these are manifestations of *māyā* alone. [YV 6/2.93.73]

यो माययेदं पुरुरूपयासृजद्-
बिभर्ति भूयः क्षपयत्यविक्रियः ।
यद्भेदबुद्धिः सदिवात्मदुःस्थया
तमात्मतन्त्रं भगवन् प्रतीमहि ॥

Being unchangeable and independent, the Lord (Brahman), by the power of *māyā*, creates, sustains and destroys this entire universe with manifold forms. Because of our ignorance, the perception of differentiation makes us perceive this entire manifestation as if it is real, different from the Lord. [SB 4.24.61]

मायामयत्वं भोग्यस्य बुद्ध्वाऽऽस्थामुपसंहरन् ।
भुञ्जानोऽपि न सङ्कल्पं कुरुते व्यसनं कुतः ॥

The wise one (who has realised the Truth) knows the illusory (unreal) nature of all enjoyment of desires. Though living in the world, the wise one withdraws (controls) the desires and ensures that no new desires arise in him. For such a one, where is the question of suffering or affliction? [PD 7.170]

* * *

40
Desires

पदं करोत्यलङ्घ्येऽपि तृप्तापि फलमीहते ।
चिरं तिष्ठति नैकत्र तृष्णा चपलमर्कटी ॥

Desire is an unsteady monkey (jumping here and there) that cannot stay in one place for a long time. Even though satiated (on fulfilment of a desire), it still wants to obtain fruits, even if it has to ascend to places not easily reachable. [YV 1.17.29]

न जातु कामः कामानामुपभोगेन शाम्यति ।
हविषा कृष्णवर्त्मेव भूय एव अभिवर्धते ॥

The desires of the mind are never fulfilled (satisfied) by the enjoyment of the desired objects. On the contrary, it is like the flame that is enhanced by the addition of clarified butter. [PD 7.147]

या दुस्त्यजा दुर्मतिभिर्जीर्यतो या न जीर्यते ।
तां तृष्णां दुःखनिवहां शर्मकामो द्रुतं त्यजेत् ॥

Desires that are the cause of all sorrows are difficult to forsake by the ignorant (and weak-minded). The desires do not fade away, even when the body decays in old age. Those who are desirous of happiness should quickly give up all these desires. [SB 9.19.16]

सर्वसंसारदोषाणां तृष्णैका दीर्घदुःखदा ।
अन्तःपुरस्थमपि या योजयत्यतिसंकटे ॥

Among all the deficiencies or evils of *samsāra*, desires are the ones which give afflictions that last a long time. These desires bring about difficult circumstances, even to the one living in the inner chambers of a palace. [YV 1.17.32]

कुटिला कोमलस्पर्शा विषवैषम्यशंसिनी ।
दशत्यपि मनाक्स्पृष्टा तृष्णा कृष्णेव भोगिनी ॥

Desires are crooked and bent like a serpent and soft to the touch. They result in the poison of misery even if slightly touched. [YV 1.17.17]

यदि रासीश मे कामान् वरांस्त्वं वरदर्षभ ।
कामानां हृद्यसंरोहं भवतस्तु वृणे वरम् ॥
इन्द्रियाणि मनः प्राण आत्मा धर्मो धृतिर्मतिः ।
ह्रीः श्रीस्तेजः स्मृतिः सत्यं यस्य नश्यन्ति जन्मना ॥
विमुञ्चति यदा कामान् मानवो मनसि स्थितान् ।
तर्ह्येव पुण्डरीकाक्ष भगवत्त्वाय कल्पते ॥

Prahlāda said to Lord Vishnu: O Lord! O most excellent among the boon-givers! If You do wish to bestow a boon, I humbly choose the boon 'that no desire for enjoyments shall arise in my heart.' Because of the birth of desires in the human being, the following are destroyed–the strength of the sense organs, the mind, the vital air (*prāṇa*, life forces), the body, dharma, will, understanding, modesty, prosperity, splendour, memory and truthfulness. O Lord, when the human gives up all desires of mind, then alone he/she becomes eligible for liberation. [SB 7.10.7-9]

भोगा न भुक्ता वयमेव भुक्ता-
स्तपो न तप्तं वयमेव तप्ताः ।
कालो न यातो वयमेव याता-
स्तृष्णा न जीर्णा वयमेव जीर्णाः ॥

The objects of enjoyment or worldly pleasures are not enjoyed, but we are the ones who are devoured by the objects of enjoyment. It is not the austerities that are endured, but we are the ones who are scorched. It is not time that passes, but it is we who pass away. It is not the desires that wither away but we who decay and perish. [VS 7]

तृणं ब्रह्मविदः स्वर्गस्तृणं शूरस्य जीवितम् ।
जिताक्षस्य तृणं नारी निःस्पृहस्य तृणं जगत् ॥

For the one who has realised Brahman, heaven is like a blade of grass. For the valorous, life is like a blade of grass. For one who has conquered the senses, the woman (the opposite gender) is like a blade of grass. And for the one who is free from desires, the entire world of objects is like a blade of grass. [CHN 6.14]

ईश्वरत्वेन किं तस्य ब्रह्मेन्द्रत्वेन वा पुनः ।
तृष्णा चेत् सर्वतश्छिन्ना सर्वदैन्योद्भवाऽशुभा ॥

If desires for the objects of the world, which are the cause of all afflictions, are completely destroyed, what is the use of sovereignty (supremacy) of everything in this universe? And then again, what is the use of attaining even the status of Brahmā (the Creator) or Indra? [US 14.28]

बहुनात्र किमुक्तेन संक्षेपादिदमुच्यते ।
संकल्पनं मनोबन्धस्तदभावो विमुक्तता ॥

What is the use of so much wordiness when all this can be succinctly expressed in just a few words, thus: "desire is the bondage of the mind, and the absence of desires is freedom." [YV 6/2.1.27]

असङ्कल्पाज्जयेत्कामं क्रोधं कामविवर्जनात् ।
अर्थानर्थेक्षया लोभं भयं तत्त्वावमर्शनात् ॥

One should conquer desires for sense enjoyments by sincerity and will. One should win over anger by giving up desires. One should win over greed by seeing the uselessness of money and wealth. And one should conquer fear by reflecting upon the truth. [SB 7.15.22]

* * *

41
Attachment and Detachment

यैस्तु चेतांसि रज्यन्ते जगत्त्रितयवर्त्तिनाम् ।
ते रागा इति कथ्यन्ते मुनिभिर्भरतादिभिः ॥

They are called attachments, by which the minds of human beings (lit., those who live in the three worlds) are delighted. This is according to Sages like Bharata and the like. [SUM]

ममेदमित्यसद्भूतमिन्द्रियार्थे भवन्मनः ।
मा निमज्जत्वमग्नः सन्मा करोतु करोतु वा ॥

"This is mine"–thinking thus, do not immerse your mind in the objects of the world, for these objects are unreal by nature. Being unattached, you may interact with them or not. [YV 4.46.18]

ॐ ईशावास्यमिदं सर्वं यत्किञ्च जगत्यां जगत् ।
तेन त्यक्तेन भुञ्जीथा मा गृधः कस्यस्विद्धनम् ॥

Om. All this–this universe of movable and immovable, sentient and insentient–is the dwelling of the Lord. By detachment, protect yourself from bondage in this world. Do not get attached to anybody's wealth, and do not covet another's wealth. [IU 1]

सङ्गी हि बाध्यते लोके निःसङ्गः सुखमश्नुते ।
तेन सङ्गः परित्याज्यः सर्वदा सुखमिच्छता ॥

The one attached to the objects of the world is the one who is distressed and miserable in this world. The one who is detached attains happiness. Therefore, anyone who is desirous of being happy in this world must always give up attachment. [PD 6.274]

काकस्यविष्ठावदसह्यबुद्धि-
भोंग्येषु सा तीव्रविरक्तिरिष्यते ।
विरक्तितीव्रत्वनिदानमाहु-
र्भोग्येषु दोषेक्षणमेव सन्तः ॥

The indifference in the sense objects, as if they are disgusting, like the excrement of a crow, is considered intense or complete *vairāgya* (detachment). The perception of defects in the objects of the world is the root cause of detachment, according to the wise. [Defects here refer to transience and the inability of the object to bestow happiness.] [SVS 24]

न ह्यङ्गाजातनिर्वेदो देहबन्धं जिहासति ।
यथा विज्ञानरहितो मनुजो ममतां नृप ॥

O King! Just as one who is ignorant of Self-knowledge does not abandon the sense of mineness (towards possessions), in the same manner, one in whom detachment has not arisen does not give up the attachment towards the body (identifying the Self with the body). [SB 11.8.29]

आत्मासङ्गस्ततोऽन्यत्स्यादिन्द्रजालं हि मायिकम् ।
इत्यचञ्चलनिर्णिते कुतो मनसि वासना ॥

The Self, by its very nature, is unattached. Everything other than the Self (the entire phenomenal universe, mind, intelligence, ego, etc.), being a display of *māyā*, is unreal and illusory. When there is a firm conviction thus, where is the question of desires appearing in the mind? [PD 9.104]

* * *

42
Action and Work

क्रियास्पन्दो जगत्यस्मिन्कर्मेति कथितो बुधैः ।
पूर्वं तस्य मनो देहं कर्मातश्चित्तमेव हि ॥

The vibration (or movement) or activity or performance is called *karma* (action) in this world by the wise. Firstly, the mind was its body (i.e., firstly, the action was born in the mind). Therefore, action is nothing but the mind. [YV 3.95.32]

कर्मणा बध्यते जन्तुर्विद्यया तु प्रमुच्यते ।
तस्मात्कर्म न कुर्वन्ति यतयः पारदर्शिनः ॥

The human being enters into bondage by means of action and is liberated by the knowledge of the Self. Therefore, the wise who have had the vision of the Supreme do not act [do not get attached to action). [MB 12.247.7]

पश्चात्तेषां स्वकर्माणि कारणं सुखदुःखयोः ।
आत्माज्ञानात्समुत्पन्नः संकल्पः कर्मकारणम् ॥

One's own actions are the cause of happiness and misery. The desire born out of ignorance regarding the knowledge of the Self is the cause for action. [YV 6/1.124.5]

संकल्पित्वं हि बन्धस्य कारणं तत्परित्यज ।
मोक्षस्तु निःसंकल्पित्वं तदभ्यासपरो भव ॥

The desire for action is indeed the cause of bondage in the world. Give up that desire. Moksha (or liberation, freedom) is, in fact, freedom from desires. Be dedicated to the practice of the renunciation of desires. [YV 6/1.124.6]

कर्माणि देहयोगार्थं देहयोगे प्रियाप्रिये ।
ध्रुवे स्यातां ततो रागो द्वेषश्चैव ततः क्रियाः ॥
धर्माधार्मौ ततोऽज्ञस्य देहयोगस्तथा पुनः ।
एवं नित्यप्रवृत्तोऽयं संसारश्चक्रवद्भृशम् ॥

Actions (work) are the cause of the association with the body (birth). In the association with the body, there are certainly pleasant and unpleasant experiences, and thus attachment and aversion are the result. And from them, follow actions, thereupon follow merits and demerits. And this again results in association with a body. Thus, this *samsāra* is continuously going on like a wheel forever. [US II.1.3-4]

कर्तव्यमस्ति न ममेह हि किंचिदेव
स्थातव्यमित्यतिमना भुवि संस्थितोऽस्मि ।
संशान्तया सततसुप्तधियेह वृत्त्या
कार्यं करोमि न च किंचिदहं करोमि ॥

In this world, I do not have any duties to perform with the aim of achieving something. "There is something that ought to be established through me"–having transcended this attitude or thinking of the mind, I live in this world. With the disposition of a thoroughly calmed mind (with a mind which is equipoised, transcending joy or grief in the event of favourable or unfavourable results) and with the mind and understanding always in a state which is free from duality (and free from the ideas of 'me' and 'mine'), I perform whatever comes my way in this world. I do all this while staying established in my actionless Self, knowing very well that even when I am apparently doing things, I do nothing (realising that there is no action possible at the level of the Self). [YV 2.10.44]

* * *

43
Happiness and Contentment

संतोषः परमो लाभः सत्सङ्गः परमा गतिः ।
विचारः परमं ज्ञानं शमो हि परमं सुखम् ॥

Contentment is the highest attainment. Company of the wise (those who have realised the Truth) is the greatest path to attaining the spiritual goal. Enquiry into one's true nature (the Self) is the highest wisdom. Restraint of the mind is the greatest happiness. [YV 2.16.19]

अकिञ्चनस्य दान्तस्य शान्तस्य समचेतसः ।
मया सन्तुष्टमनसः सर्वाः सुखमया दिशः ॥

Happiness is there for the one, everywhere and always, who is free from desires (literally, free from any possessions), who is self-restrained, who is tranquil, who is even-minded everywhere, and who is content in Me (the Supreme). [SB 11.14.13]

वयमिह परितुष्टा वल्कलैस्त्वं दुकूलैः
सम इव परितोषो निर्विशेषो विशेषः ।
स तु भवतु दरिद्रो यस्य तृष्णा विशाला
मनसि च परितुष्टे कोऽर्थवान्को दरिद्रः ॥

Here (living in a humble dwelling), we are satisfied with a garment made from the bark of a tree, and you are satisfied by a garment made of fine cloth (like silk). But the idea of contentment is the same in both cases. The external distinction (of the objects) makes no difference to the degree of contentment. He indeed is poor whose desires are extensive. If one is content in the mind, who is wealthy and who is poor! [VS 53]

नास्ति विद्यासमं चक्षुर्नास्ति सत्यसमं तपः ।
नास्ति रागसमं दुःखं नास्ति त्यागसमं सुखम् ॥

There is no eye (the sense of perception) like knowledge. There is no austerity like truthfulness. There is no suffering like attachment. And there is no happiness like sacrifice (renunciation of desires). [MB 12.174.35]

मैत्री-करुणा-मुदितोपेक्षाणां
सुखदुःख-पुण्यापुण्य-विषयाणां
भावनातः चित्त-प्रसादनम् ।

The attitude of friendliness towards the happy, compassion towards the unhappy, delight towards the good and being unbiased towards the bad leads to calmness in the mind. [PYS 1.33]

यदा ते नेन्द्रियार्थश्रीः स्वदते हृदि राघव ।
तदा विज्ञातविज्ञानः समुत्तीर्णभवार्णवः ॥

O Rama! When you come to realise that the objects of the world no longer cause any delight in your heart (i.e., you realise that happiness comes from within, independent of the objects), then you shall know that you have attained true knowledge. Then, you shall cross the ocean of *samsāra* with ease. [YV 4.46.19]

सदा सन्तुष्टमनसः सर्वाः सुखमया दिशः ।
शर्कराकण्टकादिभ्यो यथोपानत्पदः शिवम् ॥

For one who has slippers on the feet, even the path of pebbles, thorns, etc., is favourable and easy to walk on. In the same way, for one whose mind is content, there is happiness everywhere (in all directions). [SB 7.15.17]

सन्तुष्टस्य निरीहस्य स्वात्मारामस्य यत्सुखम् ।
कुतस्तत्कामलोभेन धावतोऽर्थेहया दिशः ॥

For one who is running in all directions with the aim of wealth acquisition and with the desires of objects of pleasure and enjoyment, where is the possibility of that happiness which is of a desireless person, who is content, and who delights in one's own Self. [SB 7.15.16]

कामस्यान्तं च क्षुत्तृड्भ्यां क्रोधस्यैतत्फलोदयात् ।
जनो याति न लोभस्य जित्वा भुक्त्वा दिशो भुवः ॥

The various needs of the body, by way of hunger and thirst, are met by food. Anger comes to an end by inflicting punishment on another and by the consequent reaction. But as far as greed is concerned, it does not end even after conquering all directions and enjoying everything on the earth. [SB 7.15.20]

* * *

44

Freedom from Suffering

जन्म दुःखं जरा दुःखं जाया दुःखं पुनः पुनः ।
संसारसागरं दुःखं तस्मात् जागृहि जागृहि ॥

The process of birth is one involving pain; old age is full of pain and suffering; marriage is replete with troubles and challenges. And the entire ocean of *samsāra* is full of suffering. Therefore, wake up! Wake up! [VD 2]

देहाभिमानिनो दुःखं नादेहस्य स्वभावतः ।
स्वापवत् तत्प्रहाणाय तत्त्वमित्युच्यते दृशेः ॥

Superimposition of Self with the body (i.e., identification of oneself as this body) is the cause of suffering. The suffering, by its nature, does not belong to the Self (which is devoid of the body). That is the reason, in deep sleep, one is free from suffering. [For, in deep sleep, one does not identify with the body.] Thus, the wise say, "You are That" (*tat-tvam-asi*) is the way to be free from identification with the body. ["You are That" is a statement from the Upanishads where 'That' refers to Brahman]. [US 12.5]

चित्तसत्तेह दुःखाय चित्तनाशः सुखाय च ।
चित्तसत्तं क्षयं नीत्वा चित्तं नाशमुपानयेत् ॥

The existence of the mind is the cause of sorrow; the dissolution of the mind is the cause of joy. Bringing about the attenuation of the mind, take it to its destruction. [ANU 4.15]

एतस्माद्विरमेन्द्रियार्थगहनादायासकादाश्रय
श्रेयोमार्गमशेषदुःखशमनव्यापारदक्षं क्षणात् ।
स्वात्मीभावमुपैहि संत्यज निजां कल्लोललोलां गतिं
मा भूयो भज भङ्गुरां भवरतिं चेतः प्रसीदाधुना ॥

O mind! Become detached from these dense, impervious forests of sense objects that cause sorrow and grief. Take refuge in the path of auspiciousness (beatitude) that is capable of removing all sorrows and sufferings in a moment. Attain your own real nature (realise your true Self), having renounced your ways that are fickle of the nature of unsteady waves. O mind! Do not again seek the transitory worldly enjoyments. Be happy now! [VS 63]

तावद्भयं द्रविणदेहसुहृन्निमित्तं
शोकः स्पृहा परिभवो विपुलश्च लोभः ।
तावन्ममे त्यसदवग्रह आर्तिमूलं
यावन्न तेऽङ्घ्रिमभयं प्रवृणीत लोकः ॥

The deluded sense of 'I' and 'mine' is the fundamental cause of all suffering, and as a result of the delusion (wrong perception), the human being experiences sorrow, greed and other unfavourable experiences. All these are the result of attachment to body, wealth, family, etc. The only way for a human to attain freedom from the sense of 'I', 'mine' and consequent suffering is to seek absolute refuge in the Supreme. [SB 3.9.6]

शारीरं मानसं दुःखं दैवं भूतभवं तथा ।
सर्वत्र समचित्तस्य तस्य मे जायते कुतः ॥

For me, who is even-minded everywhere, where is the question of afflictions arising from the following causes: body, mind, accidents, fate and other beings? [VP 1.19.8]

पुत्रदुःखं यथाध्यस्तं नित्यादुःखे स्व आत्मनि ।
अहंकर्त्रा तथाध्यस्तं पित्रादुःखे स्व आत्मनि ॥

The grief (or distress) of the child is superimposed on oneself by the parent, who has no grief at all. In the same manner, the ego is superimposed on the Self, which is forever free from grief and pain. [US 18.20]

इदं रम्यमिदं नेति बीजं ते दुःखसंततेः ।
तस्मिन्साम्याग्निना दग्धे दुःखस्यावसरः कुतः ॥

"This is pleasing, this is not"–these notions are the seed of your continuous sorrow. When these notions are burned by the fire of detachment towards both (what is pleasing and what is not), where is the possibility or occasion for sorrow? [ANU 5.70]

आन्वीक्षिक्या शोकमोहौ दम्भं महदुपासया ।
योगान्तरायान्मौनेन हिंसां कायाद्यनीहया ॥

Sorrow and delusion are to be overcome by discrimination between the Self and non-self (or real and unreal). Conceit (false pride) is to be overcome by offering service to noble and wise ones. Impediments or obstacles in the path of yoga are to be overcome by silence. And violence or injury may be overcome by cultivating detachment towards objects. [SB 7.15.23]

* * *

45
Fearlessness

अभयं सर्वभूतानां दानमाहुर्मनीषिणः ।
निजानन्दे स्पृहा नान्ये वैराग्यस्यावधिर्मता ॥

The wise ones say that bestowing fearlessness to all beings is the greatest charity. The desire or yearning for the bliss of one's own Self and the absence of desire in anything other than the Self is considered to be the pinnacle of *vairāgya* (detachment). [SAA 17]

स्वल्पमप्यन्तरं कृत्वा जीवात्मपरमात्मनोः ।
यः सन्तिष्ठति मूढात्मा भयं तस्याभिभाषितम् ॥

Even if a little distinction between the *jīvātmā* (the individual Self) and *paramātmā* (the Universal Self) is made, then that ignorant one shall be fear-stricken. It has been thus said in the Upanishads. [APR 52]

भोगे रोगभयं कुले च्युतिभयं वित्ते नृपालाद्भयं
माने दैन्यभयं बले रिपुभयं रूपे जराया भयम् ।
शास्त्रे वादिभयं गुणे खलभयं काये कृतान्ताद्भयं
सर्वं वस्तु भयान्वितं भुवि नृणां वैराग्यमेवाभयम् ॥

There is fear of disease in the enjoyment of sensual pleasures; there is fear of decline in the case of a lineage; there is fear of king in case of wealth and riches; there is fear of humiliation in the case of honour; there is fear of enemies in case of power; there is fear of old age in case of beauty; there is fear of wise disputant in case of learning; there is fear of the wicked in virtue;

and there is fear of death in the case of the body. All aspects of human life on earth are replete with fear. Only *vairāgya* (detachment) is fearlessness. [VS 31]

भयं यद्यभयं विद्धि अभयाद्भयमापतेत् ।
केवलं ब्रह्ममात्रत्वात् नास्त्यनात्मेति निश्चिनु ॥

If fearlessness exists, then know that fear exists. From (the notion of) fearlessness, fear is born. Because Brahman alone exists, be sure that non-Self does not exist. [RG 4.22]

यतो वाचो निवर्तन्ते । अप्राप्य मनसा सह ।
आनन्दं ब्रह्मणो विद्वान् । न बिभेति कुतश्चनेति ।

Words (speech) return along with the mind, without having reached Brahman. Having realised the bliss of that Brahman, the wise one does not fear anything. [TU 2.9.1]

यदा ह्येवैष एतस्मिन् अदृश्ये अनात्म्ये अनिरुक्ते अनिलयने अभयं प्रतिष्ठां विन्दते । अथ सोऽभयं गतो भवति । यदा ह्येवैष एतस्मिन्नुदरमन्तरं कुरुते । अथ तस्य भयं भवति । तत्वेव भयं विदुषोऽमन्वानस्य ।

When the Individual Self becomes established in the invisible, bodiless, indescribable and supportless Brahman, he becomes established in the state of fearlessness. Even if there is a slightest deviation in the oneness with Brahman, then he becomes afraid. Even if a person is wise, if he is not given to reflection (on the Supreme), then there is fear. [TU 2.7.1]

सोऽबिभेत् तस्मादेकाकी बिभेति । स हायमीक्षां चक्रे यन्मदन्यन्नास्ति कस्मान्नु बिभेमीति । तत एवास्य भयं वीयाय । कस्माद्ध्यभेष्यत् ? द्वितीयाद्वै भयं भवति ॥

He became afraid. Therefore, when one is alone, one is stricken by fear. He ruminated upon the following: "If there is nothing else other than myself, who or what am I afraid of?" Just by that alone, his fear was gone. For what is there to be afraid of? Fear comes only from a second entity. [BU 1.4.2]

यो बिम्बभूत आनन्दः स आत्मानन्दलक्षणः ।
शाश्वतो निर्द्वयः पूर्णो नित्य एकोऽपि निर्भयः ॥

That reflected happiness (which we feel from the objects of the world) is, in reality, of the nature of the bliss of the Self. That bliss of the Self is ever-lasting, non-dual, full, unchanging, one and free from fear. [SVS 655]

व्रतानि मिथ्या भुवनानि मिथ्या
भावादि मिथ्या भवनानि मिथ्या ।
भयं च मिथ्या भरणादि मिथ्या
भुक्तं च मिथ्या बहुबन्धमिथ्या ॥

Austerities are an illusion; the worlds are an illusion; the different states or conditions are an illusion; the mansions are an illusion; fear is an illusion; the various supports are an illusion; the experiences are an illusion; and the many attachments are an illusion. [RG 6.1]

देहोऽयमिति सङ्कल्पस्तदेव भयमुच्यते ।
कालत्रयेऽपि तन्नास्ति सर्वं ब्रह्मेति केवलम् ॥

The notion that "This (Self) is body" (superimposition of the body on the Self) itself is said to be fear. In all three periods of time (wakefulness, dream and deep sleep), it (the body notion) is not so. Everything is Brahman alone. [RG 8.30]

चित्तमेव महामाया चित्तमेव शरीरकम् ।
चित्तमेव भयं देहः चित्तमेव मनोमयम् ॥

The mind indeed is the great illusion. The mind alone is the one that creates the notion of the body. Mind alone is the fear of the body. Mind indeed is full with thought. [RG 18.12]

ब्रह्मैवं भेदरहितं भेदमेव महद्भयम् ।
आत्मैवाहं निर्मलोऽहमात्मैव भुवनत्रयम् ॥

Brahman is indeed devoid of any distinction; any distinction is great fear. I am the Self alone. I am pure. The Self alone is the three worlds. [RG 22.24]

अविचारो जगद्दुःखं अविचारो महद्भयम् ।
सद्योऽस्मि सर्वदा तृप्तः परिपूर्णः परो महान् ॥

The absence of enquiry (into the truth about one's own real nature) leads to suffering in the world; the absence of enquiry leads to great fear. Know that "I am content now and always; I am ever-full; I am the Supreme". [RG 35.9]

आत्मज्ञानं चित्तनाशः आत्मज्ञानं विमुक्तिदम् ।
आत्मज्ञानं भयनाशमात्मज्ञानं सुखावहम् ॥

Knowledge of the Self is the destruction of the mind; knowledge of the Self is the bestower of liberation; knowledge of the Self is the destroyer of fear; knowledge of the Self is the producer of happiness. [RG 36.18]

* * *

46
Freedom from Anger

त्रिविधं नरकस्येदं द्वारं नाशनमात्मनः ।
कामः क्रोधस्तथा लोभस्तस्मादेतत्त्रयं त्यजेत् ॥

Three-fold are the gates to hell–desire, anger and greed–that lead to the destruction of the Self. Therefore, these three should be shunned. [BG 16.21]

कामो बुद्धावुदेति प्रथममिह मनस्युद्दिशत्यर्थजातं
तत् गृह्णातीन्द्रियास्यैः तदनधिगमतः क्रोध आविर्भवेच्च ।
प्राप्तावर्थस्य संरक्षणमतिरुदितो लोभ एतत्त्रयं स्यात्
सर्वेषां पातहेतुस्तदिह मतिमता त्याज्यमध्यात्मयोगात् ॥

At first, the mind aims its attention towards the sense objects of the world. In the mind, then arises the desire to acquire the object. Then, the mind experiences that object through the sense organs. If it does not get the desired object, then anger arises. Once the object is acquired, then there is a desire to protect (or augment) the object and thus, arises greed. These three (desire, anger and greed) are the cause of the downfall (in the spiritual path) of all. Therefore, these three should be given up by the wise by means of Self-enquiry. [SS 18]

कामः क्रोधश्च लोभश्च मदो मोहश्च मत्सरः ।
न जिताः षडिमे येन तस्य शान्तिर्न सिध्यति ॥

One who has not conquered the six enemies of the mind, viz, desire, anger, greed, pride, delusion and jealousy, can never attain tranquility. [SVS 101]

काम एष क्रोध एष रजोगुणसमुद्भवः ।
महाशनो महापाप्मा विद्ध्येनमिह वैरिणम् ॥

This desire and this anger are born of *rajas*. These two are all-consuming and are great sins. Know them to be the enemies in this world. [BG 3.37]

कामक्रोधादयः शान्तिदान्त्याद्या लिङ्गदेहगाः ।
ज्वराद्वयेऽपि बाधन्ते प्राप्त्याप्राप्त्या नरं क्रमात् ॥

Desire, anger, etc., and calmness, mental and sensory restraint, etc., are of the subtle body. The affectations from both, i.e., the presence of the former (desires, anger, etc.) and the absence of the latter (calmness, etc.) cause misery to the human being. [PD 7.224]

शोकहर्षभयक्रोधलोभमोहस्पृहादयः ।
अहङ्कारस्य दृश्यन्ते जन्म मृत्युश्च नात्मनः ॥

Grief, joy, fear, anger, greed, delusion, desire, etc., as well as birth and death, are nothing but experiences that are a result of the 'I-sense' (*ahankāra*) and not of the Self. [SB 11.28.15]

कामक्रोधौ लोभमोहौ मदो मात्सर्यमेव हि ।
द्वैतदोषं भयं शोकं सर्वं नास्त्येव सर्वदा ॥

Desire and anger, greed and delusion, pride, envy (jealousy), fear and sorrow–all these are defects of duality and are always non-existent. [RG 30.42]

अहं ब्रह्मास्म्यहं मन्त्रः कामदोषं विनाशयेत् ।
अहं ब्रह्मास्म्यहं मन्त्रः क्रोधदोषं विनाशयेत् ॥

The mantra, "I am Brahman", destroys the disease of desires. The mantra, "I am Brahman", destroys the disease of anger. [RG 9.53]

ब्रह्मभावनया कामः नाशमेति न संशयः ।
ब्रह्मभावनया क्रोधः नाशमेति न संशयः ॥

By meditating upon Brahman, desires are destroyed. There is no doubt regarding this. By meditating upon Brahman, anger is destroyed. There is no doubt regarding this. [RG 39.16]

न मे देहः कदाचिद्वा न मे प्राणादयः क्वचित् ।
न मे माया न मे कामो न मे क्रोधः परोऽस्म्यहम् ॥

This body is never mine; the five vital airs (*prāṇa*, etc.) are not mine; the illusion (*māyā*) is not mine; the desires are not mine; and the anger is not mine. I transcend all these. [TJU 4.8]

नाहं योगी नो वियोगी न रागी
नाहं क्रोधी नैव कामी न लोभी ।
नाहं बद्धो नापि युक्तो न मुक्तः
साक्षी नित्यः प्रत्यगेवाहमस्मि ॥

I am not a yogi (one in pursuit of a system of philosophy), and I am not the opposite of that. I am not passionate, and I am not one who is angry. I am not desireful, and I am not greedy. I am not bound; I am not attached; I am not free. I am forever the witness, the inmost Consciousness. [SVS 839]

* * *

47

Bondage and Liberation

मन एव मनुष्याणां कारणं बन्धमोक्षयोः ।
बन्धाय विषयासक्तं मुक्त्यै निर्विषयं स्मृतम् ॥

Mind alone is the cause of the bondage and liberation of all humans. Attachment to sense objects leads to bondage; freedom from attachment to the sense objects is said to be liberation. [PD 11.117]

आशया बध्यते लोके कर्मणा बहुचिन्तया ।
आयुः क्षीणं न जानाति तस्मात् जागृहि जागृहि ॥

You are in a state of constant bondage in this world–bound by desires and expectations, actions and many anxieties. And thus, with all these fetters, you do not realise that life is ebbing away. Therefore, wake up! Wake up! [VD 1]

अत्रैकं पौरुषं यत्नं वर्जयित्वेतरा गतिः ।
सर्वदुःखक्षयप्राप्तौ न काचिदुपपद्यते ॥

Only truthful self-effort is the means, and nothing else, for attaining complete freedom (liberation) from all miseries in human life. [YV 3.6.14]

नित्यानित्यविवेकश्च देहक्षणिकतामतिः ।
मृत्योर्भीतिश्च तापश्च मुमुक्षावृद्धिकारणम् ॥

For a seeker of liberation, discrimination between the eternal and transient, the understanding that the body is transitory, the fear of death and the afflictions in life, are all the means to increase the aspiration for liberation. [SVS 248]

जाग्रत्स्वप्नसुषुप्त्यादि प्रपञ्चं यत्प्रकाशते ।
तद्ब्रह्माहमिति ज्ञात्वा सर्वबन्धैः प्रमुच्यते ॥

It is Brahman that illumines the entire universe of wakeful, dream and sleep states. When one realises that "I am that Brahman", then he is liberated from all bondages. [PD 7.213]

अद्वयानन्दरूपस्य सद्वयत्वं च दुःखिता ।
बन्धः प्रोक्तः स्वरूपेण स्थितिर्मुक्तिरितीर्यते ॥

The duality and sorrow in the context of the Self, which is non-dual and is of the nature of bliss, is called bondage. Being established in one's own nature (the Self) is called liberation. [PD 10.4]

अविचारकृतो बन्धो विचारेण निवर्तते ।
तस्माज्जीवपरात्मानौ सर्वदैव विचारयेत् ॥

Absence of *vichāra* (enquiry) into one's own real nature is bondage. And by means of *vichāra*, that bondage ceases to exist. Therefore, one should always enquire into the Individual Self and the Universal Self. [PD 10.5]

समासक्तं यथा चित्तं जन्तोर्विषयगोचरे ।
यद्येवं ब्रह्मणि स्यात्तत्को न मुच्येत बन्धनात् ॥

Just as the mind can focus on (literally, attached to) the objects of the world, in the same manner, if man were to focus the mind on Brahman, then what bondage is there that he cannot be freed from? [PD 11.115]

यस्त्वासक्तमतिर्गेहे पुत्रवित्तैषणातुरः ।
स्त्रैणः कृपणधीर्मूढो ममाहमिति बध्यते ॥

One who is attached to home (family), who is worried with thoughts of desires relating to son, wealth, and women, and who is feeble-minded is bound by the sense of 'I' and 'mine'. [SB 11.17.56]

भारोऽविवेकिनः शास्त्रं भारो ज्ञानं च रागिणः ।
अशान्तस्य मनो भारः भारोऽनात्मविदो वपुः ॥

Scriptures are a burden to one who does not have the faculty of discrimination between the real and unreal. Knowledge is a burden to one who is attached. The mind is a burden to one who is not peaceful. The body is a burden to one who has not realised the Self. [YV 1.14.13]

* * *

48

Death and Immortality

Note: Instructions from Sage Shuka to King Parikshit from Srimad Bhāgavatam, Canto 12, Chapter 5.

त्वं तु राजन्मरिष्येति पशुबुद्धिमिमां जहि ।
न जातः प्रागभूतोऽद्य देहवत्त्वं न नङ्क्ष्यसि ॥

O King, you must abandon the idea that "I will die", which is that of an animal. You are not like the body, which previously was non-existent and now has been born. You will not be destroyed. [SB 12.05.2]

न भविष्यसि भूत्वा त्वं पुत्रपौत्रादिरूपवान् ।
बीजाङ्कुरवद्देहादेर्व्यतिरिक्तो यथानलः ॥

You will not come into being in the form of a son, grandson or others like the sprout coming from the seed. You are different from the body and its parts, like the fire which is distinct from the fuel (though it is always seen together with wood or any other fuel). [SB 12.05.3]

स्वप्ने यथा शिरश्छेदं पञ्चत्वाद्यात्मनः स्वयम् ।
यस्मात्पश्यति देहस्य तत आत्मा ह्यजोऽमरः ॥

As in a dream, just as we see (or witness) the cutting of one's own head, similar is the death of the body composed of the five gross elements, etc. Therefore, the Self is indeed unborn and immortal. [SB 12.05.4]

घटे भिन्ने घटाकाश आकाशः स्याद्यथा पुरा ।
एवं देहे मृते जीवो ब्रह्म सम्पद्यते पुनः ॥

When an earthen pot is broken, the sky (space) enclosed by the earthen pot remains as the sky as it was before and joins the sky outside (the universal one). In the same manner, on the death of the body, the individual Self unites with Brahman (the Universal Self) again. [SB 12.05.5]

मनः सृजति वै देहान्गुणान्कर्माणि चात्मनः ।
तन्मनः सृजते माया ततो जीवस्य संसृतिः ॥

It is indeed the mind that creates material bodies, organs of sense and actions, qualities, etc., which are nothing but limiting adjuncts of the Self. *Māyā*, the inscrutable power to create subjective existence, creates that mind. And from this *māyā* proceeds the successive states of existence (transmigration, i.e., cycle of birth and death) of the individual Self (the *jīva*). [SB 12.05.6]

स्नेहाधिष्ठानवर्त्यग्निसंयोगो यावदीयते ।
तावद्दीपस्य दीपत्वमेवं देहकृतो भवः ।
रजःसत्त्वतमोवृत्त्या जायतेऽथ विनश्यति ॥

The status of being a lamp is maintained so long as the combination of oil, the base vessel, wick and fire is maintained. Similarly, it is due to the actions born out of *rajas*, *sattva* and *tamas* that *samsāra* (the worldly existence of the body) arises and is destroyed. [SB 12.05.7]

न तत्रात्मा स्वयञ्ज्योतिर्यो व्यक्ताव्यक्तयोः परः ।
आकाश इव चाधारो ध्रुवोऽनन्तोपमस्ततः ॥

No, there is neither destruction (at the level of the Self) nor is there a birth. The Self is self-effulgent and is beyond what is gross or subtle. Like the *ākāsha* (sky), it is the changeless substratum of everything, boundless and beyond comparison. [SB 12.05.8]

एवमात्मानमात्मस्थमात्मनैवामृश प्रभो ।
बुद्ध्यानुमानगर्भिण्या वासुदेवानुचिन्तया ॥

O King (referring to King Parikshit), by means of the discriminative intelligence pregnant with inference and by meditating upon Lord Vāsudeva, reflect upon the Self–which is situated within oneself–by oneself. [SB 12.05.9] .

अहं ब्रह्म परं धाम ब्रह्माहं परमं पदम् ।
एवं समीक्ष्य चात्मानमात्मन्याधाय निष्कले ॥
दशन्तं तक्षकं पादे लेलिहानं विषाननैः ।
न द्रक्ष्यसि शरीरं च विश्वं च पृथगात्मनः ॥

"I am Brahman, the Supreme Abode", "I am Brahman, the ultimate destination"–thus having investigated and contemplated closely and having placed the individual Self in the Universal undivided Self (practising the union of Individual Self and Universal Self), you will not even notice the serpent Takshaka, frequently licking or darting out the tongue approaching you with the mouth filled with poison and biting you in the foot. This is because you will have realised that this body and this manifested world (including the serpent and the biting) are different from your Self (which is nothing but Brahman). [SB 12.05.11-12]

* * *

49
Self-enquiry

विचारात्तीक्ष्णतामेत्य धीः पश्यति परं पदम् ।
दीर्घसंसाररोगस्य विचारो हि महौषधम् ॥

When the intellect (understanding) is sharpened by enquiry, then alone, one realises the supreme abode. For the serious disease of *samsāra*, enquiry alone is the great medicine. [YV 2.14.2]

अतोऽतुच्छमनायासमनुपाधि गतभ्रमम् ।
किं तत्स्थितिपदं साधो यत्र शोको न विद्यते ॥

Rāma's enquiry to Sage Vasishtha: O Sage! What is that state of constancy and stability in life which is non-trifling, easy to attain, free from limitations, devoid of any delusion and, above all, where there is no sorrow at all? [YV 1.30.11]

नोत्पद्यते विना ज्ञानं विचारेणान्यसाधनैः ।
यथा पदार्थभानं हि प्रकाशेन विना क्वचित् ॥

By *vichāra* alone, and not by any other means, is knowledge (Self-knowledge) attained. Just as without light, perception of any object is not possible at any time. [APR 11]

कोऽहं कथमिदं जातं को वै कर्ताऽस्य विद्यते ।
उपादानं किमस्तीह विचारः सोऽयमीदृशः ॥

Who am I? How was this world created? Who is the creator of this (creation)? What is the material used to create all this? This is how *vichāra* is to be done. [APR 12]

नाहं भूतगणो देहो नाहं चाक्षगणस्तथा ।
एतद्विलक्षणः कश्चिद्विचारः सोऽयमीदृशः ॥

I am not the body, a combination of five gross elements. I am not an aggregate of the senses. I am something other than these. This is the way of that enquiry. [APR 13]

अज्ञानप्रभवं सर्वं ज्ञानेन प्रविलीयते ।
संकल्पो विविधः कर्ता विचारः सोऽयमीदृशः ॥

Everything is a result of ignorance and dissolves when knowledge of the Self arises. The various thoughts must be the 'creator' of the entire world of experiences. This is the way of that enquiry. [APR 14]

एतोयर्यदुपादानमेकं सूक्ष्मं सदव्ययम् ।
यथैव मृद्घटादीनं विचारः सोऽयमीदृशः ॥

The material cause of ignorance and thoughts is the one (non-dual), subtle, unchanging Consciousness (*sat*). This is similar to clay being the material cause of pots and other such items. This is the way of that enquiry. [APR 15]

अहमेकोऽपि सूक्ष्मश्च ज्ञाता साक्षी सदव्ययः ।
तदहं नात्र संदेहो विचारः सोऽयमीदृशः ॥

I am the one, the subtle, the knower, the witness and the unchanging Consciousness (*sat*). There is no doubt regarding "I am That". This is the way of that enquiry. [APR 16]

कोऽहं कथमिदं चेति संसारमलमाततम् ।
प्रविचार्यं प्रयत्नेन प्राज्ञेन सहसाधुना ॥

"Who am I?" and "How did this blemish of *samsāra* emerge?" One should regularly practise enquiry into these questions with the wise. [MAU 4.21]

कालेन परिपच्यन्ते कृषिगर्भादयो यथा ।
तद्वदात्मविचारोऽपि शनैः कालेन पच्यते ॥

Just as a seed matures in the field and in the womb with the passage of time, in the same manner, self-enquiry (*ātma-vichāra*) also matures gradually in due course of time. [PD 9.37]

गच्छतस्तिष्ठतो वापि जाग्रतः स्वपतोऽपि वा ।
न विचारपरं चेतो यस्यासौ मृत एव सः ॥

While moving about in this world or while staying still in a place, while awake or lying down, if the mind is not engaged in reflecting upon the Truth, then such a one is dead indeed. [YV 5.93.15]

* * *

50
Meditation

दुःसाध्यं च दुराराध्यं दुष्प्रेक्ष्यं च दुराश्रयम् ।
दुर्लक्ष्यं दुस्तरं ध्यानं मुनीनां च मनीषिणाम् ॥
जिताहारो जितक्रोधो जितसङ्गो जितेंद्रियः ।
निर्द्वन्द्वो निरहङ्कारो निराशीरपरिग्रहः ॥

Even for those who are wise and for those who are contemplative, meditation is difficult to accomplish, difficult to overcome, difficult to conceive, difficult to practise, a difficult goal and difficult to conquer. To be successful in meditation, one should overcome desires for food, conquer anger, attachment and the temptations of the senses, be free from the pairs of opposites (like happiness and sorrow, success and failure, etc.), be free from egoism, be free from desires and be free from (attachment to) possessions. [TEJ 2-3]

अशून्ये शून्यभावं च शून्यातीतमवस्थितम् ।
न ध्यानं न च वा ध्याता न ध्येयो ध्येय एव च ॥

It (Brahman) is not void; It is mistakenly considered to be of the nature of void (non-existing). It is beyond void and firmly established (for It is the whole). It is neither the process of meditation, nor the meditator, nor the meditated upon. Yet, it is to be meditated upon. [TEJ 10]

निरोधलाभे पुंसोऽन्तरसङ्गं वस्तु शिष्यते ।
पुनः पुनर्वासितेऽस्मिन्वाक्याज्जायेत तत्त्वधीः ॥

Through meditation on Brahman, the complete destruction of the distinction between the meditator and the meditated upon takes place. Then, the Self–the unattached entity within–alone remains. By repeated meditation, by means of statements like '*tat-tvam-asi*' (You are That), the truth ("I am Brahman") is firmly established. [PD 9.127]

उपेक्ष्य तत्तीर्थयात्रां जपादीनेव कुर्वताम् ।
पिण्डं समुत्सृज्य करं लेढीति न्याय आपतेत् ॥

Abandoning spiritual practices like meditation (upon Brahman), one who indulges in pilgrimages, repetition of names (*japa*), etc., it is as if he is 'throwing away the sweetmeat and licking his hands'. [PD 9.130]

यथागाधनिधेःलब्धौ नोपायः खननं विना ।
मल्लभेऽपि तथा स्वात्मचिन्तां मुक्त्वा न चापरः ॥

(As if the Self itself is saying this to us): Just as the treasures hidden in the earth cannot be retrieved without extensive digging, in the same manner, to realise me, there is no other way but to practice deep meditation upon the Self. [PD 9.153]

देहाभिमानं विध्वस्य ध्यानादात्मानमद्वयम् ।
पश्यन्मर्त्योऽमृतो भूत्वा ह्यत्र ब्रह्म समश्नुते ॥

Abandoning the identification of the Self with the body by means of meditation (upon Brahman) and realising the non-dual Self, the mortal (the human), becoming immortal, attains Brahman here (in this world itself). [PD 9.157]

ध्यातृध्याने परित्यज्य क्रमाद्ध्येयैकगोचरम् ।
निर्वातदीपवच्चित्तं समाधिरभिधीयते ॥

In meditation, normally, there is the one who meditates, the act of meditation and the one meditated upon. When one gives up the idea of meditator and the act of meditation and becomes one with the object of meditation, that state is called *samādhi*, which is like the flame of the lamp in a breezeless condition. [PD 1.55]

अहं ब्रह्मास्मि मन्त्रोऽयं मृत्युपाशं विनाशयेत् ।
अहं ब्रह्मास्मि मन्त्रोऽयं द्वैतदुःखं विनाशयेत् ॥

The mantra "*aham brahmāsmi*" ("I am Brahman") destroys the noose or fetter of death. The mantra "*aham brahmāsmi*" ("I am Brahman") destroys the sorrow associated with duality. [TJU 3.62]

* * *

51
Self-knowledge

आत्मज्ञानं विदुर्ज्ञानं ज्ञानान्यन्यानि यानि तु ।
तानि ज्ञानावभासानि सारस्याऽनवबोधनात् ॥

According to the wise, knowledge of the Self alone is knowledge. All other forms of knowledge are false and are merely knowledge in appearance, because they do not result in the perception of the Truth. [YV 6-2.21.7]

ज्ञानादेव तु कैवल्यमिति श्रुत्या निगद्यते ।
ज्ञानस्य मुक्तिहेतुत्वमन्यव्यावृत्तिपूर्वकम् ॥

"By knowledge of the Self alone, one attains final beatitude (liberation)"–it is thus said in the Vedas. By negating all other means, knowledge as the means to liberation is described. [SVS 170]

संसारोत्तरणे जन्तोरुपायो ज्ञानमेव हि ।
तपो दानं तथा तीर्थमनुपायाः प्रकीर्तिताः ॥

For human beings, Self-knowledge is the only means to cross the ocean of *samsāra*. Austerity, charity and visiting places of pilgrimage are not considered to be means to cross *samsāra*. [YV 2.10.22]

शीतवातातपादीनि द्वन्द्वदुःखानि राघव ।
ज्ञानशक्तिं विना केन सह्यतां यान्ति साधुषु ॥

Knowledge of the Self alone is the means by which the wise forbear the difficulties and find *samatva* (sameness) in the pairs of opposites (like heat and cold, favourable and unfavourable) in this world. [YV 2.11.39]

किं वेदैः स्मृतिभिः पुराणपठनैः शास्त्रैर्महाविस्तरैः
स्वर्गग्रामकुटीनिवासफलदैः कर्मक्रियाविभ्रमैः ।
मुक्त्वैकं भवदुःखभाररचनाविध्वंसकालानलं
स्वात्मानन्दपदप्रवेशकलनं शेषैर्वणिग्वृत्तिभिः ॥

What is to be gained by the study of Vedas, *smritis*, *purāṇas* and other scriptures? What is the use of whirling about with various rites and ceremonies prescribed in the Vedas that bestow results like a residential cottage in heaven? All these are like the transactions of traders, meaning they are mere activities. Being free from all these, resort to that One, which is the means to attain the abode of the bliss of the Self, which is the fire of knowledge that destroys the heavy burden of the sorrow of worldly existence. [VS 71]

सर्वेषामपि चैतेषामात्मज्ञानं परं स्मृतम् ।
तध्यग्र्यं सर्वविद्यानां प्राप्यते ह्यमृतं ततः ॥

Among all the forms of knowledge, Self-knowledge is said to be the most supreme. It is the foremost because, as a result of this, one attains immortality. [MS 12.85]

करोतु भुवने राज्यं विशत्वम्भोदमम्बु वा ।
नात्मलाभादृते जन्तुर्विश्रान्तिमधिगच्छति ॥

While one may rule over the entire earth or the other worlds, the human being does not attain peace of mind except through the realisation of the Self. [YV 4.57.34]

प्राज्ञं विज्ञातविज्ञेयं सम्यग्दर्शनमाधयः ।
न दहन्ति वनं वर्षासिक्तमग्निशिखा इव ॥

Afflictions of the mind do not affect the wise one who has realised what is to be known and has the right understanding (*viveka*) to assess everything (as real or unreal) in this world, just as the fire does not burn the forest wetted by rain. [YV 2.11.41]

तिलेषु तैलं दधनीव सर्पिरापः स्रोतःस्वरणीषु चाग्निः ।
एवमात्माऽत्मनि गृह्यतेऽसौ सत्येनैनं तपसा योऽनुपश्यति ॥

Just as oil is hidden in the sesamum seeds, clarified butter in curd, water in the flowing currents and fire in firewood, so is the Self within. One who seeks this (the Self) through truthfulness and austerity (one-pointedness of the mind) realises the Self. [SU 1.15] .

निर्वाणं नाम परमं सुखं येन पुनर्जनः ।
न जायते न म्रियते तज्ज्ञानादेव लभ्यते ॥

The supreme happiness called *nirvāṇa* (liberation) is attained only through knowledge of the Self. Once *nirvāṇa* is attained, there is no birth or death after the death of the body. [YV 2.10.21]

मुक्तिस्तु ब्रह्मतत्त्वस्य ज्ञानादेव न चान्यथा ।
स्वप्रबोधं विना नैव स्वस्वप्नं हीयते यथा ॥

Just as the dream state does not end until and unless we wake up, in the same manner, liberation, that is realisation of the oneness of the Self with Brahman, is not attained through anything but knowledge. [PD 6.210]

मय्येव सकलं जातं मयि सर्वं प्रतिष्ठितम् ।
मयि सर्वं लयं याति तद्ब्रह्माद्वयमस्म्यहम् ॥

In me, everything is born; in me, alone, everything exists; in me, everything attains its dissolution. I am that non-dual Brahman. [KAI 19]

अहं ब्रह्मास्म्यहं मन्त्रः दृष्टादृष्टं विनाशयेत् ।
अहं ब्रह्मास्म्यहं मन्त्र आत्मज्ञानप्रकाशकम् ॥

The mantra “I am Brahman” destroys all seen and unseen. The mantra “I am Brahman” enlightens one with the knowledge of the Self. [RG 9.58]

***

52
Advaita
(Non-duality)

सर्वत्र सन्तोषसुखासनोऽसि
सर्वत्र विद्वेषविवर्जितोऽसि ।
सर्वत्र कार्यादिविवर्जितोऽसि
ब्रह्मासि पूर्णोऽसि परावरोऽसि ॥

You are forever blissfully established in the seat of contentment. You are forever devoid of hatred. You are forever free from activity, etc. You are Brahman. You are Full, Complete. You are all-embracing. [RG 5.8]

सर्वोऽसि सर्वहीनोऽसि शान्तोऽसि परमो ह्यसि ।
कारणं त्वं प्रशान्तोऽसि त्वं ब्रह्मासि न संशयः ॥

You are everything. You are devoid of everything. You are peaceful. You are verily the Supreme. You are the cause of everything in this universe. You are actionless. You are Brahman. There is no doubt regarding this. [RG 5.14]

स्वस्मिन् सुखे स्वयं चासि स्वस्मात् किञ्चिन्न पश्यसि ।
स्वात्मन्याकाशवद्भासि त्वं ब्रह्मासि न संशयः ॥

You are established in the bliss of your own Self. You do not perceive anything besides yourself. You shine like the space within your Self. You are Brahman. There is no doubt regarding this. [RG 5.24]

कर्ता नास्ति क्रिया नास्ति करणं नास्ति पुत्रक ।
केवलं ब्रह्ममात्रत्वात् नास्ति नास्त्येव सर्वदा ॥

There is no doer (performer). There is no action. There is no instrument of action. Brahman, being the Only one, all these are forever void. [RG 5.33]

श्रवणं मननं नास्ति निदिध्यासनविभ्रमः ।
केवलं ब्रह्ममात्रत्वात् नास्ति नास्त्येव सर्वदा ॥

There is no listening to (or study of) scriptures. There is no reflection or introspection. There is no meditation. There is no delusion. Brahman, being the Only one, all these are forever void. [RG 5.35]

गङ्गा गया तथा सेतुर्व्रतं वा नान्यदस्ति हि ।
केवलं ब्रह्ममात्रत्वात् नास्ति नास्त्येव सर्वदा ॥

There is no Ganga; there is no Gayā; and there is no Rameshwaram (literally *setu*, Rama's bridge). There is no austerity or other such things. Brahman, being the Only one, all these are forever void. [RG 5.40]

इह नास्ति परं नास्ति न गुरुर्न च शिष्यकः ।
सदसन्नास्ति भूर्नास्ति कार्यं नास्ति कृतं च न ॥

There is no concept of 'here' (this world). There is no 'hereafter' (life after, heaven, etc.). There is no guru and there is no disciple. There is no concept of real and unreal. There is no existence, duty (things to be done) and there are no performed actions (accomplishments). All these are void. [RG 5.43]

नित्यपूर्णस्वरूपोऽस्मि सच्चिदानन्दमस्म्यहम् ।
केवलाद्वैतरूपोऽहमहं ब्रह्मास्मि केवलम् ॥

I am of the nature of ever-completeness (ever-fullness). I am Existence-Consciousness-Bliss (*sat-chit-ānanda*). I am of the nature of non-duality alone. I am Brahman alone. [RG 4.39]

न बोधरूपं बोध्यं वा बोधकं नात्र यद्भ्रमः ।
न बाध्यं बाधकं मिथ्या त्रिपुटीज्ञाननिर्णयः ॥

There is nothing by way of instruction; there is nothing to be instructed; there is no instructor. All this is illusory. There is nothing to be restrained (suppressed); there is none to restrain (suppress). All this is illusory. There is no affirmation by way of the triad of knowledge (knowledge, knower and knowing). [RG 26.33]

सर्वं चैतन्यमात्रत्वात् केवलं ब्रह्म एव सः ।
आत्माकारमिदं सर्वमात्मनोऽन्यन्न किञ्चन ॥

Everything being Consciousness, there is Brahman alone. All this (the phenomenal world) is of the form of the Self alone. There is nothing besides the Self. [RG 38.29]

अस्मद्रूपसमाविष्टः स्वात्मनात्मनिवारणे ।
शिवः करोतु निजया नमः शक्त्या ततात्मने ॥

Let Siva (the Auspicious One), who is verily my own nature, having entered me of His own volition, offer salutations through His own effort, to His own Nature, when He Himself hinders the realisation of His own Self. (Worshipper and the obstacles, for which this worship is offered, are both Siva Himself.) [SID 1.1]

यत्र हि द्वैतमिव भवति तदितर इतरं पश्यति तदितर इतरं जिघ्रति तदितर इतरं रसयते तदितर इतरमभिवदति तदितर इतरं शृणोति तदितर इतरं मनुते तदितर इतरं स्पृशति तदितर इतरं विजानाति ।

When there is duality, then one sees another, smells another, tastes another, speaks of another, hears another, thinks of another, touches another and knows something else. [BU 4.5.15]

यत्र त्वस्य सर्वमात्मैवाभूत् तत्केन कं पश्येत् तत्केन कं जिघ्रेत् तत्केन कं रसयेत् तत्केन कमभिवदेत् तत्केन कं शृणुयात् तत्केन कं मन्वीत तत्केन कं स्पृशेत् तत्केन कं विजानीयात् ?

But when everything is nothing other than the Self, then what shall one see and through what, what shall one smell and through what, what shall one taste and through what, what shall one speak and by what, what shall one hear and through what, what shall one think and through what, what shall one touch and through what? [BU 4.5.15]

येनेदं सर्वं विजानाति तं केन विजानीयात् ? स एष नेति नेत्याऽऽत्मा अगृह्यो न हि गृह्यते अशीर्यो न हि शीर्यते असङ्गो न हि सज्यते असितो न व्यथते न रिष्यति ।

Through what shall one know That (Self) by which all this is known? This Self is That which has been described as "not this, not this". It is incomprehensible (imperceptible), for it cannot be comprehended (perceived). It is indestructible (undecaying), for it does not decay. It is unattached, for it is never attached to anything. It cannot be restrained (bound). It is never agitated or disturbed. It is never injured. [BU 4.5.15]

***

53

Tattvamasi (Thou art That)

Note: The Mahāvākya, तत्त्वमसि appears in the Chāndogya Upanishad (6.8.7). The Upanishadic statement says, "You, the (Individual Self), are nothing but the Universal Self". The following verses are from Tattvamasi Pañcakam.

निस्तमसि नीरजसि निर्गलितसत्वे
तेजसि विवेकजुषि भेदमतिशून्ये ।
निर्वचनमानसपदातिगमचिन्त्यं
तत्त्वमसि तत्त्वमसि तत्त्वमसि राजन् ॥ 1 ॥

O King! That which is beyond the three *guṇas*, That which is of the nature of spiritual essence dwelling in true knowledge, That which is free from the perception of distinctions, That which is the abode that is beyond interpretation and imagination, and That which is incomprehensible, Thou art That. Thou art That. Thou art That.

यज्जनितमेतदखिलं जगदनित्यं
स्वप्नजगदभ्रगजवारिवनतुल्यं ।
अप्रमित मूर्तिरहितं परसुखं यत्
तत्त्वमसि तत्त्वमसि तत्त्वमसि राजन् ॥ 2 ॥

That from which is born this entire universe, That which is transient like the world in a dream, like an elephant seen in the cloud and like a forest seen in the waters, That which is unbounded and not established by authority, That which is devoid of material form or embodiment, and That which is of the nature of supreme happiness, O King! Thou art That, Thou art That, Thou art That!

देहगुणजालमतिलीलमतिलोलं
येन लसितं भवति धीपुरशतञ्च ।
अद्वयमनन्तकमपारमतिसूक्ष्मं
तत्त्वमसि तत्त्वमसि तत्त्वमसि राजन् ॥ 3 ॥

That presence by which this web of the body and sense organs becomes manifested, and appears sportful and transient, That which is beyond the purview of the intelligence, That which is non-dual, eternal, unbounded and extremely subtle, O King! Thou art That, Thou art That, Thou art That!

कोशमयपञ्चकमिदञ्च सविकारं
यत्र वियदादि विमलस्फुरितमेतत् ।
अस्ति न कदाचिदपि रज्जुवदनन्तं
तत्त्वमसि तत्त्वमसि तत्त्वमसि राजन् ॥ 4 ॥

That which is enveloped by five sheaths (the food sheath, the vital air sheath, the mental sheath, the knowledge sheath and the bliss sheath), That in which the elements like ether, etc., with all their modifications, appear, That which is pure brilliance, That which is not like the rope (superimposed as a snake) and That which is eternal, O King! Thou art That, Thou art That, Thou art That!

भेदमतिजातमवधूतमनुभूतं
येन विदितं ततं परात्परसुखं च ।
तद्भवति सोहमिति यच्छ्रुतिषु चोक्तं
तत्त्वमसि तत्त्वमसि तत्त्वमसि राजन् ॥ 5 ॥

That by which everything is pervaded, knowing which the mendicant transcends duality, which when experienced as "I am That", results in Supreme Bliss, and That which is spoken of in the Vedas (Upanishads), O King! Thou art That, Thou art That, Thou art That!

***

54

The Knower of Truth

द्वैतावज्ञा सुस्थिता चेदद्वैते धीः स्थिरा भवेत् ।
स्थैर्ये तस्याः पुमानेष जीवन्मुक्त इतीर्यते ॥

When the notion of duality is ignored, the intellect becomes firm and unwavering in the notion of non-duality. Such a one who is thus steadfast and unwavering in the notion of non-duality is called a *jīvan-mukta* (liberated while living). [PD 2.102]

यस्य नेच्छा न वानिच्छा ज्ञस्य कर्मणि तिष्ठतः ।
न तस्य लिप्यते प्रज्ञा पद्मपत्रमिवाम्बुभिः ॥

The wise one, doing whatever is supposed to be done, neither desires anything nor wishes to abandon anything. Because of the absence of desires, the wisdom of this wise one is untainted, just as the lotus is not smeared by the water droplets. [YV 4.46.16]

अयं बन्धुरयं नेति गणना लघुचेतसाम् ।
उदारचरितानां तु वसुधैव कुटुम्बकम् ॥

"This is my relative", "this is not"–such is the reckoning of those who are small-minded. But for the wise ones (the ones who have realised the Self), the entire world itself is a family. [MAU 6.71]

आनन्दं ब्रह्मणो विद्वान्न बिभेति कुतश्चन ।
एतमेव तपेन्नैषा चिन्ता कर्माग्निसम्भृता ॥

The wise one, who has experienced the bliss of Brahman, never fears anything in this world. Also, any thoughts relating to merit or demerit born out of the fire called action do not torment or affect the wise one. [PD 11.5]

कौपीनं शतखण्डजर्जरतरं कन्था पुनस्तादृशी
नैश्चिन्त्यं निरपेक्षभैक्षमशनं निद्रा श्मशाने वने ।
स्वातन्त्र्येण निरङ्कुशं विहरणं स्वान्तं प्रशान्तं सदा
स्थैर्यं योगमहोत्सवेऽपि च यदि त्रैलोक्यराज्येन किम् ॥

If one has a loin cloth torn in numerous places and has a patched garment (wrapped around the body) again in the same condition, if he is free from anxiety, if food is available obtained unexpectedly by begging, if he is able to sleep in a cremation ground or a forest, if he wanders freely by his own free will, if he is tranquil within, and if he is established in the festivity of the union with the Supreme, then what is the use of even the kingdom of the three worlds! [VS 91]

प्राप्तकर्मकरो नित्यं शत्रुमित्रसमानदृक् ।
ईहितानीहितैर्मुक्तो न शोचति न काङ्क्षति ॥

One who performs the actions that providence (chance) brings, who always looks upon friends and enemies alike, and who is free from likes and dislikes, such a one is free from grief and longing. [MAU 6.64]

देहन्यासो हि संन्यासो नैव काषायवाससा ।
नाहं देहोऽहमात्मेति निश्चयो न्यासलक्षणम् ॥

Renunciation of the body (i.e., renunciation of the desires) alone is *sannyāsa* (renunciation), not adorning the robe dyed in ochre. "I am not the body, but I am the Self"–this conviction is the true character of *sannyāsa* (renunciation). [SAA 16]

अक्षरत्वाद्वरेण्यत्वाद्धूतसंसारबन्धनात् ।
तत्त्वमस्यादिलक्ष्यत्वादवधूत इतीर्यते ॥

One is called AVADHŪTA because his real nature is immutable or imperishable (***A**-kshara*); he is excellent (***VA**-renya*); he has shattered all the bondages and attachments regarding the world (***DHU**-ta-samsāra-bandhana*), and he characterises the message of the cardinal statements like ***TA**-ttvamasi* ("You are That"). [AVU 2]

त्यज धर्ममधर्मं च उभे सत्यानृते त्यज ।
उभे सत्यानृते त्यक्त्वा येन त्यजसि तत्त्यज ॥

Renounce *dharma* and *adharma*; renounce truth and falsehood. Then, renounce that by which you have renounced truth and falsehood. [SNU 2.17]

नारायणोऽहं नरकान्तकोऽहं
पुरान्तकोऽहं पुरुषोऽहमीशः ।
अखण्डबोधोऽहमशेषसाक्षी
निरीश्वरोऽहं निरहं च निर्ममः ॥

I am Nārāyaṇa; I am the destroyer of the daemon Naraka. I am Siva, the destroyer of the cities of daemon Tripura. I am the Supreme Being. I am the unfragmented awareness. I am the infinite (unbounded) Witness. I am the most Supreme (without someone who is my lord). I am free from 'I' and 'mine'. [KDU 23]

सर्वात्मकोऽहं सर्वोऽहं सर्वातीतोऽहमद्वयः ।
केवलाखण्डबोधोऽहं स्वानन्दोऽहं निरन्तरः ॥

I am the Self of all (the Universal Self). I am everything. I transcend all. I am non-dual, without a second. I am the one indivisible Existence (Awareness). I am the bliss of my Self. I am undivided (without parts). [KDU 32]

आत्मवत्सर्वभूतेषु यः समत्वेन पश्यति ।
सुखं दुःखं विवेकेन तस्य चित्तं प्रसीदति ॥

The one who, through *viveka* (discrimination), sees happiness and sorrow in all beings with equanimity, as in one's own case, then the mind of such a one attains tranquility. [SVS 366]

निराशता निर्भयता नित्यता समता ज्ञता ।
निरीहता निष्क्रियता सौम्यता निर्विकल्पता ॥
धृतिर्मैत्री मनस्तुष्टिर्मृदुता मृदुभाषिता ।
हेयोपादेयनिर्मुक्ते ज्ञे तिष्ठन्त्यपवासनम् ॥

Desirelessness, fearlessness, constantly dwelling in the Truth, equanimity, knowledge of the Self, freedom from attachment, actionlessness (free from desires to act), gentleness, complete freedom from doubt, resoluteness, friendliness, contentment of the mind, tenderness and softspokenness–these are the qualities of the Knower of the Truth, who is free from desires and who is free from notions of acceptance and rejection. [YV 5.13.28-29]

***

55

Transcendence

Note: These verses are from Śukāṣṭakam. This is a composition of Sage Śuka, the son of Sage Vyāsa. This version has been taken from the book Subhāshita-Ratna-Bhandāgāra, which is a collection of over 10,000 verses.

भेदाभेदौ सपदि गलितौ पुण्यपापे विशीर्णे
मायामोहौ क्षयमुपगतौ नष्टसंदेहवृत्तेः ।
शब्दातीतं त्रिगुणरहितं प्राप्य तत्त्वावबोधं
निस्त्रैगुण्ये पथि विचरतः को विधिः को निषेधः ॥ 1 ॥

For one who has realised the Supreme Reality, which is beyond words and is devoid of the three *guṇas*, the sense of distinction and identity is instantly destroyed, the idea of virtue and vice is shattered, the idea of *māyā* and delusion falls, and all doubtful dispositions disappear. For such a one who wanders in the path beyond the three *guṇas*, where is the question of any injunctions or prohibitions?

यद्वात्मानं सकलवपुषामेकमन्तर्बहिःस्थं
दृष्ट्वा पूर्णं खमिव सततं सर्वभाण्डस्थमेकम् ।
नान्यत्कार्यं किमपि च ततः कारणाद्भिन्नरूपं
निस्त्रैगुण्ये पथि विचरतः को विधिः को निषेधः ॥ 2 ॥

Having realised the all-wonderful non-dual Self, residing inside and outside, that is always full like space, residing in all the bodies, which has no other cause, and because of which all different forms exist–for one who wanders in the path beyond the three *guṇas*, where is the question of any injunctions or prohibitions?

हेम्नः कार्यं हुतवहगतं हेममेवेति यद्वत्
क्षीरे क्षीरं समरसगतं तोयमेवाम्बुमध्ये।
एवं सर्वं समरसतया त्वंपदं तत्पदार्थे
निस्त्रैगुण्ये पथि विचरतः को विधिः को निषेधः ॥ 3 ॥

A product made of gold, on entering fire, results only in gold; milk being added to milk becomes milk alone; water being added to water becomes water. In the same manner, on account of the sameness of attributes, the Individual Self is nothing but that Supreme Reality. Thus, for one who wanders in the path beyond the three *guṇas*, where is the question of any injunctions or prohibitions?

यस्मिन्विश्वं सकलभुवनं सामरस्यैकभूतं
उर्वी ह्यापोऽनलमनिलखं जीवमेवं क्रमेण।
यत्क्षाराब्धौ समरसतया सैन्धवैकत्वभूतं
निस्त्रैगुण्ये पथि विचरतः को विधिः को निषेधः ॥ 4 ॥

Just as salt in the ocean attains to the ocean-ness, owing to the sameness in attributes (saltiness), in the same manner, the entire universe, including the worlds, earth, water, fire, wind, space and living beings are one with the Supreme Reality (or Brahman). For one who wanders in the path beyond the three *guṇas*, where is the question of any injunctions or prohibitions?

यद्वन्नद्योदधिसमरसौ सागरत्वं ह्यवाप्तौ
तद्वज्जीवालयपरिगतौ सामरस्यैकभूतौ।
भेदातीतं परिलयगतं सच्चिदानन्दरूपं
निस्त्रैगुण्ये पथि विचरतः को विधिः को निषेधः ॥ 5 ॥

After having merged into the ocean, the river becomes the same as the ocean since the river and the ocean have the same essential substance. In the same manner, going beyond the body, being of the same essence, the individual self is one with the Universal Self. Transcending any distinctions and transcending death, it is verily of the nature of Existence-Consciousness-Bliss (*sat-chit-ānanda*). For one who wanders in the path beyond the three *guṇas*, where is the question of any injunctions or prohibitions?

दृष्ट्वा वेद्यं परमथपदं स्वात्मबोधस्वरूपं
बुद्ध्वात्मानं सकलवपुषामेकमन्तर्बहिःस्थम् ।
भूत्वा नित्यं सदुदिततया स्वप्रकाशस्वरूपं
निस्त्रैगुण्ये पथि विचरतः को विधिः को निषेधः ॥ 6 ॥

Having realised the Supreme abode which is to be known and is of the nature of Self-knowledge, and having realised the One Self seated inside and outside of all embodied beings–thus forever attaining the self-effulgent nature as a result of the dawning of the Supreme Truth–for such a one who wanders in the path beyond the three *guṇas*, where is the question of any injunctions or prohibitions?

कार्याकार्ये किमपि सततं नैव कर्तृत्वमस्ति
जीवन्मुक्तस्थितिरवगतो दग्धवस्त्रावभासः ।
एवं देहे प्रविलयगते तिष्ठमानो विमुक्तो
निस्त्रैगुण्ये पथि विचरतः को विधिः को निषेधः ॥ 7 ॥

In action and inaction, there is certainly no sense of doership. Having realised the state of *jīvanmukti* (liberation while still living), one gives an appearance of scorched or tattered clothes (unmindful of external appearance). Thus, having attained complete dissolution, seated in a body, for the one who is liberated, who wanders in the path beyond the three *guṇas*, where is the question of any injunctions or prohibitions?

कस्मात्कोऽहं किमपि च भवान्कोऽयमत्र प्रपञ्चः
स्वं स्वं वेद्यं गगनसदृशं पूर्णतत्त्वप्रकाशम् ।
आनन्दाख्यं समरसघने बाह्यमन्तर्विहीने
निस्त्रैगुण्ये पथि विचरतः को विधिः को निषेधः ॥ 8 ॥

What or where have I come from? Who am I? Who are you? What is this visible phenomenon here? That which is to be known, that which resembles the sky, which is the effulgence of the fullness of Supreme Reality, and which is called *ānanda*, is the unchanging essence devoid of outside and inside. For one who wanders in the path beyond the three *guṇas*, where is the question of any injunctions or prohibitions?

सत्यं सत्यं परमममृतं शान्तिकल्याणरूपं
मायारण्ये दहनममलं ज्ञाननिर्वाणदीपम् ।
तेजोरूपं निगमसदनं व्यासपुत्राष्टकं यः
प्रातःकाले पठति मनसा याति निर्वाणमार्गम् ॥

This Śukāṣṭakam is the Supreme Nectar, which is of the nature of peace and auspiciousness, that burns the impurities in the forest of illusion (this *samsāra*), which is the lamp of knowledge and liberation, which is of the form brilliance, and the seat of the Vedas. One, who, early in the morning, sincerely studies this text, attains the path to liberation. It is true indeed. It is true indeed.

* * *

56
A Great Performer

Note: A conversation between Sage Vasishtha and Sri Rama from Yogavāsishtha.

धर्माधर्मौ महाभाग शङ्काविरहिताक्षयः ।
यः करोति यथाप्राप्तौ महाकर्ता स उच्यते ॥

Lord Siva said: O Illustrious one! He is said to be a great performer who does whatever presents (occurs by) itself, whether right or wrong, established in a state of freedom from fear or doubt. [YV 6/1.115.11]

रागद्वेषौ सुखं दुःखं धर्माधर्मौ फलाफले ।
यः करोत्यनपेक्षेण महाकर्ता स उच्यते ॥

One who performs the activities without any desire regarding the outcome of the action, with indifference towards likes or dislikes towards the action, pleasure or pain, right or wrong and regarding the productive or unproductive nature of the action, is called a great performer. [YV 6/1.115.12]

मौनवान्निरहंभावो निर्मलो मुक्तमत्सरः ।
यः करोति गतोद्वेगं महाकर्ता स उच्यते ॥

One who performs actions without any agitation or anxiety, who is taciturn, is free from egoism, pure-minded and free from envy or greed is called a great performer. [YV 6/1.115.13]

शुभाशुभेषु कार्येषु धर्माधर्मैः कुशङ्कया ।
मतिर्न लिप्यते यस्य महाकर्ता स उच्यते ॥

One whose mind is not tainted by the wrong notions regarding actions being right or wrong and auspicious or inauspicious is called a great performer. [YV 6/1.115.14]

सर्वत्र विगतस्नेहो यः साक्षिवदवस्थितः ।
निरिच्छं वर्तते कार्ये महाकर्ता स उच्यते ॥

One who is free from attachment everywhere (towards everything), who is abiding as the witness and who is free from desires regarding action and its outcome is called a great performer. [YV 6/1.115.15]

उद्वेगानन्दरहितः समया स्वच्छया धिया ।
न शोचते यो नोदेति महाकर्ता स उच्यते ॥

One who is free from anxiety and delight, who neither grieves nor exults, possesses clarity of understanding and is with equanimity is called a great performer. [YV 6/1.115.16]

यथार्थकाले मतिमानसंसक्तमना मुनिः ।
कार्यानुरूपवृत्तस्थो महाकर्ता स उच्यते ॥

One who is wise and unattached, and who is indrawn (i.e., the mind is established in the Self), yet as the situation demands, is established in action in accordance to what needs to be done, is called a great performer. [YV 6/1.115.17]

उदासीनः कर्तृतां च कर्माकर्माचरंश्च यः ।
समं यात्यन्तरत्यन्तं महाकर्ता स उच्यते ॥

One who, while engaged in action or non-action (**), is free from the sense of doership (performing it as an offering to God) and who is indifferent (i.e., unattached to action and its outcome), but in all cases internally extremely remains even-minded, is called a great performer.

(** Sometimes interpreted as prescribed action and forbidden actions on certain occasions. This is because the wise one acts based on situations and actions as they present themselves and not out of desires.) [YV 6/1.115.18]

स्वभावेनैव यः शान्तः समतां न जहाति वै ।
शुभाशुभं ह्याचरन्यो महाकर्ता स उच्यते ॥

One who, while engaged in pleasant or unpleasant actions (agreeable or disagreeable actions), is calm by one's innate disposition and never gives up the evenness of the mind is called a great performer. [YV 6/1.115.19]

जन्मस्थितिविनाशेषु सोदयास्तमयेषु च ।
सममेव मनो यस्य महाकर्ता स उच्यते ॥

In birth, existence and death (destruction), and in one's own rise and fall, one whose mind is even (equanimous) is called a great performer. [YV 6/1.115.20]

* * *

57

A Mighty Enjoyer

न किंचन द्वेष्टि तथा न किंचिदभिकाङ्क्षति ।
भुङ्क्ते च प्रकृतं सर्वं महाभोक्ता स उच्यते ॥

One who does not hate anything, also does not long for anything and experiences everything that presents itself, without any reservation, is called a mighty "enjoyer" (Note: The word *bhoktā* in *māhābhoktā* literally means 'experiencer'). [YV 6/1.115.21]

नादत्तेऽप्याददानश्च नाचरत्याचरन्नपि ।
भुञ्जानोऽपि न यो भुङ्क्ते महाभोक्ता स उच्यते ॥

One who, though receiving (taking), does not receive (take) anything, though acting (performing), does not act (perform) and though experiencing (enjoying) does not experience (enjoy), is called a great enjoyer. [YV 6/1.115.22]

साक्षिवत्सकलं लोकव्यवहारमखिन्नधीः ।
पश्यत्यपगतेच्छं यो महाभोक्ता स उच्यते ॥

One who sees all affairs of the world as a witness with an unwearied mind and who is free from desires is called a great enjoyer. [YV 6/1.115.23]

सुखैर्दुःखैः क्रियायोगैर्भावाभावैर्भ्रमप्रदैः ।
यस्य नोत्क्रामति मतिर्महाभोक्ता स उच्यते ॥

One who is not dislodged from the evenness of the mind in pleasure and pain, in victory and defeat, in gain and loss and remains steady in all tribulations is called a great enjoyer. [YV 6/1.115.24]

जरा मरणमापच्च राज्ये दारिद्र्यमेव च ।
रम्यमित्येव यो वेत्ति महाभोक्ता स उच्यते ॥

One who considers old age, death, misfortune, kingdom (sovereignty) and poverty, as equally beautiful (agreeable) is called a great enjoyer. [YV 6/1.115.25]

महान्ति सुखदुःखानि यः पयांसीव सागरः ।
समं समुपगृह्णाति महाभोक्ता स उच्यते। ॥

One who receives and accepts completely with even-mindedness both the great pleasures and the great pains, just as the ocean receives the waters of the rivers, is called a great enjoyer. [YV 6/1.115.26]

अहिंसा समता तुष्टिश्चन्द्रबिम्बादिवांशवः ।
नोप यस्माच्चोपयाता महाभोक्ता स उच्यते ॥

One from whom the qualities of non-hurtingness (non-violence), the vision of equality and contentment radiate like the cool rays from the orb of the moon is called a great enjoyer. [YV 6/1.115.27]

कट्वम्ललवणं तिक्तममृष्टं मृष्टमुत्तमम् ।
अधमं योऽत्ति साम्येन महाभोक्ता स उच्यते ॥

One who eats the bitter, the sour, the salty, the pungent, the not-so-delicious, the sweet and tasteless items with the attitude of sameness is a great enjoyer. [YV 6/1.115.28]

सरसं नीरसं चैव सुरतं विरतं तथा ।
यः पश्यति समं सौम्यो महाभोक्ता स उच्यते ॥

The gentle one, who treats the juicy and flavourless (tasteless) alike and sees the pleasant and the unpleasant with equal vision, is called a great enjoyer. [YV 6/1.115.29]

क्षारे खण्डप्रकारे च शुभे वाप्यशुभे तथा ।
समता सुस्थिरा यस्य महाभोक्ता स उच्यते ॥

One whose equanimity is firm (stable) in the pungent items and various kinds of candied sugar, as also in the pleasant (agreeable) and in the unpleasant (disagreeable), such a one is called a great enjoyer. [YV 6/1.115.30]

इदं भोज्यमभोज्यं चेत्येवं त्यक्त्वा विकल्पितम् ।
गताभिलाषं यो भुङ्क्ते महाभोक्ता स उच्यते ॥

"This to be enjoyed and this is prohibited (not to be enjoyed)"– having given up such doubts or distinctions, one who enjoys without any desires is called a great enjoyer. [YV 6/1.115.31]

आपदं संपदं मोहमानन्दमपरं परम् ।
यो भुङ्क्ते समया बुद्ध्या महाभोक्ता स उच्यते ॥

One who experiences misfortune (calamity, distress), success (or prosperity), wonder, and superior and inferior happiness, with evenness of the mind, is called a great enjoyer. [YV 6/1.115.32]

* * *

58

A Great Tyāgī (Renunciate)

धर्माधर्मौ सुखं दुःखं तथा मरणजन्मनी ।
धिया येनेति संत्यक्तं महात्यागी स उच्यते ॥

One who has completely relinquished from the mind any thoughts regarding *dharma* and *adharma*, happiness and sorrow, and so also regarding death and life, is called a great renouncer. [YV 6/1.115.33]

सर्वेच्छाः सकलाः शङ्काः सर्वेहाः सर्वनिश्चयाः ।
धिया येन परित्यक्ता महात्यागी स उच्यते ॥

One who has completely forsaken all desires, doubts, activities (efforts) and resolutions of the mind is called a greater renouncer. [YV 6/1.115.34]

देहस्य मनसो दुःखैरिन्द्रियाणां मनःस्थितेः ।
नूनं येनोज्झिता सत्ता महात्यागी स उच्यते ॥

One who is not disturbed by the pains of the body, mind and sense organs and by whom all troubles of existence are verily cast off is called a great renouncer. [YV 6/1.115.35]

न मे देहो न जन्मापि युक्तायुक्ते न कर्मणी ।
इति निश्चयवानन्तर्महात्यागी स उच्यते ॥

"The body is not mine; even this life is not mine, and I do not have any notions of injunctions or prohibitions regarding actions"–one who has this kind of firm inner resolve is called a great renouncer. [YV 6/1.115.36]

येन धर्ममधर्मं च मनोमननमीहितम् ।
सर्वमन्तः परित्यक्तं महात्यागी स उच्यते ॥

One is called a great renouncer, who has completely forsaken the bodily functions (in terms of *dharma* and *adharma*), all the inner functions, including those of the mind, and functions like speech, etc. [YV 6/1.115.37]

यावती दृश्यकलना सकलेयं विलोक्यते ।
सा येन सुष्ठु संत्यक्ता महात्यागी स उच्यते ॥

One by whom all thoughts regarding the visible phenomena in this world have been completely relinquished (having perceived the Truth) is called a great renouncer. [YV 6/1.115.38]

* * *

59
Cardinal Statements

The Four *Mahāvākyas* (the great statements from the Upanishads):

अहं ब्रह्मास्मि ।

I am Brahman. [BU 1.4.10]

तत्त्वमसि ।

You are That. [CHU 6.8.7]

अयमात्मा ब्रह्म ।

This Self is Brahman. [MDU 2]

प्रज्ञानं ब्रह्म ।

The knowledge by which the Truth is known, is Brahman. [ATU 3.3]

* * *

एकं सद्विप्रा बहुधा वदन्ति ।

The Truth is one; the wise address it variously. [RV 1.164.46]

आ नो भद्राः क्रतवो यन्तु विश्वतः ।

May noble thoughts come to us from all directions. [RV 1.89.1]

सत्यं वद । धर्मं चर । स्वाध्यायान्मा प्रमदः ।

Speak the truth. Follow the path of dharma. Do not be careless about the study of the scriptures. [TU 1.4]

तदेतत्त्रयं शिक्षेद् दमं दानं दयामिति ।

One should learn the three cardinal values of self-restraint, charity and compassion. [BU 5.2.3]

न वित्तेन तर्पणीयो मनुष्यः ।

The human being is never satisfied with wealth. [KU 1.1.27]

आत्मा वा इदमेक एवाग्र आसीत् ।

In the beginning, this was the one Self, alone. [AT.U 1.1]

सत्यं ज्ञानमनन्तं ब्रह्म ।

Brahman is Truth, Infinitude and is of the nature of knowledge. [TU 2.1]

एकमेवाद्वितीयम् ।

One alone without a second. [CHU 6.2.1]

आत्मैवेदं सर्वम् ।

The Self, indeed, is all this. [CHU 7.25.2]

सर्वं खल्विदं ब्रह्म ।

All this is indeed Brahman. [CHU 3.14.1]

एको देवः सर्वभूतेषु गूढः ।

It is the One Supreme that is residing (hidden) in all beings. [SU 6.11]

इदं सर्वं यदयमात्मा ।

All these are nothing but the Self. [BU 2.4.6]

ब्रह्मविदाप्नोति परम् ।

The one who realises Brahman attains the Supreme. [TU 2.1]

ब्रह्मैवेदं विश्वमिदं वरिष्ठम् ।

This Universe is indeed the Supreme Brahman. [MUU 2.2.11]

ओमिति ब्रह्म । ओमितीदं सर्वम् ।

Om is Brahman. All this, the universe, is Om. [TU 1.8]

द्वितीयाद्वै भयं भवति ।

Fear comes only from a second entity (from duality). [BU 1.4.2]

नायमात्मा प्रवचनेन लभ्यः ।

The Self is not attained through discourses. [MUU 3.2.3]

नायमात्मा बलहीनेन लभ्यः ।

This Self is not attained by those with a weak heart. [MUU 3.2.4]

ॐ तत्सदिति निर्देशो ब्रह्मणस्त्रिविधः स्मृतः ।

Om Tat Sat is regarded as a triple indicator of Brahman. [BG 12.23]

यो वै भूमा तत्सुखं नाल्पे सुखमस्ति भूमैव सुखं ।

That which is infinite is happiness. In the finite, there is no happiness. Infinite alone is happiness. [CHU 7.23.1]

असङ्गो ह्ययं पुरुषः ।

This Supreme Being is unattached indeed. [BU 4.3.15]

कर्मणा बध्यते जन्तुर्विद्यया च विमुच्यते ।

Man becomes bound by actions and liberated by knowledge. [MB 12.241.7]

आत्मानमेव प्रियमुपासीत ।

One should meditate upon the Self alone as dear. [BU 1.4.8]

ब्रह्मविद्यया सर्वं भविष्यन्तः ।

Through the knowledge of Brahman, we become the infinite existence. [BU 1.4.8]

तरति शोकमात्मवित् ।

The knower of the Self goes beyond sorrow. [CHU 7.1.3]

आत्मा वा अरे द्रष्टव्यः श्रोतव्यो मन्तव्यो निदिध्यासितव्यः ।

The Self should be realised, studied, reflected upon and meditated upon. [BU 2.4.5]

उदारचरितानां तु वसुधैव कुटुम्बकम् ।

For the ones who have realised the Self, the entire world itself is a family. [MAU 6.71]

यः ब्रह्म वेद सः ब्रह्मैव भवति ।

One who knows (realises) Brahman, becomes Brahman. [MUU 3.2.9]

सत्यमेव जयते नानृतम् ।

Truth alone prevails, not untruth. [MUU 3.1.6]

शान्तं शिवमद्वैतं चतुर्थं मन्यन्ते स आत्मा स विज्ञेयः ।

That which is tranquil, Siva (auspicious), Non-dual, the Fourth, know that to be the Self. [MDU 7]

सा विद्या या विमुक्तये ।

Knowledge is that which liberates. [VP 1.19.41]

ब्रह्म सत्यं जगन्मिथ्या ।

Brahman alone is truth, and the entire universe is unreal. [NU 35]

देवो भूत्वा देवानप्येति ।

Being divine, he becomes divine. [BU 4.1.2]

आशा हि परमं दुःखं नैराश्यं परमं सुखम् ।

Desire is the source of the most poignant sorrows and desirelessness of the most intense delight. [SB 11.8.44]

यत्र विश्वं भवत्येकनीडम् ।

Where (in the one who has realised the Self) the whole world meets in a single nest. [MNU 1.14]

ऐतदात्म्यमिदं सर्वम् ।

All this is this Self. [CHU 6.8.7]

न कर्मणा न प्रजया धनेन त्यागेनैके अमृतत्वमानशुः ।

They have not attained immortality (liberation) by action, progeny, or by wealth. They have attained it only by renunciation. [MNU 12.14]

ममेति बध्यते जन्तुर्निर्ममेति विमुच्यते ।

The human is bound by the idea of 'mine' and is liberated when free from the idea of 'mine'. [MAU 4.72]

* * *

Appendix

Key to Transliteration and Pronunciation

Sanskrit	*Transliteration*	*Sounds like*
Vowels		
अ	a	o in son, not sat
आ	ā	a in master
इ	i	i in if
ई	ī	ee in feel
उ	u	u in full, put
ऊ	ū	oo in boot
ए	e	a in evade
ऐ	ai	y in my
ओ	o	o in over
औ	au	ow in now, down
ऋ	ṛ	somewhat between r and ri
Consonants: Guttural		
क	ka	cu in cup
ख	kha	ckh in blockhead
ग	ga	ga (hard)

घ	gha	gh in log-hut
ङ	ṅa	ngue in tongue

Palatal

च	ca	ch (not k), c in cello
छ	cha	chh in catch him
ज	ja	ju in just
झ	jha	dgeh in hedgehog
ञ	ña	n (somewhat)

Lingual

ट	ṭa	tu in tub
ठ	ṭha	th in ant-hill
ड	ḍa	du in dull
ढ	ḍha	dh in godhead
ण	ṇa	n in under

Dental

त	ta	French t
थ	tha	th in thumb
द	da	th in then
ध	dha	theh in breathe here
न	na	nu in nurse

Labial

प	pa	pu in pun
फ	pha	ph in loop-hole

ब	ba	bu in bun
भ	bha	bh in abhor
म	ma	mu in mud

Semi-vowels

य	ya	you in young
र	ra	ru in run
ल	la	lo in love
व	va	v in avert

Sibilants/Aspirate

श	śa	sh in shine
ष	ṣa	sh in show, wish
स	sa	su in sun
ह	ha	hu in hunger

Others

अं	ṃ	ng
अः	ḥ	half h in huh!
क्ष	kṣa	ctio in action
त्र	tra	thr in three
ज्ञ	jña	gn in gnosis
श्र	śra	shra in ashram
ऽ	'	Replaces a leading vowel in compound words

***

Glossary

Note: The meaning and interpretations for all the terms in this glossary have been presented in the context of a spiritual pursuit.

āchārya

A teacher or preceptor (in general); a spiritual guide or preceptor. Yājñavalkya Smriti gives the following definition to the term: "One who acquires knowledge by the study of scriptures, establishes them in one's conduct and behaviour, and practises them oneself is called an *āchārya*."

Adi Shankarāchārya

A great philosopher and theologian who consolidated the doctrine of Advaita Vedanta. He wrote commentaries on the Brahma Sutras, the principal Upanishads and the Bhagavad Gīta. Also referred to as Adi Shankara.

advaita

In the context of spirituality, it means non-duality—the idea that Brahman alone is the One Reality and that the phenomenal universe is a mere appearance of Brahman; also, the Self is not different from Brahman.

ahankāra

The I-sense in all of us: Sense of 'I', 'me' and 'mine' (egotism); The mistaken notion of the self; Mistakenly identifying the Self with the body-mind-senses. Sometimes, it is also spelt as '*ahamkāra*'.

āshrama

In common parlance, it refers to a hermitage, or dwelling or abode of ascetics. More specifically, it refers to the orders or stages of life. There are four ashramas: (1) *brahmacharya* or student-hood, (2) *gārhasthya* or the role of a householder, (3) *vānaprastha* or the life of an anchorite, and (4) *sannyāsa* or monkhood.

ātmā

The most used meaning of the word is 'the Self', the Individual Self, the Soul. Depending on the context, the following meanings are also used: oneself, essence, nature, character, mind and intellect.

bhagavān

It means the lord, the illustrious one, the divine one. According to the scriptures, the Lord (*bhagavān*) has the following six qualities: overlordship of the all, strength, fame, wealth, knowledge and detachment.

bhakti

It means devotion, pious faith, faithfulness, belief or reverence. It is usually in the context of a deity, God or preceptor.

brahman

Brahman denotes the highest Cosmic Principle, the Universal Principle and the Ultimate Reality in the universe. It is the ultimate cause of all that exists. It is the all-pervasive, genderless, infinite, changeless and eternal truth. It is the single unity in all the diversity that exists in the universe. It refers to the Supreme Being, regarded as impersonal and free of all quality and action. In the spiritual pursuit, it is Brahman that is sought after as the highest goal in life. Brahman is different from Brahmā (the deity associated with creation). This term is completely different from the term *brāhmaṇa*, which refers to one who is engaged in the pursuit of knowledge or acts of rituals, ceremonies and sacrifices.

buddhi

Refers to intellect, understanding or intelligence. It refers to the faculty of reason, cognition or comprehension. In some contexts, it could also be used to refer to the mind.

chit

It refers to Consciousness itself, distinct from 'being conscious of something'; awareness.

deeksha

Initiation in general; Initiation (from a guru to the disciple) into the spiritual path, including receiving the initiation mantra. Investiture with the sacred thread.

dharma

This is one of those words which has a number of interpretations, even as used in spiritual texts. The following are a few meanings, depending on the context: * Body of law, usage, practice, custom, ordinance, statue, morals, ethics, etc., that sustain a society, nation and globe. The maxim (from Manu Smriti)–"dharma protects those who protect dharma". * Duty, prescribed course of conduct. * Nature, disposition, character. * An essential quality, peculiarity, characteristic property and attribute.

dhyāna

In simple terms, it refers to meditation. There are various kinds of meditation, and varies across traditions. Here is one perspective: Meditation is a mind-based activity involving constant dwelling upon the Supreme Brahman, and the culmination of meditation lies in attaining the state where one realises the oneness of the meditator and the meditated upon, i.e., the Self.

duhkha

Refers to sorrow, unpleasant, grief, unhappiness, affliction, distress, pain, agony, trouble or difficulty. Typically juxtaposed with *sukha* (happiness, pleasure). Sometimes also used to mean difficult. There are three kinds of *duhkha*: (1) Afflictions from supernatural agencies, the divine and influence of planets; (2) Afflictions from terrestrial, all beings, material things and from the elements; (3) Afflictions relating to body and mind.

dvandva

It means the pairs of opposites we experience in life–heat and cold, favourable and unfavourable, pleasure and pain, success and failure, happiness and sorrow, honour and dishonour, etc. All our experiences in life are within these pairs of opposites.

guṇa

Literally, it means quality, attribute or property. Nature consists of three *guṇas–sattva*, *rajas* and *tamas*. Everything or everyone is a combination of these three *guṇas* existing in various proportions, and the balance of these three may change from time to time. The three qualities are: (1) *sattva* refers to the quality of harmony, goodness, purity, virtue, etc.; (2) *rajas* refers to passion, activity, drive, egoism, dynamism, movement, etc.; (3) *tamas* refers to ignorance, inertia, lethargy, dullness, disorder, delusion, etc.

guru

While this word has many meanings, we will be using it to mean a spiritual preceptor who instructs and guides a disciple on the spiritual path towards attaining the spiritual goal of liberation.

indriya

It refers to a sense organ or faculty of the senses. There are two kinds of sense organs: (a) organs of knowledge: ear, skin, eye, tongue and nose; and (b) organs of action: hand, foot, larynx, organ of reproduction and excretion). In the context of spirituality, the sense organs are often compared to restive horses, which, if not properly checked, will lead one astray.

Īshvara

Literally, it means lord or master. We will use it to mean God or the Supreme Being.

jñāna

In simple terms, it means knowledge, learning, knowing or understanding. In the context of spirituality, it does not typically refer to the knowledge of the world around us, like sciences, mathematics, astronomy, medicine, etc. In spirituality, it refers to the knowledge that will help us understand our own nature.

jīva

In simple terms, it refers to a living being, a creature. In the context of spirituality, it refers to the individual Self enshrined in the human body. Also referred to *jīvātma*, the individual self, while the *Paramātma* refers to the Universal or Supreme Self.

kāma

It is desire, longing, wishing, wanting, yearning or craving for something that brings enjoyment or pleasure. Desires are not only about acquiring what we like but are also about not wanting what we dislike. In simple terms, it is an expectation.

karma

In simple terms, it means action, work or deed. It also refers to rituals or rites. The concept of karma is also closely tied to the idea of the cycle of birth and death (transmigration). Karma is of three kinds: *āgāmi*, *sanchita* and *prārabdha*. Karma, here, refers to the unseen fruits of action (as opposed to the objective, tangible outcomes). *āgāmi karma* is future karma, which are effects that are the fruit of our current actions and decisions. *Sanchita karma* is all the accumulated karmas of the past, which are in seed form and will take effect in future. It is the portion of the *sanchita karma* which is influencing the present is called *prārabdha*. Having given birth to this body, the actions which give results in this very world, in the form of happiness or misery, and which can be destroyed only by enjoying or suffering them, is called *prārabdha karma*.

manana

Manana refers to thinking, reflection, cogitation or introspection. It also means an inference arrived at by means of reasoning.

In Vedanta, the spiritual pursuit consists of three steps that lead the seeker to the goal of self-realisation: *shravaṇa* (listening), *manana* (rumination) and *nididhyāsana* (meditation).

manas

The mind.

māyā

In simple terms, it is an illusion of magic, an unreal or illusory image, a phantom, an illusion, unreal apparition. In Vedanta, maya refers to the illusion by virtue of which one considers the unreal universe as really existent and as distinct from the Supreme Being or Brahman.

mithyā

Sometimes, in a badly lit place, a rope lying on the floor is mistaken for a snake. The snake appears and feels real. But when the rope's presence is known, it is found that the snake never existed. So, the snake appears to be real, so long as the substratum (i.e., the rope) is not known. Once the knowledge of the rope is had, it is realised that the snake was never real. In this context, the snake is *mithyā*. Literally translated, one may use words like false, untrue unreal.

moha

It means "delusion of the mind which prevents one from discerning the truth". It refers to the state of being deluded or having a wrong perception about who we are, what this world is, our relationship with this world, etc. Delusion is considered to be one of the causes of sorrow, misery, etc. Also referred to as *ajñāna*, *avidyā*–both meaning ignorance.

moksha

See Mukti.

mukti

In simple terms, *mukti* means liberation, deliverance, emancipation or freedom. In spirituality, mukti is used to refer to the final beatitude or emancipation or absolution of the soul from metempsychosis or the cycle of births and deaths. *Mukti* is also used to refer to the state of uninterrupted cessation of sorrow or attainment of permanent or eternal happiness.

nididhyāsana

It refers to meditation on a mantra or the sacred utterances of the Upanishads, leading to the goal of self-realisation. In Vedanta, the spiritual pursuit consists of three stages that lead the seeker to the goal of self-realisation: listening (or study), rumination (introspection) and meditation.

paramātma

Refers to the Supreme Self, the Universal Self, the Supreme Being, considered as the Self of the entire universe, the Supreme Brahman. Compare with *jīvātma*.

praṇava

The sacred syllable Om is nothing but the name or symbol representing the Supreme Self.

prāṇa

In simple terms, it refers to the breath of life, the air inhaled, vitality, the life force or vigour. It also refers to the five-fold vital forces that enable to physiological functioning of the human body: *prāṇa* (respiration), *apāna* (elimination), *vyāna* (circulation), *samāna* (digestion) and *udāna* (upward movement; e.g., vomiting).

purushārtha

There are four-fold objects of human pursuit called *purushartha*. These are: *dharma*, *artha*, *kāma* and *moksha*. While leading a life based on *dharma*, acquire the necessary wealth and resources (*artha*), then fulfil various desires and wishes for enjoyment (*kāma*), and finally turn the attention to the goal of attainment of *moksha* (liberation).

rajas

Refer to *guṇa*. Also referred to as *rajo-guṇa*.

sādhana

It refers to the means of effecting or accomplishing something, any agent or instrument. In spirituality, it refers to the means to achieve the goal of spiritual pursuit. *Sādhana* refers to the pursuits, practices, disciplines, techniques, etc., aimed at achieving the goal of realising the self, liberation, etc.

samatva

Literally, it means sameness, equality or uniformness. However, in the context of spirituality, it means being even-minded in pleasure and pain (happiness and sorrow), success and failure, favourable and unfavourable circumstances, honour and dishonour and all pairs of opposites (*dvandva*).

samskāra

From the religious point of view, it commonly refers to a purificatory rite, a sacred rite or ceremony. For example, a sacred thread ceremony is a *samskāra*. In the context of spiritual literature, it refers to the mental impressions or psychological imprints formed in the mind as a result of our actions. It is also synonymous with the term *vāsana*.

samsāra

In simple terms, it refers to the course of life in this world, the mundane or worldly existence. In certain contexts, it also refers to the passage through the cycle of birth and death or metempsychosis or transmigration. It is also referred to as the wheel of *samsāra* or the cycle of births and deaths. The illusory experience of the world is also referred to as *samsāra*.

sanga

Literally, it means 'association'. In spirituality, it is more often used in the sense of 'attachment'. Patanjali Yoga Sutras (aphorism 2.7) define attachment as that which dwells upon pleasure.

sannyāsa

It refers to the act of leaving or abandonment. It also refers to one of the four stages of human life–*brahmacharya*, *gārhasthya*, *vānaprastha* and *sannyāsa*, where *sannyāsa* refers to the complete renunciation of the world and its possession, and taking to a life of austerity, mendicancy and isolation. See *āshrama*.

sannyāsin (or sannyāsi)

Literally, one who has renounced. We will use it to mean one who has completely renounced the attachments in the world, an ascetic. One who has taken to the fourth order or stage of life. See *sannyāsa*.

sat

In Vedanta, this term is mostly used for Existence, Reality and Truth. The following meanings are also common: good, virtuous, noble, right, proper, respectable and wise.

satsanga

Association with good and wise people. In a spiritual seeker's life, the association with the wise is of very great importance. *Satsanga* also means 'association with the Truth'–which could be attained by even 'interaction or association with reading Texts that reveal the Supreme Truth'. In the term *satsanga*, '*sanga*' refers to association.

sattva

Refer to *guṇa*. Also called *sattva-guṇa*.

shraddhā

Loosely, it means faith, trust, belief or confidence. In the context of any pursuit, *shraddhā* refers to a mental attitude that includes faith or confidence, sincerity of purpose, commitment of heart and utmost diligence to the undertaking. Bhagavad Gīta says: "A man is what his *shraddhā* is".

shravaṇa

Literally, it refers to the act of listening. In spirituality, it refers to the acquisition of knowledge by means of listening, reading or studying. In Vedanta, the spiritual pursuit consists of three stages that lead the seeker to the goal of self-realisation: listening (or study), rumination and meditation.

sukha

Happiness, pleasure, delight, agreeable. Sometimes also used to mean easy.

tamas

Refer to *guṇa*. Also called *tamo-guṇa*.

tapas

It refers to the 'inner heat' created by the practice of physical austerities. *Tapas* is a religious or spiritual self-disciplined practice, abstinence, or ascetic practice voluntarily carried out to achieve some object. It is also associated with disciplines meant to purify the mind in preparation for higher spiritual practices, leading to the final goal of liberation. *Tapas* could be physical (bodily), like fasting, abstinences, renouncing certain pleasures, etc. or mental (mind-based), like service to others, study, meditation, etc. However, both are aimed at the mind.

tyāga

It refers to the act of leaving, forsaking, abandoning, giving up or renouncing. In the context of spirituality, these are the usual meanings. For example, abandoning desires, giving up greed for wealth, etc. One who has renounced is referred to as a *tyāgi*.

vāsana

It refers to past impressions in the mind that influences thoughts and behaviour. These impressions are unconsciously left behind in the mind as a result of past actions, present consciousness of past perceptions, or knowledge derived from memory. It can also mean a wish, desire, expectation and inclination.

vairāgya

It refers to the absence of desires or passions for the enjoyment of the objects of the world. It is also defined as the desire to give up all worldly enjoyments ranging from bodily to other worldly. In the context of spirituality, it would be a mistake to translate *vairāgya* as indifference, aversion, disgust or distaste. The word indifference shows a lack of concern, whereas a person with *vairāgya* may have concern towards something but will not be attached to that or may not be interested in that. So, *vairāgya* can also be seen as indifference to the world, where indifference does not mean 'lack of concern'.

vedanta

Literally, it refers to the end portion of the Vedas. It refers to the philosophies contained in the Upanishads. The basis of Vedanta is contained in the following texts: Brahma Sutras, Upanishads and Bhagavad Gīta.

vichāra

This is a term commonly used in the context of spirituality to refer to the process of reflection, deliberation, thought, investigation and examination. The term *ātma-vichāra* is used to refer to Self-enquiry.

vidyā

It means knowledge, learning, education, science or any branch of knowledge. In spirituality, it commonly refers to the Self-knowledge or knowledge of the self. The opposite of *vidyā* is *avidyā* or ignorance.

vishaya

The objects of sense-perception; the objects of the world that are perceived by the senses; the term object refers to anything that we perceive, like things, people, events, etc. These are the objects of our day-to-day experience, which lead to favourable and unfavourable experiences.

viveka

It is the faculty of distinguishing, discriminating, discretion or discernment of things by their real and not apparent nature. In spirituality, it is applied to the faculty of discriminating the real (Brahman) from the unreal or the permanent from the transient.

yajña

In simple terms, it is an act of worship, any pious or devotional act. It is also a sacrifice, sacrificial rite or any offering or oblation. In the context of spirituality, it is NOT the offering of an animal, plant or human life, as in propitiation or homage. Every householder has the following five responsibilities (*pancha-mahā-yajña*): (1) *deva-yajña* – offering to the gods; (2) *pitr-yajña* – homage to forefathers and ancestors; (3) *bhoota-yajña* – offering of food and care to all beings–plants and animals; (4) *manushya-yajña* – caring for all fellow human beings; (5) *brahma-yajña* – study of sacred texts constitutes offering to Brahman, the Supreme Reality.

yoga

In simple terms, yoga means union or the act of yoking. In spirituality, yoga refers to the union with the Supreme Being by means of contemplation, meditation, etc. Yoga also refers to the system of philosophy which deals with the union of the individual self with the Supreme Being, Brahman or God. For example, *karma-yoga*, *bhakti-yoga*, *jñāna-yoga*, etc.

***

Abbreviations

Abbreviation	*Name of Text*
ANU	Annapurṇa Upanishad
APR	Aparokṣānubhūti
ATU	Aitareya Upanishad
AVU	Avadhūta Upanishad
BG	Bhagavad Gīta
BU	Brihadāraṇyaka Upanishad
CHN	Chāṇakya Nīti
CHU	Chāndogya Upanishad
IU	Īśāvāsya Upanishad
KAI	Kaivalya Upanishad
KDU	Kuṇḍika Upanishad
KU	Kaṭha Upanishad
MAU	Mahā Upanishad
MB	Mahābhārata
MDU	Māndukya Upanishad
MNU	Mahānārāyaṇa Upanishad
MS	Manu Smṛti
MUU	Muṇḍaka Upanishad
NU	Nirālamba Upanishad

PD	Panchadashī
PP	Padma-purāṇam
PYS	Pātañjali Yoga Sūtrās
RG	Ribhu Gītā
RV	Rig Veda
SAA	Sadācārānusandhānam
SB	Śrīmad bhāgavatam
SID	Śiva-dṛṣṭi
SNU	Sannyāsa Upanishad
SS	Śataśloki
SU	Śvetāśvatara Upanishad
SUM	Subhāṣitam
SVS	Sarva-vedānta-siddhānta-sāra-saṅgrahaḥ
TEJ	Tejabindu Upanishad
TJU	Tejobindu Upanishad
TU	Taittirīya Upanishad
US	Upadeśa-sāhasrī
VC	Viveka-chūḍāmaṇi
VD	Vairāgya-Dindima
VP	Viṣṇu-purāṇam
VS	Vairāgya-śatakam
VSA	Vedānta-sāra
YV	Yoga-vāsiṣṭhaḥ

* * *